Way Too Cool

Way Too Cool

SELLING OUT RACE AND ETHICS

Shannon Winnubst

Columbia University Press New York

COLUMBIA UNIVERSITY PRESS
Publishers Since 1893
New York Chichester, West Sussex
cup.columbia.edu

Library of Congress Cataloging-in-Publication Data

Winnubst, Shannon.
Way too cool : selling out race and ethics / Shannon Winnubst.
pages cm
Includes bibliographical references and index.
ISBN 978-0-231-17294-3 (cloth : acid-free paper) — ISBN 978-0-231-17295-0 (pbk. : acid-free paper) — ISBN 978-0-231-53988-3 (e-book)
1. Advertising—Social aspects—United States—History. 2. Minorities in advertising—United States—History. 3. Commodification—United States. 4. Neoliberalism—United States. 5. United States—Race relations. I. Title.

HF5813.U6W55 2015
306.3'4—dc23 2015004862

Columbia University Press books are printed on permanent and durable acid-free paper.
This book is printed on paper with recycled content.
Printed in the United States of America

Cover design: Julia Kushnirsky
Cover art: Portrait of Andries Stilte II (2006) © Kehinde Wiley. Used by permission. Courtesy of the artist and Stephen Friedman Gallery, London; Sean Kelly, NY; Roberts & Tilton, Culver City, CA; and Galerie Daniel Templon, Paris.

IN MEMORY OF

Patricia Lou LeGer Winnubst

1932–2011

CONTENTS

ACKNOWLEDGMENTS

This book has seen many twists and turns over several years of research and, accordingly, I have many individuals and audiences to thank for engaging various aspects of the project: for indulging all kinds of inchoate musings and speculations about neoliberalism, late liberalism, biopolitics, Foucault, precarity, pain, pleasure, and the social contract, Ladelle McWhorter, Jana Sawicki, Falguni Sheth, Kimberly Springer, Mary Thomas, Matt Coleman, Phillip Armstrong, Becky Mansfield, Marc Spindelman, Michael Bray, and graduate students in Women's, Gender, and Sexuality Studies and Comparative Studies at Ohio State, especially Meredith Lee, Matt Brenn, and Divya Sundar; for thinking about race and all its damning contortions, bell hooks and Kimberly Springer; for persistent thinking and work on ethics, bell hooks, Lynne Huffer, and Cynthia Willett; for helpful suggestions and feedback on thinking through Lacan, Andrew Cutrofello and Tim Dean; for indulging a stream of random questions on Marx, Amy Wendling; for disabusing me of pursuing apathy as a neoliberal affect, Falguni Sheth; for priceless help in navigating the contemporary world of cool, J. Brendan Shaw; for helping me sort through the difficulty of writing about New Orleans, Thom McClendon; for encouraging me to embrace charts and tables (to say the least), Alison Kafer; for brainstorming cool titles, Andy Cavins, Lynaya Elliott, and Tess Pugsley; and for inspiring cheerleading, Marie Draz, Perry Zurn, and Andrew Dilts. I also offer a special thanks to Kehinde Wiley for allowing me to use his artwork on the cover and in the fifth interlude, which captures real cool now. At Columbia University Press, I thank Wendy Lochner for believing in this project for so long and Christine Dunbar for tireless assistance. I thank an anonymous reviewer for generously reining in parts of my argument regarding Marxism and pushing me to think more seriously about social cathexis. Finally, I thank Lynne Huffer for believing in this project with such enthusiasm and becoming an important voice in my final thinking about it: your generosity and fierce insight are inspiring.

The book was also written across several profound transitions in my life and I am grateful to many for seeing me through these joyous and difficult times. Without this kind of support, I could never have found a way to sustain the focus or spirit of this project. For catching us in Columbus, I am forever grateful to Sandra Macpherson, Luke Wilson, Roma Cady, and Margo Lucy; Mary Thomas, Mat Coleman, and Tom Cosmo; Mollie Blackburn, Mindi Rhoades, Blais and Dottie Grey; Tanya Erzen, Bill Quigley, and Tilda; and my wonderful colleagues in the Department of Women's, Gender, and Sexuality Studies. For hanging on to us in Austin, I remain deeply grateful to Kris Hogan and Milly Gleckler, Kathleen Juhl, Alison Kafer and Dana Newlove, and Thom McClendon and Nancy Schmechel McClendon. And for always being there, for such a long time now, I thank Ton Winnubst, Kimmy Dee Winnubst and Sue Rivers, Mark, Shelbi, Morgan, Rachel and J. Willies Winnubst, bell hooks, Eric Selbin, Helen Cordes, Jesse Cordes Selbin, Zoe Cordes Selbin, Erin FitzGerald, Craig Irvine, John Spooner, Jennifer Byrne, Mark Hersh, Margaret and Jay Suchland, Mary and John Grundy, and all my fantastic extended Winnubst (and Stammetje) family on both sides of the Atlantic.

Both the Department of Women's, Gender, and Sexuality Studies and the College of Arts and Sciences at Ohio State University have offered generous institutional and financial support of this project. I particularly thank Jill Bystdyzienski for her steadfast and generous support: she has helped me make sense of my move to the Department of Women's, Gender, and Sexuality Studies and to Ohio State time and time again. I also thank the amazing staff in WGSS, Lynaya Elliott, Andy Cavins, and Tess Pugsley, all of whom inspire me, keep me honest, and make my life and work much richer and easier. Additionally, I thank Nikki Engel and

Debanuj DasGupta for early assistance with research and the College of Arts and Sciences for a semester research leave that allowed me to complete the manuscript. Finally, I thank my remarkable colleagues in the Department of Women's, Gender, and Sexuality studies for the relentless pursuit of all forms of resistance and justice, especially those that draw across disciplinary boundaries: this book is the fruit of landing in this amazing intellectual space.

I have also benefited from presenting various parts of the book to generous and rigorous audiences at the following organizations and institutions: the Department of Philosophy at Emory University, hosted by Cynthia Willett; a scholarly session arranged by Gail Weiss at the International Association of Philosophy and Literature; the Gloria Anzaldúa Speakers Series at University of Texas-Pan America, arranged by Adriel Trott; a scholarly session arranged by Alia Al-Saji at the American Philosophical Association, with a response by Falguni Sheth; a panel at the Society of Phenomenology and Existential Philosophy, with a response by Peter Gratton; the Women, Gender, and Sexuality Program at the University of Richmond; the "Queer Places, Practices, and Lives" conference at Ohio State; a plenary panel arranged by Marc Spindelman at the "Race, Sexuality, and Social Justice" conference at the Moritz College of Law at Ohio State; the "Queerly Political/Politically Queer" Speakers Series at Trent University, initiated by Emilia Angelova; and a plenary panel arranged by Shannon Sullivan at the *PhiloSOPHIA* conference at the Pennsylvania State University. I am very grateful to the hosts and audiences of these various talks, where I received invaluable feedback that has shaped much of my thinking in the book.

Finally, I must put words to the impossible task of thanking Jennifer Suchland and Micah Simone Suchland-Winnubst for the many wonders of our shared world, along with Phaedrus, MoZoe, and Sir Walter. Micah Simone, a force for joy in the world, has taught me aspects of play, pleasure, space, and time I could have never imagined: I hope you remain forever uncool. Jennifer Suchland has lived through this book and all the events that have surrounded it with a sheer will to flourish that refuses any neoliberal reduction. Our traveling together has, across all these years, become a bumpy, raucous ride that I cherish. I am deeply grateful for her patience, insight, laughter, perseverance, sharp wit, and grounding: this book would not exist without her.

I dedicate this book to my mother, Patricia Lou Leger Winnubst, who passed away in the middle of my writing and reinvigorated my commitment to thinking about these problems in the register of ethics. Despite all kinds of impassioned disagreements with me about politics, she has always been my first teacher of ethics.

Way Too Cool

Introduction

A VERY UNCOOL BOOK

This is a very uncool book.

Despite the unavoidably cool irony of such a claim, I offer a warning from the outset: filled with suspiciously structuralist analyses, close readings of texts long ago mastered, an argument that runs the length of the book, a critique of ideological analyses, and several ridiculously detailed charts, the book just plain ain't cool. Even the Interludes of Cool aren't very cool in their annoying brevity. But perhaps worse of all, I don't lament or regret it. I may even find some sliver of ethical respite in it.

My primary concern in this book is, obviously, not actually with coolness. (Or at least not with being cool.) This book is driven by a persistent sense that, living in the materially affluent northern-western hemisphere of the early twenty-first century, we have no meaningful language for social difference, especially race, or ethics—a twinned pair of phenomena that feeds and informs each other. Increasingly inhabiting a lexicon filled with economic metaphors, we seem to assume that the genre of economics can aptly answer any question of difference or value. Or perhaps we're just losing any sense that things might be otherwise: the repeated response to my writing on neoliberalism and ethics is an immediate dismissal—"isn't that an oxymoron?"

While analytic philosophers such as Ronald Dworkin and Debra Satz have framed such questions as a problem of the limits of markets, I am asking a very different set of questions. Rather than assume the inevitability of the incursion of an economic form of rationality into all areas of living, I understand neoliberalism as a particular historical formation, with specific sets of not only economic and political transformations, but also epistemological, social, and subjective transformations. Extrapolating from a very close reading of Michel Foucault's 1979 lectures on neoliberalism, *The Birth of Biopolitics*, I aim to understand how this particular form of economic rationality that is called "neoliberalism" has become a dominant social rationality over the last three decades or so, especially in mainstream culture of the United States. Arguing against a dominant conceptualization of it as an ideology, I aim to map precisely what is "new" about the much circulated—and consequently overdetermined—constellation of concepts, theories, and practices that we call "neoliberalism." I focus on the transformations in processes of subject formation, conceptualizations of race alongside other forms of social difference, and understandings of ethics.

The history of cool in the United States provides the cultural vehicle for these arguments. While we may think of "cool" as hip and ironic, various advertising machines and markets have been packaging and selling it to us for some time. Since at least the 1970s, we in the United States have been incited across a broad array of media and markets to embrace "coolness" as a metric for a wide range of evaluations, spanning from the aesthetic to the political. But "coolness" is not just one among many poses of youth culture. "Cool" was birthed in the post–World War II black aesthetics of jazz and blues. Accordingly, it harbors very specific and highly charged connotations of resistance to both white supremacy and the exploitation of globalized capital. As the work of bell hooks demonstrates, the pose, aesthetics, and even ethics of "cool" have deep roots in black US culture as long-standing resources of resistance and protection. To be cool has, indeed, always included a pose of ironic detachment, but it has also nurtured the skill, as hooks puts it, to take the hardships of life in a racist world and "alchemically turn the pain into gold."[1] "Cool" in black culture carries a long history of cultivating the strength to withstand the psychological and physical violence of racism and come out even stronger, even more centered and grounded.[2] Both these long historical roots in black culture and the enshrining of ironic detachment render cool a particularly incisive and generative cultural disposition through which to trace the transformation in modes of cathexes and concepts of race, as well as other forms of social difference, in neoliberal social rationalities.

When neoliberal markets sell "coolness," they are not only bastardizing nonconformity into a hollowed-out, generic posture; they are also commodifying black resistance in the process. As an aesthetic that originates in US black culture, "cool" offers resources for resistance and rebellion through access to "something better." This racialized character of "something better"—or what we can also call *jouissance*—marks black culture as both alluring and dangerous in the white imaginary. But as coolness is gradually co-opted, first into white masculinist postures of detachment and irony (James Dean, Marlon Brando) and then, through the advertising machines of the 1970s, into contemporary white, consumer-class aesthetics of hipster rebellion, it becomes commodified.[3] This commodification entails not only a distancing from the roots of cool in black aesthetics of resistance, but also a deeper erasure of any historical connotation of resistance at all. This more widespread emptying of historical meaning exemplifies the kind of formalization of social difference itself that, I argue, is central to neoliberal social rationalities—a formalization that I call the fungibility of difference.

As is well documented by now, neoliberal social rationalities spawned the language of multiculturalism in the late 1980s and its even more aestheticized child, diversity, in the late 1990s as the new, preferred vocabulary for social difference. As the work of Lisa Duggan, Henry Giroux, and Elizabeth Povinelli shows so forcefully, this language has aided and abetted the emergence of neoconservative politics in the United States and, with different permutations, in the United Kingdom and northern-western Europe. Buzzwords such as "multiculturalism," "diversity," and "color-blindness" are clearly not the antiracist, antixenophobic mantras that they purport to be. My focus on cool affords a deepening of these analyses to grasp how the categories and concepts of social difference have transformed from a long-standing, historical cathexis with xenophobia in the times of classical liberalism into an aestheticized, ahistorical cathexis with o so cool forms of fungible difference in the social rationality of neoliberalism.

Across the detailed readings and analyses of the book, I argue that one of the fundamental social transformations enacted in and through neoliberalism as a social rationality is the rendering of social difference for the barometer of fungibility, the ultimate metric of the market. A formalizing of differences, fungibility refers to the kinds of formal units of measurement that undergird markets, monetary systems, and many forms of legal adjudication: the bushel of wheat produced "here" is fungible with the bushel of wheat produced "there"; the $5 note in my pocket is fungible with the $5 note in the cash register; and the harm inflicted by "x" is fungible with the reparation offered to "y." To render social differences fungible is to scrub them clean of any historical, political, or ethical valences. It is, as I show in great detail across this book, at the heart of the deracialization of the social field toward which neoliberal social rationalities aspire (and that we hear in its mantras of diversity and color-blindness). With deracialization as one of its primary effects, this fungibility of social difference is at the heart of our inability to think meaningfully about ethics.

The historical transformation in the meanings of cool offers a condensed snapshot of this rendering of social differences into "cool" stances that are wholly fungible units. Once linked to a politics of resistance in black culture, coolness has become the aestheticizing motor of modes of living. That is, coolness itself has been stripped of any historical, political, or ethical meaning. The commodification of cool thereby becomes not merely a generic operation of capitalism, but a performance of the very evacuation of history, especially histories of conflict such as those that animate racialization and racism. That the erasure in cool is precisely the erasure of race makes it exemplary for the arguments of this book. The historical transformation of cool enacts the slide from social difference as antagonistic to social difference as purely aesthetic, formal, and fungible. This slide, in turn, enacts a central axis of the transformations from liberalism to neoliberalism that I map across the book. In contemporary neoliberal culture, coolness allows difference to proliferate and intensify in a purely formal and thus purely superficial manner. Unhinged from any historical or ethical barometer, social difference-as-fungibility cannot be a source of conflict. And this is precisely how it becomes one of the most insidious transformations of our neoliberal social worlds, enacting a slow torsion on our concepts of race and ethics that is gradually choking off any meaningful cathexes to them.

CATHEXIS: SUBJECT FORMATION BEYOND INTERPELLATION

Coined in psychoanalysis, cathexis captures a broad set of sociopsychic dynamics about what makes us feel connected to the world and its stunning variety of phenomena. Cathexis can refer to both individual and social phenomena, throwing any strict boundary between the two into fuzzy disarray. For example, while we might find biographic explanations for an arachnologist's particular fascination with exotic spiders in Australia, she is always also oriented toward such objects by complex social formations that encourage such kinds of obsessions. The concept of cathexis focuses attention on these shared, overlapping dynamics that make us—as a collective and as individuals—find some phenomena fascinating and others boring. It describes why we feel connected to some bodies and not others, why we care about some questions and not others. It's what makes us tick. Freud called it "libidinal preoccupation." Neoliberals call it "personal investment." (Sound familiar now?)

Leaving the infinite regress of the question of individual cathexes to psychoanalytic practice, I focus on the transformation of social cathexes underway in cultures (especially in the United States) where a neoliberal social rationality is taking root. By social cathexis, I mean the kinds of social investments (in neoliberal parlance) that enliven particular issues, questions, values, phenomena, and ways of living as the ones a society deems worth pursuing. Social cathexes refer to broadly shared proclivities that orient us toward particular kinds of social preferences. The objects of these shared preferences are thus easily captured, for example, by a taxonomy of the values over which a society debates, argues, and votes. But as emotional and libidinal, social cathexes also function without our consent or knowledge. They circulate unconsciously, orienting us toward a broad set of possible objects of interest and then leaving us to feel as if we choose our particular path. The taxonomy of values that a society explicitly and directly advertises, therefore, does not capture the full range of circulating cathexes. We are also cathected more obliquely to values we do not even acknowledge—the kinds of unspoken values, for example, for which a society imprisons and even kills.

The psychoanalytic lexicon initiated by "cathexis" thereby enables me to account for processes of subject formation beyond the dominant analytic lens of interpellation. Derived from Althusserian accounts of ideology, interpellation provides a powerful account of how hegemonic social discourses regulate and incite specific forms of subjects. It is little wonder that the concept has been and continues to be used across so many fields of social theory, particularly those focused on analyzing social power and its normalizing, constraining effects. Given the changes in the functions of social authority underway in neoliberal social rationalities, however, I argue (with great specificity) that interpellation may no longer capture the processes of subject formation in neoliberal cultures such as the United States. Interpellation, as Althusser develops it, hinges on a coherent set of practices and concepts (the school, the church, the family, the press, and so on) that function with sufficient authority to bind persons of a culture together and to police those who do not readily assent. The central mechanism in this process is identification, however unconscious, with that set of practices and concepts. Theorists such as Jodi Dean and Slavoj Žižek, however, have argued persuasively that this kind of cohesive social authority is being eclipsed in neoliberal cultures. In Lacanian terms, the symbolic function is being eclipsed, setting social life largely loose across the plane of the imaginary. If this is so (and I argue through many examples that it is), then we need accounts of subject formation that do not fall back on Althusserian interpellation and identification.

By turning to the psychoanalytic concept of cathexis, along with a more robust Lacanian lexicon, I specify and analyze some of the new processes of subject formation—or what Foucault calls "subjects of interests"—that are underway in these neoliberal social rationalities. I understand and use social cathexes as historically developed complex patterns of social attachments—and thus also as detachments, though usually unnoticed. For example, the (apparently ever growing) contemporary social attachment in the United States to competitive sports derives from a historical sedimentation of a broad variety of cathexes: advanced capitalist competition, long-standing Protestant individualism, the post–Cold War intensification of US exceptionalism, the increasing masculinizing of mainstream culture, the neoliberal embrace and intensification of depoliticized entertainment, vicarious enjoyment of victory, and so on. The list is impossible to delineate exhaustively, disturbing once more a singular, universal account. But as the cathexes to this set of particular values are intensified, other values lose traction in the broad social fabric: artistic creativity, speculative thinking, and historical curiosity, for example, serve as intriguing exceptions to the general societal will (indeed, mania) to compete in the United States. I focus on changes in social cathexes to map transformations in both the modes of social attachments and the objects of the values we hold, both explicitly and implicitly. *How* we connect to particular ideas, values, and ways of living indicates not only what we care about most deeply, but also the limits of such caring at all.

By taking cool as my heuristic for the social transformations underway in neoliberal social rationalities (and US mainstream culture), I focus not only on the objects of our cathexes, but also on the transforming modes of our cathexes. Coolness connotes an ironic detachment: one is too cool for school, for bourgeois niceties, for legal restrictions, for the banal responsibilities of everyday working life. (It is little wonder that it has largely been coded as a masculinist attitude.)[4] Once more, to strike the pose of cool is to lay claim to "something better, something more." This invocation of a *jouissance* that is beyond the reach of mundane lives is profoundly racialized in the United States, making the commodification of coolness from black culture itself all the more generative for the thinking I undertake in this book. But the precise manner through which coolness has become deracialized also displays itself in the changing mode of cathexis itself.

As I have already noted, the deracialization that occurs in the changing meanings and postures of cool occurs through the stripping of any historical or politicized connotation from the posture of being cool. It empties coolness of any content, rendering it a formal stance of ironic detachment that does not materially stake any claim to "something better, something more." It is stripped of cool's (historical and racialized) *jouissance*. One acts cool, but in a way that is stripped of any historicized meanings; one does not thereby gesture toward any concrete alternative to the dominant attitude from which the posture is allegedly detached. Being cool becomes a purely formal, empty gesture: cool becomes detachment for detachment's sake.

Thinking about these aspects of coolness in relation to the processes and modes of cathexis, then, exposes remarkable transformations underway in our very modes of social cathexis. If we are becoming more and more cool, with less and less sense of the racialized meanings that it has historically connoted, then we are cathecting more and more with detachment (qua detachment). This leads to a pairing of the mode of cathexis with the limits of its reach: we do not care about particular kinds of values, bodies, and lives because of the *cool* manner through which we do care about other values, bodies, and lives. Our modes of cathexes erect and enforce the limits of those cathexes. Becoming what Foucault called "subjects of interests," we may be undergoing a profound change in the very mode through which we cathect any value, thing, person, or idea at all. The ultimate warning of the analyses and arguments put forward in this book may be that, living in these dizzying neoliberal times, we might be well on our way to becoming way too cool.

NEOLIBERALISM IN THE MODERN EPISTEME

Before turning to the detailed development of these various arguments, I must attempt the vexed, extraordinarily thorny project of locating the plane of my analysis with some precision. Trying to write about neoliberalism increasingly feels like trying to catch a moving train, several miles out of the station. Something of a blur, neoliberalism is only more and more difficult to pin down, especially if we assume fixity as a necessary condition for precision—an anachronistic assumption, at best, in the world of hypertechnological speed. Indeed, a remarkably elastic and proliferating set of meanings attaches to the word "neoliberalism" itself in both academic and nonacademic literature. It is, in the early twenty-first century, a quintessentially floating signifier.

Running the gamut of political fealties, it can refer, for its advocates, to the enlightened state of a free market that is the essence of democracy or, for its critics, to the evils of the economic doctrines of globalization, particularly as linked to the IMF and World Bank.[5] These buzzwords of "free market," "regulation," and even "neoliberalism" have undergone that strange process Nietzsche describes in his very early essay "On Truth and Lying in an Extramoral Sense," whereby concepts lose their constructed character through repeated use, just as the distinguishing marks of coins fade, with repeated use, into mere lumps of precious metals. Emptied of content, the categories function as Rorschach figures, soaking up whatever sets of connotations that the particular (pro or con) ideology projects upon them.[6]

The connotations put into circulation are thus the products of the category's ideological development and history, rather than descriptions of historical and material phenomena.[7] The categories function as idealized modes of language, shorn further and further away from the material practices and phenomena they portend to describe with each repeated use. But enlivened by the contemporary political energy around these economic categories, these buzzwords—"neoliberalism," "free market," "regulation"—also harbor a performative power that carries these contrary ideological projects forward, shaping values and lives in unnoticed and pervasive ways. Whether the words connote a set of "naturalized" economic principles that is helping to democratize the world and raise the global standard of living or a set of politicized economic principles that is causing widespread environmental destruction and increased global poverty, whole sets of ideological reverberations are set into play that then reinforce the idealized standpoint from which they originated. This idealized language positions all subjects, despite one's ideological dwelling, as holding sufficient epistemological distance from sociohistorical conditions to proclaim some views as "bad" (perhaps even as "evil," depending on the intensity of the debate) and others as "good"—or, again following Nietzsche's early essay, as "false" and "true." The problem becomes, as Althusser presciently argued in 1970, ideology all the way down.[8] Hermetically sealed in a structurally solipsistic hall of mirrors, these ideological accusations can ricochet back and forth endlessly—and often viciously, as the polarized contemporary politics of the United States shows all too poignantly. We become trapped, again in Lacanian terms, at the strictly binary plane of the imaginary, with its endless battles of ego-driven comparisons.

This project aims to intercede in this idealizing and obfuscating logic of ideology that structures so many of our analyses of this Rorschach figure, "neoliberalism." If we remain in an exclusively ideological mode of analysis, we will fail to see this idealizing effect of the language of neoliberalism and thereby mistake the category for the thing. One of the central problematics obscuring our analyses of neoliberalism is thereby an overreliance on ideological analytics. That is, if we frame neoliberalism exclusively as a matter of ideological manipulation, we may inadvertently naturalize the very phenomena (say, the free market or the savvy consumer) we are hoping to call into question. In an effort to short-circuit this ideological warfare, I frame neoliberalism as a late iteration of the modern episteme Foucault excavates in *The Order of Things*.

In that remarkable, groundbreaking work, Foucault develops the concept of the episteme as a description of new forms of knowledge that reflect and initiate material shifts across a range of social registers. The framework of an episteme refers both to systems of representation (for example, the norm, the rule, the system as he locates them in biology, economics, and philology) and to the material iterations of those systems. It embraces multiple registers of dominant rationalities (economic, sociological, educational, medical, subjective, political, and so on) without getting sidetracked by classically nineteenth-century concerns about the origins or dialectical development of such rationalities. In an episteme, dominant rationalities proliferate across multiple registers in ways that duplicate, contradict, overlap, and stand alone as unique iterations. When Foucault examines, for example, the emergence of the human sciences, he locates multiple modes of representing and analyzing "man" that bring this category into widespread focus. The schematic of the episteme affords an emphasis on both differentiating rationalities (for example, the rationality of demography and that of the individual) and common sets of categories (for example, "man").

By reading neoliberalism as a late and still developing iteration of the modern episteme, I disaggregate and analyze the new epistemic and material practices that go under this name, "neoliberalism." Neoliberalism emerges from multiple sites, ranging from economic theorists and the practices they influence to the technologically enabled globalized routes of trade and education that emerge in the late twentieth century. When Foucault locates neoliberalism at the center of biopolitics in his 1979 lectures, he pushes us to see how it operates in innumerable social registers. The schematic of the episteme allows us to see how neoliberalism functions in multiple registers beyond those of the economic and the political—or the market and the state. It allows us to see that the "new" aspects of neoliberalism constitute new modes of not only economic rationality, concepts, and practices, but also social rationality, concepts, and practices.

In the United States, as I analyze and demonstrate across this book, the language of neoliberalism has taken and is continuing to take root in the social fabric, both explicitly and unwittingly. For example, in the midst and subsequent wake of the economic downturn of 2008, the mantras of privatization, deregulation, and the free market abounded in public discourse, encouraging us all to debate, with varying degrees of ignorance and intuitive insight, whether and how the federal government should intervene in the crashing of industries, the freezing of credit markets, and the skyrocketing of unemployment. But more implicitly and insidiously, the noneconomic language and social values of neoliberalism, such as individual interests, entrepreneurial schemes, and maximizing choices, have become part of the lingua franca of mainstream culture in the United States: they are circulating unconsciously as constitutive elements of this new iteration of the modern episteme that we can name "neoliberalism." The schematic of the episteme allows us to analyze these particular normative terms and social rationalities. It allows us to analyze, as I do in chapters 1 and 2, how neoliberalism initiates new representations of social authority that alter processes of subject formation. It allows us to analyze, as I do chapters 3, 4, and 5, how cultural practices within this neoliberal social rationality transform our modes of social cathexes that subsequently empty categories of social difference (race, gender, sexuality, class) of their critical historical reference and weight. And it allows us to analyze, as I do in chapter 6, how these neoliberal social rationalities erode our traditional understandings of ethics, demanding fresh imaginings to salvage any meaningful sense of the ethical. Consequently, in the analyses and arguments that follow, I call neoliberalism by the shorthand of an episteme and approach it through the multiple social rationalities that constitute this late and still developing iteration of the modern, liberal, and capitalist episteme.

To derive this episteme, I begin with a focus on theoretical accounts of neoliberalism, especially those of Foucault's 1979 lectures, the texts of early theorists of neoliberalism (especially the Chicago School), and contemporary theoretical critiques of neoliberalism. This kind of theoretical approach sets clear parameters around the kinds of claims I can and cannot make. I understand this problematic as the unavoidable requirements of intentionality and demarcation, whereby we must foreground, background, and delimit our objects of analyses at the expense of other objects. Framing the location of my analysis in theoretical accounts as a kind of phenomenological horizon, I understand my methodology as undertaking what Husserl called an eidetic reduction, whereby we can artificially strip away the richly variegated, material instantiations of neoliberal practices in an effort to distill the "essence" of the thing-in-itself. Such a methodology is clearly not in vogue in these post-poststructuralist times, especially with the thorough critiques of essentialism from queer, antiracist, and decolonial feminists (myself included). I do not intend to take us back to any kind of flatfooted universalism; rather, I invoke a Husserlian eidetic reduction to indicate how my embrace of the theoretical clearly renders this account abstracted from the kinds of materialist analyses of neoliberalism widely underway across contemporary scholarship. Knowing that the alleged "thing-in-itself" is always already the thing-as-it-exists, I frame this as an examination of the "essence" of neoliberalism to indicate how, taking various theoretical accounts as the point of departure, I develop a careful taxonomy of the dominant categories and operative modes of rationality enacted in this late iteration of the modern episteme neoliberalism.

A SLOW FUGUE: RACE AND ETHICS

With a focus on the transformations in subject formation, race and other forms of social difference, and ethics, the complexity of my analyses of this neoliberal episteme expands and intensifies considerably. First of all, as I elaborate at great length in chapter 1, Foucault's lectures on neoliberalism are also remarkable lectures on classical liberalism: he insists, over and over, that theories and practices we might call "neoliberal" emerge out of the intensifying of theories and practices of classical liberalism. Taking that as my point of departure, I add several historical and epistemological periods to my analysis of the neoliberal episteme. Riffing on the fabulous title page of Elizabeth Povinelli's *Economies of Abandonment*, where she sketches various historical moments and registers of this neoliberal iteration of the modern episteme as a musical score, I understand the work of this book as an analysis of a rich historical fugue.

An appropriately eighteenth-century musical form, the fugue is made up of two or more voices that take up the central theme or melody of the composition at different pitches. These then develop into distinct iterations of the same melodic thread that recur frequently throughout the composition. I invoke this as a loose metaphor for the many historical threads of this book. As such, the many voices of the fugue under analysis here include the following phenomena: the transatlantic slave trade in the eighteenth and nineteenth centuries; classical liberalism; the psychosexual history of chattel slavery; the Civil Rights Movement, feminist movement, and the emergence of identity politics in the 1960s; Marxist theories of social change, especially Althusser's accounts of ideology and interpellation; multiculturalism in the 1980s; diversity and color-blindness from the 1990s through the 2010s; the attack on the United States known as "9/11" (2001); the layered debacles leading to and emergent from Hurricane Katrina (2005); and, finally, the #BlackLivesMatter movement that is literally emerging as I send this book to the final stages of publication (December 2014). These are the sociopolitical and epistemic frameworks as well as the historical benchmarks that structure this book and often serve as the objects of analysis. By placing my analyses in this fugue, I argue that the most pressing transformation underway in the neoliberal episteme is the twinned erasure of race and ethics from our social lexicon.

While I have sketched how the transformations in cool indicate a deracializing of social life, the mechanisms through which I make that argument in the book have remarkable reach. The particular details of the transformations in processes of subject formation that I excavate and analyze (for example, changing concepts of the individual, of the subject, of social authority, of freedom, of arbiters of truth, of binding social fantasies, of normativity, and of metrics of meaning) directly impact our concepts of social difference and, concomitantly, our understandings of ethics. First of all, given the ascendancy of fungibility as a social metric that alters the dominant concepts of social difference (gender, class, race, sexuality, ability), I argue that the erasure of race and racialization functions on a different historical axis from other modes of social difference. Consequently, as a thinker grounded in both a feminist and a post-Hegelian lineage of thinking about ethics, where the figure of the Other constitutes the ethical scene, this also means that the erasure of race is foundational to the erosion of the very possibility of a meaningful language of ethics in the contemporary United States. The central concern of this book is to decipher this twinned erasure and, more urgently, to speculate what it might even mean to live ethically.

Once again, to do so has required a very careful step beyond the ideological analyses that abound regarding neoliberalism, including those emergent out of leftist social theory. While I frame neoliberalism as a late iteration of the modern episteme and focus on its manifestations as a social rationality, it clearly did emerge as a set of economic doctrines. My emphasis on social rationalities and subject formation does not imply that there is nothing ideologically afoot in the materialization of neoliberal economic principles. Indeed, given the dire consequences of the last three decades (using the historical benchmarks of Thatcherism and Reaganomics to track its ascent), we must heed the critical appraisals of neoliberalism as an economic doctrine that has resulted in a vast array of political and ethical problems.

The list of topics can be dizzying: structural, gross disparities in wealth and poverty, globally and locally; long-term resource depletion and environmental destruction; human rights violations in and around the workplace; the persistent economics of racism and the dismantling of public education; and so on. Led particularly by astute work by feminist and critical race theorists, this scholarship is calling out one of the central ethical dilemmas of our neoliberal times, namely, the structured production of gendered and racialized poverty, along with horrific human rights violations, by the widespread embrace of neoliberalism's economic mantras of deregulation and privatization.[9] Early neoliberal theorists, most famously perhaps Milton Friedman, argued that a truly free market and the triumph of pure entrepreneurial opportunity would ultimately erase any such structural poverty.[10] For overdeveloped countries that have embraced these neoliberal practices and principles, the exposure of these structured socioeconomic disparities presents an aporia, a true failure of neoliberal modes of reflection to address, much less solve, the fundamental violence against human lives exposed by the scholarship.

Rather than analyze them as ethical problems, however, these examples of structural violence are most often conceptualized in one of these two ways: (a) for defenders of the free market economics of neoliberalism, the problems are framed in exactly the manner that early neoliberal theorists conceptualized such problems, namely, as merely contemporary misfortunes that the long-term work of the free market will eventually solve; (b) for critics of the free market of neoliberalism, the analysis is most often constrained by an implicitly Marxist framework, advancing an ideological analysis that conceptualizes neoliberalism strictly within the confines of the economic and the political.[11] Consequently, while the critical scholarship exposes these ethical problems of structural deleterious effects and thereby stirs intense affective responses to them, it fails to offer conceptual resources for engaging them explicitly as ethical problems: invoking anger, indignation, and sometimes rather ugly self-righteousness, these leftist critiques most often fuel ideological warfare, not ethical reflection. The aim of this project is, through the excavation of the formal transformations of the category of social difference (especially race) and our cathexis to it, to develop a taxonomy of the shifts implicated in and producing these deep ethical aporia of these neoliberal times. And this problem, which seems to be spreading and worsening constantly, is urgent.

But this does not mean it is a crisis, the dramatic temporality that seems to be absorbing our understandings of change, turmoil, and even emergency. To be a crisis is to enter a completely different temporality than that of everyday, banal life. In crisis, everything accelerates: decision processes, communication modes, resource procurement of whatever sorts. Extraordinary demands are levied and, bending to the genre and temporality of crisis, are met with no questions. It puts us into overdrive. Entering this extra-ordinary time and space, we are expected to suspend all regular activity to meet these extra-ordinary demands. Ironically, however, while the break from the ordinary defines crisis, the response to crisis demands one of our most ordinary habits in the overdeveloped world: problem-solving. We are, it seems, made for crisis. It should be unsurprising, then, that we seem to thrive in crisis so intensely. Out of crises come heroes—those who meet the crisis with courage and, in true superhero form, wrangle it, manage it, and lay it to rest. Crises make our adrenaline flow, giving us the hyperaesthetic stimulation that makes life meaningful in the overdeveloped world: may we all have the opportunity to be Superman—or, at least, to catapult him into action. Crises feed our craving for spectacle, complete with its clear narrative arc of beginning, middle, and end. Reduced to these formal qualities, crises are now fed to us serially by our multiple media screens in the overdeveloped world.

But the logic of crisis also has deep roots in leftist social theory. Marxist and neo-Marxist theorists continually write toward the historical moment when capitalism will find itself in crisis, engaging the future-anterior temporality as the horizon of critique. The language of revolution is almost always the language of crisis, which is one way that the language of crisis has absorbed our notions of social change. This came through particularly clearly in the kinds of reflections we heard in the media and blogosphere when the Occupy Wall Street movement erupted in the fall of 2011. Cynics of various ideologies (left, right, center) mused over how this could be a "revolution" when the participants were using i-Technology to telecast their happenings and communicate with one another, while stopping by Starbucks for a quick jolt. The hyperboles aside, the point in this kind of rhetoric is the demand that social change look like revolution—with its drama, violence, and demand for abrupt, clearly demarcated, directly contradictory change. And the language of that change is crisis. (If the #BlackLivesMatter movement is to develop a critically new antiracist lexicon, it must avoid the temporality of crisis.)

The problems I am excavating here do not track along these temporal, social, or affective registers of crisis. Given Milton Friedman's direct embrace of crisis as the moment that neoliberal economic-political theorists should await and then seize, we should at least pause before embracing it as the temporal horizon of critique.[12] Subsequently, the analysis I develop here of the shifts in our categories of social difference and ethics over the last forty to eighty years (depending on the preferred time chart) operates in a much slower time frame, despite the hypertechnological accelerations of the last couple of decades.[13] It is a slow, rich fugue that I invoke and analyze across these pages. In this slower rhythm, the accounts I develop are not trying to track or analyze dramatic social change, such as that which we might find in moments of crisis—or hope for in revolutionary garb. I am not a theorist of social movements, although I analyze contemporary social phenomena, especially those involving race. Rather, I aim to analyze subtle shifts in subjectivity that are the epiphenomena of the encroachment of neoliberal market rationalities upon the various social spheres in which we in overdeveloped countries live—from education and popular culture to personal modes of reflection and decisions ranging from romance to career to religious practices to childbirth. Following out a Foucaultian analysis, which I will develop in great detail, I contend that the cultural transformations underway are remarkably slow. Involving intensifications of previously existent categories, values, and practices, the alterations emerge out of and layer upon existent social formations, sedimenting into a kind of glacial formation that is most legible in its crevices, thresholds, and fault lines. And, needless to say, glacial time is far from the time of crisis.

I thus agree with Elizabeth Povinelli's reorientation of our analytic focus in *Economies of Abandonment* from crises, catastrophes, and events to forms of living that she describes as "ordinary, chronic, and cruddy" (13). I agree that it is only through this kind of reorientation that we can begin to understand what is happening ethically in neoliberal social rationalities. When crisis invokes the transcendence of the ordinary, it locates the ethical as an extra-ordinary moment detached from the banal activities and values of our lives. As such, whether emerging out of ideological critiques generated by the political right or left (including leftist social theory), such an understanding of ethics tends to be projective, rather than intro-jective or even self-reflective. It is a continuation of the Rorschach effect of idealized categories, now tricked out in the truly blinding dazzle of crisis. It is about pointing fingers, finding others at fault, claiming a (if not the) higher moral ground—indeed, it is about morality and all of its self-righteous certainty; it is not about ethics and an abiding reflection on the deep histories of the categories through which we govern and modes through which we cathect relationships to ourselves and others.

For example, the recurrent refrain so often used in these serial crises comes in the language of morality: villain and victim; corrupt and innocent; and, increasingly, terrorist and civilian. As a moralism serving ideological warfare, these categories assume moral qualities that simultaneously bear the labor of racializing the social world in facially neutral terms. That is, the categories used to call out "moral evils" also enact racializing schemes, depending once more on one's left or right ideological dwelling to determine the assignments at one end of the spectrum or the other of the clearly bifurcated zone of judgment. This elision of ethics and racializing schemas in the language of morality enacts some of the central mechanisms, especially erasure and disavowal, of the neoliberal episteme that I analyze across this book.

This book thereby attempts to offer an account of one of the most pressing problems in contemporary overdeveloped cultures that are materially benefiting from the incursion of neoliberal social rationalities into so many areas of living, namely, ethics. While I agree with

Povinelli's situating of these social transformations in the spaces of ordinary lived experiences, I depart considerably from both the affective registers and the geopsychic locations of her analyses. As with so many critiques inspired by Agamben and his rich concept of bare life, Povinelli locates her analyses in the sociopsychic space of the "ordinary, chronic, and cruddy" suffering of the abandoned. The proliferation of scholarship on this broad affective register has produced a fairly extensive lexicon to name various aspects and emphases of these disturbing phenomena: precarity, abandonment, dispossession, vulnerability, austerity, and the like.[14] These incisive analyses are a crucial part of excavating the kinds of ethical aporia I am describing. But I am forging a different path.

By investigating cool as a transforming aesthetics, I focus on the changing experiences, representations, and politics of pleasure, not pain. In this, I agree with Tim Dean's curiosity about the trend in scholarship on biopolitics to emphasize, in broad terms, the Agamben-inspired registers of bare life, precarity, abandonment, and so on. As Dean puts it, "There is plenty of pain and injustice but very little pleasure" in these critiques.[15] While I agree with Dean that part of this occlusion may be caused by the difficulty of thinking pleasure—indeed, of experiencing it, as Foucault noted so often—I also think it has much to do with the geopsychic location of these proliferating critiques of biopolitics. Ironically, this pervasive focus on the violently destructive effects of contemporary power is often driven, at least partially and sometimes explicitly, by Foucault's searing analyses of the myriad forms of biopower's normalizing functions.[16] But well beyond Foucaultian scholarship, critical theorists trained in a variety of leftist social theory traditions focus on the material damages wrought by biopolitics, even if also charting its psychosocial, affective registers. As critique, this scholarship apparently must expose unseen, sometimes unrecognized violence. And this, in turn, leads one to focus *outward*—whether to other geographic regions of the world, nation, city, or neighborhood—from the first-world position of "the typing left," as Jodi Dean so wonderfully calls critical theorists. It leads critical theorists to turn to "other" experiences of biopolitics, often following the well-worn rut of calling out the "victims."

Examining the neoliberal episteme in its most ordinary of iterations, I insist that we must also analyze it in its first-world instantiations. To do so, I follow Foucault's provocations and examine the transformations in one of the first world's most vaunted spoils: pleasure. No longer those delicious transgressions that we once called "guilty pleasures," the experiences that we now call "pleasurable" in the overdeveloped world feed on the endless stimulation of the most superficial sort. They spin us, as I develop in psychoanalytic language in chapter 3, endlessly in the kinetic circuit of the drive. This transformation in how we understand and practice "pleasure" has profound implications. In the history of cool I have already sketched, for example, racism in the United States is animated by an unspoken suspicion that the Other possesses greater *jouissance*; to render pleasure superficial is thus to occlude the capacity to cathect this long historical social dynamic, thereby falling unconsciously into the pernicious postrace mantras of color-blindness. Subsequently, this transformation in concepts and practices of pleasure also enables the aestheticizing of ethical atrocities of the late twentieth and early twenty-first centuries in all their most banal iterations. This transformation in our concepts and practices of "pleasure," I argue, is at the heart of how we seem to be well on our way to becoming way too cool.

By rooting my cultural analyses in the mainstream contemporary United States, I am trying to grasp these banal transformations that are underway where neoliberalism as an economic policy is materially benefiting many lives, albeit in starkly stratified manners, and where neoliberalism as a social rationality is increasingly the lingua franca. Trying to think from the perspective where we are all arguably becoming neoliberal in our modes of reflection and cathexes, I argue we cannot rely upon invoking guilt or shame as a mode of ethical response. If my analysis of coolness is at all correct, such modes of social cathexes have eroded, if not evaporated, across the variegated social fabric of the United States. Nor can we remain within the realm of the strictly political, given my protracted argument against ideological interpellation as a sufficient analytic for neoliberal social rationalities. Therefore, we must also consider the transformations in our modes of ethical reflection from the changing sociopsychic position of those who are, albeit still in starkly stratified ways, empowered and privileged by neoliberalism. Speaking from that position, it seems to me, drastically attenuates our ability to reflect ethically on issues, questions, and modes of living. To reflect ethically is virtually an aporia in contemporary cultures under the sway of neoliberal social rationalities.

Granted, this does not mean that we realize or admit this. To the contrary, as ethics centers proliferate across universities and ethics boards continue to grow in hospitals and corporations, we have apparently become quite proficient at "doing ethics." Or, as Nietzsche might correct us, in "doing morals." We neoliberals have no hesitation in delineating and then laying claim to the higher moral ground. We have no hesitation in calculating the goods and evils attached to a wide variety of issues and interventions, whether medical, military, economic, legal, or penal. But this kind of neoutilitarian mode of calculation, often unreflectively reliant on statistics, never questions the normative edifice upon which "moral problems" are culturally cast: it is not what I mean by thinking ethics. To think, reflect, and perhaps even live in a register that we might deem "ethical" requires a kind of speculative thinking that asks questions beyond the habitual epistemological frameworks of one's culture. Uninterested in neat or tidy calculations of "good" or "correct" behaviors, this kind of speculation challenges the terms in which such questions are cast by asking them from a very different angle. A kind of fulcrum that shifts the focus of thinking and cathexis, it opens onto different fields of values, where economic productivity, in whatever alluring guise, is not the final arbiter or constitutive epistemology.

NEOLIBERAL TALK

Neoliberalism has become, as I have said, one of those floating signifiers that mean everything, and consequently nothing. A kind of overdetermined Rorschach figure, it is freighted with a wide array of fears, hopes, desires, and politics. By locating it as a still ascending social rationality in the mainstream culture of the United States, I am interested in both how neoliberalism speaks and where it sputters.

Across this book, I argue that this sly, new social rationality speaks in the language of cool. It seduces us to see ourselves as living across a smooth, cool façade that is remarkably interesting, endlessly stimulating. This language of cool bends the history of coolness to its particular iteration and thereby enacts some of the most important transformations of this new social rationality: the aestheticizing of living itself and all its messiness (love, politics, violence, pleasure, and so on); the erasure of histories, especially those of violence and conflict, and the evacuation of their force or meaning in this dazzling space of the present; and the aspiration to flatten all other social evaluations to this singular metric, coolness.

I have tried to stir some of our social cathexes to this aesthetics of cool and to map some of its stammerings. To do so, I have interspersed "Interludes of Cool" between each chapter. Not any kind of history of cool, these serve as snapshots of various historical representations of cool across the last sixty years in the United States. My hope is that they will conjure both these social memories of and cathexes to this changing aesthetics of cool. Rhetorically, they serve as epigraphs to the chapters that immediately follow and I recommend reading them as such. They follow the argument of the book, not any linear or even scattered account of the development of cool.

The argument itself follows this outline. In chapter 1, I offer a careful reading of Foucault's 1979 lectures on neoliberalism, *The Birth of Biopolitics*. While these lectures are well circulated and known, I insist on a careful reading of them both to complicate our readings of Foucault and to lay the groundwork for the analyses I develop across the book. Locating myself in Foucault's texts, I explore the implications of a nonideological approach to neoliberalism. More specifically, I excavate the central categorical and epistemological transformations that, Foucault argues, occur in the shifts from classical liberalism to neoliberalism: the sites and mechanisms of truth (from the contract to the market; from the protection of ownership to the expansion of maximizing interests); dominant social values (from utility to human capital); concepts of freedom (from Rights of Man to subjects of interests); concepts of subjectivity (from "citizen" to "entrepreneur"); and modes of rationality (from juridical to calculative). This may be the most uncool chapter of the book, but the analyses executed across the rest of the book rely entirely upon it.

Chapter 2 then explores the stakes of a nonideological analysis of neoliberal social rationalities and practices. As such, I understand these analyses as accentuating and elaborating, rather than proving "wrong" in some facile manner, the rich scholarship of ideological critique of neoliberalism. The focus of the chapter is Althusserian interpellation, which continues to serve as the primary framework for most readings of subject formation, social discourses, and possibilities of resistance in neoliberalism. By following out the argument that the classic social authority of the symbolic function is waning in the neoliberal episteme, I argue that Althusserian interpellation fails to capture the kinds of subject formation underway in it. I then draw the connection directly to the Althusserian conceptualizations of social difference that we inherit from early theorists of queer theory, specifically Judith Butler and José Esteban Muñoz. By tracing the Althusserian roots of these two theorists, I demonstrate how the dominant understandings of gender and race spawned by queer theory may be insufficient for thinking resistance in the neoliberal episteme. This intervention thereby accentuates the emergent line of critique of queer theory's long-standing fealty to antinormativity, especially as a problematic way of conceiving resistance in the neoliberal episteme.[17] Having problematized Althusserian interpellation as a sufficient framework for reading neoliberal subject formation, I conclude the chapter with an examination of the carceral state as a contemporary social site where the Althusserian reading of Repressive State Apparati still captures the racism of this institution. This initiates my rethinking of race away from the legacies of identity politics, which Antonio Viego places in the Lacanian imaginary, and toward reading race as the real that jams the neoliberal machine.

Chapter 3 shifts gears entirely into the Lacanian lexicon to examine precisely how the dominant fantasies of classical liberalism, tolerance and neutrality, are transforming in the neoliberal episteme and its embrace of the fantasy of instant wealth. Developing Jodi Dean's provocation that subjective formation in neoliberalism is structured by a shift from desire to the drive, I show how this manifests in a gradual social tendency toward formalizing social difference itself. Specifically, I show how the neoliberal embrace of the fantasy of instant wealth turns on a waning social cathexis to both utility and xenophobia, the respective bedrocks (*objet a*) of the doubled liberal fantasies of neutrality and tolerance. With a focus on how this formalizes the concepts of social difference, I conclude the chapter with the implications of these transformations for meanings, modes, and cathexes to normativity in the neoliberal social rationality of calculation, especially in the exemplar of statistics, and with the implications of the transformation of concepts of social difference into units of fungibility. While this is also not a particularly cool chapter, it is only after clearing this ground that I can begin turning toward rethinking race as the real.

In chapter 4, I turn to the category of social difference that carries out this neoliberal formalization into fungible units most clearly: gender. I begin with a protracted discussion of the racialized history of cool to schematize what this means for the neoliberal transformations in concepts of social difference per se. I then focus on two contemporaneous examples from the United States in the late twentieth century, one from popular culture, the other from academic culture: metrosexuality and the theory of gender performativity. First, I return to the Althusserian concept of gender that we inherit from early queer theory, especially the infamous text *Gender Trouble* by Judith Butler. By bringing Tim Dean's work on the imaginary status of gender in Butler's work to bear on my Foucaultian call for a nonideological analysis of the neoliberal episteme, I explore whether the remarkable popularity of this text exposes it as a kind of neoliberal playbook. Drawing explicitly on Milton Friedman's celebrations of nonconformity, I then turn to the cultural example of metrosexuality to argue that gender has become a kind of playground for neoliberal social rationalities and practices. Gender offers up superficial spaces that are easily evacuated of any historical meanings and that are thus served up for endless self-enhancement and manipulation. Intensified through a transformation of class into consumerism, gender has become an o so cool accessory. It aestheticizes cultural representations of nonnormative sexuality, especially those that go under the now fully legible categories of gay and lesbian. I conclude the chapter with speculations on what forms of social difference may still harbor the long-standing "somatic xenophobia" that the neoliberal episteme aspires to repress.

Chapter 5 answers this question directly: race. With theoretical roots in various strands of queer theory and the Lacanian analyses of neoliberalism, I argue that we must read race as the real. Consequently, this intervenes in these theoretical fields in the following manner: (1) it extends and problematizes the Lacanian-Marxian analyses of neoliberalism (especially those of Žižek and Jodi Dean), which read race as (merely) a problem of ideology in the register of the imaginary; (2) it insists that the psychoanalytic work of queer theory (especially that of Bersani and Tim Dean) must attend to the racializing aspects of the drive and the real; and (3) it accentuates and deepens the sociological and historical work of queer of color critique (especially that of Muñoz, Ferguson, Shah, and Reddy) by bringing forth the transforming dynamics of social cathexis, along with a fundamental challenge to liberal and Althusserian concepts of consciousness, embedded in the reading of race as the real.

Following the elaboration of these theoretical interventions, I turn to the persistence of racism in the contemporary United States to argue, through analyses of "the ghetto tax" and the racialized wealth gap, that the limits to the neoliberal transformation of class into consumerism turn on one obstinate historical vector: race. I develop this argument further through analyses of Barack Obama's two most important speeches (prior to August 2014) on race and racism, "A More Perfect Union" of 2008 and the response in 2013 to the verdict in the Trayvon Martin murder case, as well as through an analysis of the responses to the murder of Trayvon Martin.[18] I then turn directly to the mutual constitution of sexuality with race and place the meteorite ascendancy of the political movement to legalize same-sex marriage in the United States in a crucial and crucially overlooked contemporaneous institutional emergence: the carceral state. By analyzing (and graphing) the simultaneous historical emergence of the racist carceral state and the political movement to legalize same-sex marriage, I argue that this contemporaneous expansion of rights to a particular kind of same-sex relationship and contraction of rights from a clearly racialized portion of the population capture the kinds of transformations underway in gender, sexuality, class, and race in these dizzying neoliberal times. The historical simultaneity of these two phenomena exemplifies a biopolitics of cool, wherein the malleability to become the neoliberal cool allows the expansion of social life and the incitement to make one set of people live (in very particular and normal ways), while the failure to become the neoliberal cool, despite having birthed cool, becomes a mode of social abandonment that lets another set of people die. Consequently, I conclude by elaborating my fundamental conviction and provocation that, amid these confusing and kinetic neoliberal times, a singular vector of social difference in the United States remains, obstinately, at the level of the real: race.

This initiates the final meditation of the book: the doubled, deeply intertwining aporia of race and ethics in the neoliberal episteme. Having argued that race functions differently from other modes of social difference in neoliberal social rationalities and practices, I articulate it in chapter 6 explicitly in the Lacanian register of the real. My hope is to stir some awareness of the asignifying, persistent force of the long violent history of racism in the slow fugue that is the complex social field of the contemporary United States—a history that I name the censored chapter of our American grammar. With the help of Lacan's 1962–63 seminar, *Anxiety*, I draw out the depersonalizing aspects of anxiety as it signals the real to argue, through a meditation on the contemporary cultural anxiety regarding race, for a reconceptualization of race away from identity categories and politics. I then develop a Lacanian reading of Kantian ethics, extending what Alenka Zupančič calls "an ethics of the Real," to argue that ethics in the neoliberal United States must always be an ethics of race. The erasure of race and ethics is a doubled erasure. To develop this in a cultural mode, I conclude with a meditation on New Orleans, a city that helped to birth cool so long ago, and the nonevent of Hurricane Katrina as an illuminating site of this doubled aporia and what it might mean to approach both race and ethics as the real.

To do all this work, we must become adept at reflecting on both our modes and our objects of social cathexes. In the idiom of this book, we must become adept at reflecting on how and when and where we speak the language of cool. The Interludes of Cool that punctuate this book-length argument are my effort to speak in this neoliberal idiom and to stir some cathexes with it. My hope, in so doing, is not simply to interrupt it. Interruption requires a firm and clear stance outside of the conversation underway, and I am deeply skeptical that we can lay claim to any such space or language, enmeshed as we are in the neoliberal episteme. My hope, rather, is to speak in the language of neoliberalism just fluently enough to find where it sputters, stammers, comes to a halt. Given the sly powers of this new social rationality's seduction, stirring this cathexis and speaking in this language are dangerous. But I see no other option. And so I hope to strike the pose, to speak in the language of cool, while still remaining so uncool.

CHAPTER ONE

Excavating Categories

FOUCAULT'S *BIRTH OF BIOPOLITICS*

Of all the work on neoliberalism, I have chosen Foucault's 1979 lectures, *The Birth of Biopolitics*, as the most valuable point of departure for two basic reasons. First and foremost, the analyses Foucault undertakes in these lectures reorient current approaches to neoliberalism historically and epistemologically. Historically, as I will elaborate, he begins not in the 1970s or even the 1920s, but in the eighteenth century. This longer historical arc brings his discussion of neoliberalism into the sociohistorical fugue that frames this book. Epistemologically, Foucault does not analyze sociological and historical effects of economic practices. Rather, he analyzes the transformations of the categories central to the reworking of the economic, political, and social worlds by neoliberal theorists. This excavation of the central, constitutive categories of neoliberalism, especially as produced through an intensification of the central, constitutive categories of classical liberalism, grounds my thinking about this current historical present. It initiates the Husserlian eidetic reduction that I described in the introduction.

Second, as is well known by now, Foucault argues in these lectures that neoliberalism expands its market rationality beyond the strictly economic domain to create a new social rationality with the causal power to produce new enterprising subjectivities—what he calls "subjects of interest." This emergent account of subject formation in the early neoliberal theorists partially grounds Foucault's insistence that neoliberalism does not function (solely) as an ideology. Calling it "one of the most important theoretical transformations in Western thought since the Middle Ages," Foucault emphatically proclaims this new account of subject formation to be a profound alteration in the modern episteme.[1] In what I fear is but another mark of our neoliberal times, however, we seem to have reduced this radically new subject formation to a banal truism. The claim that neoliberalism turns us all into enterprising entrepreneurs seems to roll off our tongues without a single flinch. By turning to these lectures in great detail, I hope to reignite some of the awe in which Foucault held this transformation in subject formation (and, by extension, in social cathexes). I hope to begin mapping the full impact of this kind of profound transformation in subjectivity and subject formation.

While not wanting to add yet another exegesis of these lectures to the already robust body of such valuable scholarship,[2] I offer this close reading of them to excavate the exact categories that frame my larger project here. For readers already familiar with the lectures, parts of this reading may seem elementary or even pedantic; it may also read as an exegesis. (This is definitely the most uncool chapter of the book.) As with so much scholarship engaging Foucault, however, I argue that careful, detailed attention to the complexity of his analyses generates remarkably fruitful avenues of inquiry. Through a selective excavation of some of the dominant categories at work in Foucault's 1979 lectures, I locate those sites where the emergence of neoliberalism intensifies categories of liberalism that subsequently do not track along the trajectories of (loosely Marxian) ideological analyses. This then sets the framework for my larger investigation into the transformation in the categories and processes of subject formation, social difference, and subsequently ethics.

"IT'S NOT AN IDEOLOGY!"

Despite the title of the lectures, *The Birth of Biopolitics*, Foucault never turns to biopolitics at all. Apparently caught in the complexity of its birthing, the entire course at the Collège de France is dedicated to a detailed account of neoliberalism, which he positions as the birth-site of contemporary biopolitics. Standing at an interesting juncture in his writing—between the analyses of power offered in *Discipline and Punish* and *The History of Sexuality*, volume 1, and the turn to the care of the self in volumes 2 and 3 of *The History of Sexuality*—these lectures on neoliberalism offer a fascinating lynchpin, of sorts, to the complex questions of the subjectivation of power as well as to the shift in Foucault's thinking about subjectivity and ethics that we also see in this transitional period of his work. Over thirty years later, they feel remarkably timely, even urgent, for deciphering Foucault's most persistent object of study—our historical present.

Unlike David Harvey's self-avowed "brief" history of neoliberalism, Foucault situates his discussion in a much longer historical arc than the majority of scholars currently writing about this new form of economics. Rather than tracing the emergence of neoliberalism to the 1960s of the Chicago School or even to the mid-twentieth-century debates of Karl Polyani, Foucault begins with mid-eighteenth-century French and British economists. While still arguing that neoliberalism is a qualitatively new and different kind of social rationality that takes hold, with shades of different emphases, in Germany, France, and the United States in the early (not mid- or late) twentieth century, he nonetheless locates some of its roots in practices and values of liberalism in the mid-eighteenth century. This broader historical orientation, which Foucault explicitly marks as echoing his approaches to madness, criminality, and sexuality, sets his discussion of neoliberalism in a historical time frame that is incommensurate with the ideological framework that dominates so much of the scholarship critical of neoliberal policies and practices.

While neoliberalism undoubtedly functions very much like an ideology, particularly in areas of the world where it arrives in the explicitly marked western form of neocolonialism in economic policies, the conceptual framework of ideology limits our understanding of it and thereby dangerously narrows our vision of possible resistances to it. David Harvey's account, along with the work of critics such as Henry Giroux, David Theo Goldberg, and Lisa Duggan, falls into this limited framework, arguing that neoliberalism is driven by a fairly conscious, intentional, and structural effort to restore class power to the elite wealthy, both nationally and globally. While that ideologically framed critique functions quite valuably as a mode of consciousness-raising regarding the pernicious effects of neoliberalism, such work is (as we also see in the history of feminist and antiracist praxis) intellectually, politically, and, most of all, psychologically necessary—but it is also insufficient. As Beatrice Han notes, "Foucault rejects the [Marxist] hypothesis that only an increase in awareness could liberate the oppressed class from ideological fictions."[3] As I will elaborate throughout this project, the mode of subjectivation at work in neoliberalism no longer succumbs to the principles of interpellation that undergird the hopes of these kind of consciousness-raising analyses. In a move that deepens and extends, without contesting or antagonizing, the political work of these ideological critiques of neoliberalism, I turn to Foucault's lectures in an effort to develop a differently situated approach to these widespread phenomena that we are labeling "neoliberalism." We need a more robust analysis of neoliberalism—one that includes attention to vectors such as ethics, affect, social difference, and subjectivity—to understand, not to mention to uproot or actively dislodge, this powerfully subtle *episteme*.

Consequently, as Thomas Lemke, Wendy Brown, and Jeffrey Nealon have all recognized, perhaps the most strident and provocative aspect of Foucault's reading of neoliberalism is precisely his insistence that we not take it up as an ideology. This is also arguably the most difficult task presented to us, given my introductory discussion of the current discursive terrain and its valorization of the very categories of neoliberalism, such as the "free market," as part of "the natural order." But Foucault warns us in "Truth and Power" that ideological critique activates three epistemic habits that are, in turn, central to the biopolitics of normalization, namely, concepts of a truth, a subject, and an economic structure that all claim to transcend historico-political mutations.[4] The transformation of each of these concepts becomes the foci of his account of neoliberalism in *The Birth of Biopolitics*. Attuning us to the fine contours of their historical mutations, he clearly wishes to disabuse us of these epistemological habits. But, as Foucault also well knows, they are not purely or exclusively epistemological habits. And so ridding ourselves of them is not purely an intellectual—or ideological—matter.

The lectures are sprinkled with explicit remarks about the confines of a Marxist analysis. Never framed as "wrong" or "false," Marxist analyses are critiqued and avoided because the kinds of conceptual demarcations that they assume and enact no longer hold the same kind of traction in the neoliberal iteration of the modern episteme. So, for example, concepts such as the critique of capitalism as creating a "standardizing, mass society of consumption and spectacle" (BB, 149) or the abstraction of the infra-/superstructure apparatus that divides the economic from the juridical (BB, 163) or the analysis of labor via alienation (BB, 220–24) or, perhaps most damning, the insistence on a single "logic of capital and its accumulation" (BB, 165) no longer function in the same critical manner in the widespread, multiplying, diffuse practices of neoliberalism. These major conceptual breaks from Marx come as no surprise for readers of Foucault,[5] but are particularly critical to his approach to neoliberalism and its considerable difference from contemporary scholarship.

We can begin by grouping these primary breaks in the schema suggested by his comments in "Truth and Power." First, there is the concept of a transcendental truth, which takes on many of its possible guises in the lectures, including concepts of History as a Hegelian-Marxist unfolding of Capital (BB, 313), liberatory ideas of freedom as overcoming the alienation of labor (BB, 240–42), or even economic rationality itself à la Adam Smith (BB, 279–82); it also undergirds the infra-/superstructure division that relegates discourse to a secondary epiphenomenon.[6] Second, there is the concept of a transcendental, nonhistorical, or prehistorical subject, which is taken up through the discussion of liberalism's subject of rights in the lectures (BB, 40–43, 273–78) and which undergirds the assumptions of interpellation and consciousness-raising noted in Marxist analyses (Lisa Duggan's analyses is exemplary here). And, third, there is a transcendental economic structure that directs economic practices from an abstracted ontological causal plane; this also feeds the infra-/superstructure apparatus, but even more so directs our critical attention away from the specificity of disciplinary mechanisms that are the lifeblood of neoliberalism (BB, 89–92, 222–24).

For readers of Foucault, from *The History of Madness* and *The Archaeology of Knowledge* (and its appendix, "The Discourse on Language") to *Discipline and Punish*, all three volumes of *The History of Sexuality*, and various essays, especially "Nietzsche, Genealogy, History," the breaks from these dominant epistemological habits are the hallmarks of Foucault's thinking. But in the case of these lectures on neoliberalism, these serve as explicit arguments against a Marxist analysis that demarcates neoliberalism as just the latest, most clever, most widespread ideology of capitalism. The point is so important that Foucault, a quintessentially French thinker of nuance and innuendo, even goes so far as to state it explicitly, arguing that the historical framework within which German neo-liberalism ("Ordoliberalism")[7] takes place "is something other than a political calculation. . . . *No more is it an ideology*" (BB, 94, my emphasis). Operating in a qualitatively different register and thus requiring a different dimension of analysis, neoliberalism is not an ideology.

And so, what is it? What exactly does Foucault think neoliberalism is? Why are these three breaks from transcendental structures so important for the particularities of neoliberalism? What shifts in subjectivity and authority—the constitutive parts of any ethics—occur in this adamant argument that neoliberalism is not an ideology? What is at stake here, exactly?

LIBERALISM AND NEOLIBERALISM: FROM CONTRACTUAL RIGHTS TO MARKET INTERESTS

Foucault's overarching argument is that, through processes of intensification, neoliberalism transforms the categories, practices, and values that it inherits from eighteenth-century liberalism into substantively new categories, practices, and values. In the language of the complex sociohistorical fugue that I am investigating, that is, neoliberalism repeats the themes of liberalism in a different voice.

When Foucault locates himself in the mid-eighteenth century to begin this genealogy, he immerses himself in a period in which three conceptual actors dominate the epistemological and cultural scene in Europe: the Church, the State, and the Economy. Classic Enlightenment narratives about the triumph of liberalism have locked most attention on the strife involved in separating the Church from the State, thereby fixating us on a conceptual framework that pits one sovereign actor (the Church) against another sovereign actor (the State). The upshot is a static concept of power as sovereign, paired interestingly with a narrow understanding of Protestantism that frames secularism as a primary barometer of modernity.[8] In focusing his discussion of liberalism on the struggles and shifts between the State and the Economy, rather than the State and the Church, Foucault begins to reorient our conceptual framework of power toward his concepts of biopolitics. Following his arguments in part 5 of *The History of Sexuality*, volume 1, that biopower emerges alongside sovereign power, without displacing it, we can approach these lectures as analyzing precisely this shift.[9]

Beginning in liberalism, Foucault then turns to the transformations in governmental practices in the mid-eighteenth century to examine a new kind of politico-economic rationality that he calls "political economy" (BB, 13). Situated against the kind of political self-reflection at work in practices of government in the sixteenth and seventeenth centuries, when the law emerged to limit the domain of the state, political economy does not exist in "the kind of external position occupied by juridical thought" (BB, 14). Lodging itself, rather, within governmental reason, political economy locates the principle of political self-limitation internally. And this alters all barometers of judgment, including the modes of self-reflection possible in such a rationality.

Rather than referring to an external "nature" or "law" to determine the legitimacy/illegitimacy of its actions, political economy analyzes governmental practices to determine whether the *effects* of its actions will be successful. It brings a utilitarian rationality to bear on all practices of the government and thereby transforms the very meaning of "nature." Displacing the premodern metaphysics of a transcendental nature that, whether divine or human, hovers over and hems in the realm of politics, the mid-eighteenth-century emergence of political economy refers only to the specific logic internal to governmental practices for its evaluative barometers. Politics thus becomes the singular horizon of judgment and, within that singularity, the epistemological mechanisms of the economy become the practice of judgment: "success replaces legitimacy" (BB, 16) as the criteria for governmental action. All the questions formerly posed by and for the art of governing, especially those of its ethical contours and limitations, are transformed. For Foucault, this new form of governmental practice, which he locates in eighteenth-century liberalism, becomes the basis for grasping biopolitics.

Consequently, Foucault focuses on the mechanism that causes this crucial shift in the relations between politics and economics, namely, the market. In a further distancing from Marxist analysis, he does not frame this emergence of the market as the advent of capitalism. Approaching it as a new kind of rationality and resisting, as ever, the possibility of a singular cause of its emergence, Foucault suggests "a polygonal or polyhedral relationship" (BB, 33) between a number of economic, demographic, technical, theoretical, and governmental shifts to try to understand how this new market rationality emerges. He argues that, displacing the role of the law as a juridical structure to limit the power of the state, the market becomes a site of veridiction that, in turn, begins to saturate the field of the political writ large.

In the middle of the eighteenth century, Foucault argues, "the market no longer appeared as, or rather no longer had to be the site of jurisdiction" (BB, 31). Framed as following "natural" mechanisms, the market emerges—*as both a concept and a practice*[10]—as a site of "truth" that governmental practices need to leave alone. As Foucault explains, "Inasmuch as it enables production, need, supply, demand, value, and price, etcetera, to be linked together through exchange, the market constitutes a site of veridiction" (BB, 32). *Laissez-nous faire* becomes the logic of this market rationality that, in the mid-eighteenth century, emerges as a counterpoint to the juridical rationality of the government. But as the market saturates the political per se, the relation between economics and politics is subsequently flipped: no longer is it the government's duty to rein in the market to ensure "fair" prices; rather, "to be good government, government has to function according to truth" (BB, 32), and it is the market that is the site of veridiction. "The market must tell the truth (*dire le vrai*)" (BB, 32), and thereby shape, enliven, and regulate exactly what it means to live *dans le vrais*, as we and Mendel all must do.[11]

This results in a fundamental split in the modes of rationality dominant in practices of liberalism. While Foucault traces the changes as historical developments in the relations between politics and economics, it is important to read them also as transformations in the fields and modes of rationality itself, namely, the split between the juridical and the calculative modes. That is, while Foucault frames his discussion here as an analysis of "the birth of this dissymmetrical bipolarity of politics and the economy" (BB, 20)—a dissymmetry that neoliberalism virtually tosses overboard, as the economic becomes the singular mode of judgment—we must also realize that the transformations, occurring at the level of deciphering the true from the false, are transformations in the very mechanisms of judgment. Thus, while Foucault traces the historical emergence of "two absolutely heterogeneous conceptions of freedom, one based on the rights of man, and the other starting from the independence of the governed" (BB, 42), he is also beginning to turn to the fundamental changes in rationality itself that come to dominate the neoliberal iteration of the modern episteme. As we begin to see the erosion of juridical authority in neoliberalism, we also find the lapsing of modernity's epistemology of certitude and a slide toward the neoliberal epistemology of calculating success.

When the market begins to function as a site of veridiction, it becomes a kind of social rationality with sufficient causal power to produce competitive, atomistic subjectivities with specifically demarcated sets of values, concerns, and interests. Foucault cites Condillac, writing in 1776, to explain how this regulation of prices in markets, rather than through transcendental concepts of a "just price," functions only on the condition of the public character of the market: "Prices can only be regulated in markets, because it is only there that the gathered citizens, by comparing their interests in exchanging, can judge the value of things relative to their needs . . . it is only in markets that one can judge the relationship of abundance and scarcity between things that determines their respective prices" (BB, 48n6). The kind of rationality attendant to this particular form of subjectivity alters accordingly, setting an economic calculation of success and failure into motion as the primary horizon upon which value must be determined. Other forms of judgment, especially juridical appeals to transcendental principles such as those we find in contractual logic, are displaced as possible modes of evaluative discernment: only the calculation of private interest, which is the final barometer of acceptable profit and loss, becomes the acceptable mode of evaluation. Still dependent on the liberal concept of a split between public and private, the public domain shifts from the regulatory mechanism of the contract to the ateleological mechanism of the market: the market, not the contract, becomes the site of veridiction—and this is necessarily a public site.

Foucault locates the emergence of these new kinds of material and rational regulatory principles in the development of liberalism. Eventually, however, neoliberalism intensifies these political, economic, and epistemological shifts and schisms in liberalism. As the new social rationality of neoliberalism emerges on top of or in the midst of, as it were, the older ones of liberalism, the framework of the rights-bearing citizen invested in contracts of ownership no longer captures the characteristics of subjectivity enacted in neoliberalism: we become what Foucault calls "subject of interests," entrepreneurs extraordinaire, intensifying our interests in and through markets of any and all stripes.

ENTERPRISING SUBJECTS

The neoliberal aim, across all of these early theorists, is to transform society itself into a mode of enterprise, of entrepreneurial and productive activities, of creative and competitive subjects. While Foucault argues that the German ordoliberal model achieves the extension of principles of market economy into the overall exercise of political power, it is the model of neoliberalism in the United States that enacts this radically new kind of social epistemology at the level of the individual. With appropriate irony, Foucault locates the foothold for this neoliberal epistemological transformation in the very thing that Marxist analysis claims as its own, although its roots are also found in the ontology of liberalism, namely, labor.[12] Foucault argues that "the *essential epistemological transformation* of these neoliberal analyses is their claim to change what constituted in fact the object, or domain of objects, the general field of reference of economic analysis" (BB, 222, my emphasis). No longer the analysis of mechanisms of production, exchange, distribution, or consumption, economic analysis under neoliberalism takes up a new kind of object—the activity of labor.[13]

The process of this transformation is crucial to map carefully. Foucault frames the neoliberal concerns as invested in the general question of how "individuals allocate . . . scarce means to alternative ends" (BB, 222). In this, it would seem that the logic of efficiency and utility that already dominated liberalism in the eighteenth century is fully in play. However, as the object of analysis changes, the operative mode of rationality also shifts. When neoliberals try to understand *how* individuals make these choices among scarce means, they begin to ask *why* individuals make such choices. The question of economics shifts not only from processes to activities, but concurrently from structural questions about "what choices are made" to the individuating and subjectivating questions "why did you choose this?" and, ultimately, "who are you?" The anchor of this activity is not labor as an abstracted category, but the point of view of the person who works: "We will have to study work as economic conduct practiced, implemented, rationalized, and calculated by the person who works. What does working mean for the person who works? What system of choice and rationality does the activity of work conform to?" (BB, 223). Just as we find in Foucault's work on madness, criminality, and sexuality, here we have the emergence of a new kind of social epistemology that does not displace the eighteenth-century economic epistemologies of efficiency and utility, but lays alongside and on top of them a heterogeneous, irreducible, disparate logic of enterprise.

Moving into the heart of the matter, Foucault follows out the neoliberal reflection on labor from the worker's point of view and explains how the worker transforms into an "enterprise-unit" (BB, 225). As such, the worker is conceptualized not so much as a partner of exchange, as in classical conceptions of *homo economicus*, but rather as "an entrepreneur, an entrepreneur of himself" (BB, 226).[14] Neoliberalism does not draw on the liberal logic of "utility based on a problematic of needs" (BB, 225) and its endless calculation of the utility of exchange. Breaking from this limited economy of scarcity, neoliberalism enacts a different logic, wherein productivity and intensity, rather than utility and exchange, become the barometers of evaluation. In a further indication that we are no longer dealing with juridical rationality and its application of transcendental principles, this transformation of logic occurs at the level of the subject: it is internalized. When the early neoliberal theorists approach the worker as "being for himself his own capital, being for himself his own producer, being for himself the source of [his] own earnings" (BB, 226), they frame the worker as an actor and producer of his own wealth: the worker becomes "human capital" (BB, 227), the phrase that Gary Becker uses as one of his best- known titles.

With this category, neoliberals are off to the races: "They are led to study the way in which human capital is formed and accumulated, and this enables them to apply economic analyses to completely new fields and domains" (BB, 227). Human capital becomes the barometer for all of life's activities: reproduction, as well as the choice of partners to be involved, becomes a matter of genetic calculation of future human capital; childrearing—"time spent, care given, as well as the parents' education" (BB, 229)—become a form of investment in human capital; medical care, public health and hygiene, and even migration all become matters for careful calculation of "investments we have made at the level of man himself" (BB, 231).[15] As neoliberalism takes root as a widespread social rationality, economic calculation becomes the dominant mode of self-reflection and the barometer for individual success.

Initially, this appears to be the same kind of process Foucault had traced in his previous genealogical work, wherein a complex set of mechanisms slowly coalesces to produce an identity with very particular contours of interiority. For example, in the passages from *The History of Sexuality*, volume 1, that have become so crucial, if problematically so, to the emergence and early development of queer theory in the United States,[16] Foucault demonstrates how the category of sexuality took root as a normative category of identity, which then came to be internalized into the questions of sexual orientation that still dominate our cultural milieu, providing a crucial lynchpin for biopolitics of normalization. And in roughly parallel ways, his work on madness, delinquency, and criminality also trace similar moves, wherein a typology of identities and individuals emerges to set alongside the older typology of acts and practices (BB, 248). In each of these fields, a different register is thereby enacted, as I already indicated, in which the questions of interiority and identity can gain traction, thereby giving the groundwork necessary for the ensuing judgments of normativity: "who are you?" emerges and then enables the damning "are you normal?"

While it may at first appear that a similar transformation is at work here in the discourses of neoliberalism, the logic of enterprise functions differently from that of the contract, which frames the liberal understanding of market transactions and is, arguably, also at the root of the normative judgments at work in madness, criminality, and sexuality. As the long tradition of contract theory shows, the stakes of the contract are explicitly ethical: the contract delineates clear terms of agreement that each party promises to fulfill, thereby constituting one's duty. Of course, as Kantian ethics (and especially Lacanian readings of them)[17] teach us, it is impossible to discern motivations that are ethically aligned with duty from those that merely conform to duty: this is the lasting aporia of modern ethics. But the tension that grabs Foucault's attention in his readings of the emergence of political economy in eighteenth-century theorists of liberalism is the uneasy relation that emerges between this kind of contractual duty, with its ethical barometer of right and wrong, and the rationality of the market, which functions purely through the efficient barometer of success and failure.

As the practices of political economy take root, Foucault writes, "Success or failure, then, will replace the division between legitimacy and illegitimacy" (BB, 16) as the barometer by which to judge "good" governmental practices and—by intensification and extension into a new, *neo*-liberal social rationality—"good" human lives. This tension maps onto the split subjectivity that Foucault locates at the heart of modern ontologies of liberalism, namely, the split between the contractually mitigated Rights of Man and the economically calculated "subject of interests." The former falls under the rationality of normative judgment that governs the contract, while the latter is driven by the economic calculations that determine success and failure in the market: the former is ethical, the latter is efficient.

Foucault argues, then, that the ontology of liberalism develops across the eighteenth century into two major branches: the contract and the market. Each of them functions according to different rationalities: the juridical and the efficient. And each of them stakes different social domains: the ethical and the economic. The subjectivities attendant to these two branches of liberalism consequently also shift from the interiority of the autonomous subject that purports to control his or her behavior to the socially scripted self that seeks to navigate the market's vacillations and thereby maximize his or her interests. Tracing this along Foucault's various inquiries prior to the 1979 lectures, I suggest that the normative judgments at work in the discourses of madness, criminality, and sexuality follow out the logic of the contract and its subjectivity of interiority, which eventually becomes the normalizing judgment of identity. The practices and theories of neoliberalism then intensify and extend the logic of efficiency that constitutes success and failure on the market and renders us "subjects of interest."

Consequently, as the neoliberal concept of human capital takes root through the social rationality of enterprise, the question of identity slides from the ability to articulate a deep interior desire into the socially externalized barometer of success. The framework of the rights-bearing citizen invested in ethical contracts of ownership, however construed, no longer captures the sociopsychic dynamics of subjectivity enacted in neoliberalism. The rights-bearing citizen no longer functions as the regulative ideal of subject formation, publicly or privately. Unlike the other discursive fields of madness, criminality, and sexuality, the neoliberal social rationality no longer demarcates identities through the bifurcation of normativity and nonnormativity: neoliberalism operates through the scalar social rationality of success, not identity. One cannot ask *whether* one is a neoliberal in the same way that one can ask *whether* one is a pervert or a criminal or a madman. The question of identity, which involves laying claim to a substance, is turned inside out, becoming a matter of process that is calibrated by this neoliberal grammar of success. In neoliberalism, one does not ask, "who are you?" Rather, one asks, "how good are you at what you do? How successful are you?" And the true bottom line: "*how much and how well do you maximize your interests?*"

SUBJECT OF INTERESTS: BEYOND THE CONTRACT

In his admittedly very brief genealogy of *homo economicus*, that "basic element of the new governmental reason formulated in the eighteenth century" (BB, 271), Foucault returns to English empiricists such as John Locke and David Hume to trace the emergence of what is, fundamentally, a split subjectivity at the heart of modern discourses of the Rights of Man. Framing it as "one of the most important theoretical transformations in Western thought since the Middle Ages" (BB, 271), Foucault sketches the introduction of a subject of *interests* at the heart of the contractual logic that drives the subject of rights. Drawing on Hume's discussion of that irreducible, nontransferable experience of pain or pleasure that drives all choices, Foucault characterizes interests as the bedrock for all decisions: "this principle of an irreducible, non-transferable, atomistic individual choice which is unconditionally referred to the subject himself" (BB, 272). Interests are those irrational and sometimes ineffable connections, whether positive or negative, we have to experiences; they are the reasons we care about things; they are what psychoanalysis comes to call cathexes. And for Foucault, they are a radically new way of conceptualizing the subject. He insists that this idea of a subject as the source and site of a mechanism of interests "reveals something which absolutely did not exist before" (BB, 273), namely, "a form of both immediately and absolutely subjective will" (BB, 273).

For Foucault, this early conception of subjectivity as driven by interests, which he locates in the contractarian tradition of classical liberalism associated with Locke, produces a dynamic that cannot be subsumed by the contractual logic of the subject of rights and its juridical will. As he puts it, "Individuals entered the contract because they have an interest"

(BB, 273): they are cathected to its stakes, hopes, risks, dreams. They enter the contract because something about it speaks to them—something about it matters. But as the contractual logic then takes hold, the subject becomes framed purely as a juridical will (as a subject of rights), effectively erasing by allegedly subsuming this originary subject of interests.

As the juridical evaluation of rationalized ends and means begins to totalize the horizon of subjective deliberation, the subject of interests is allegedly subsumed into this purified state of satisfaction. But, as Foucault interestingly notes, the logic of subsumption seems to fail. While the subject of interests and the juridical will may be reconciled, they "are not governed by the same logic" (BB, 274) and "cannot be completely assimilated to each other" (BB, 273). A fundamental heterogeneity lies at the core of liberalism's schemas of subjectivity, which extends into the heterogeneous juridical and calculative modes of rationality: the subject of interests and the subject of rights are different animals.

Positioned as the psychological condition of possibility of the subject of right's functioning, the subject of interests overflows and outstrips the subject of rights. While the subject of rights gives in to a logic of renunciation, the subject of interests never does. As Foucault sketches, upon entering the contract, the subject of rights undergoes a self-splitting whereby he becomes, "at one level, the possessor of a number of natural and immediate rights, and, at another level, someone who agrees to the principle of relinquishing them and who is thereby constituted as a different subject of right superimposed on the first" (BB, 275). Once more in strikingly psychoanalytic terms, we have a split subject animated by a relationship of negativity, renunciation, and limitation between its two parts: the juridical contract initiates, as it were, a Freudian superego or Lacanian Symbolic that enforces a law of obligation and renunciation upon the Freudian libido or the Lacanian Real—or what I will frame in the following chapter as the drive. To quicken the psychoanalytic spin, Foucault quips, "It is in this movement [the self-splitting that entrance into the contract precipitates] that law and the prohibition emerge" (BB, 275).

Strikingly, Foucault emphasizes that the subject of interests seems to be quite indifferent to this incipient logic of sacrifice and prohibition. Given voice through the eighteenth-century economists' analyses of the market, the subjects of interests are encouraged to pursue their own interests to the utmost, maximizing their egoistic pursuits to the greatest extent possible.[18] Precisely through the suspension of any juridical limit to such expansiveness, these economists give a nascent account of what will become neoliberalism's moral rationalization and lasting charge, namely, that the pursuit and intensification of egoist interests will, eventually, benefit all.

In a classic trickle-down argument, for example, Foucault describes how this neoliberal economic analysis of the grain market encourages sellers to pursue their own interests to the fullest and rush the grain to the countries where there is dearth and the price is high. Casting aside all concern for causing shortages in one's own country, the egoist mechanism will, without intention or purposeful design, magically benefit all, resulting in the increase of interests and returns to all. According to these eighteenth-century economists' analysis of the inner workings of the subject of interests, there is "an egoistic mechanism, *a directly multiplying mechanism without any transcendence* in which the will of each harmonizes spontaneously and as it were involuntarily with the will and interest of others" (BB, 276, my emphasis).

As Foucault goes on to emphasize in his reading of Adam Smith's infamous invisible hand (BB, 278–86), it is the invisibility of capital's mechanisms that matters most here, not the mere intervention that is usually highlighted. With a fascinating foreshadowing of Kant's noumenal and all of its epistemological and ethical force, Smith renders fundamentally invisible, opaque, and unknowable the economic mechanisms that ensure this trickle-down moral rationalization, that is, the economic mechanisms by which all are eventually benefited through the pursuit of each subject's egoist interests. The benefit to all simply emerges, without design or rational pursuit. Consequently, of course, political power must not ever interfere: no government, no sovereign, no human can ever have a totalizing point of view on the economic mechanism. Foucault quotes Smith: "No human wisdom or knowledge could ever be sufficient" (BB, 282) for the task of supervising the economic mechanisms of capital. The market and the contract function in two fundamentally heterogeneous logics, one of which cannot be known.

It is this split in subjectivity and the modes of social authority that neoliberalism exacerbates. By intensifying the subject of interests, neoliberal practices exacerbate this heterogeneity at the heart of liberalism. Neoliberalism intensifies the subject of interests as an ever-expansive mode of maximizing interests via boundless economic calculation until it eclipses the contractual law and juridical rationality that govern the subject of rights in classical liberalism. The fundamental heterogeneity of a contractual subject of rights and a libidinal subject of interests thereby intensifies in this neoliberal iteration of the modern episteme into an incommensurability that, among other alterations, results in the following, mutually constituting transformations: (1) it exposes and then feigns to disavow the racializing schemas endemic to the liberal social contract ontology; (2) it enables and encourages exteriorizing practices of subjectivity, effectively devaluing the treasured interiority of liberalism; (3) it formalizes modes of social cathexes (to histories, cultures, values) into a purified process emptied of content; (4) it transforms the category of social difference itself into a formal category empty of all meaning, value, and history; (5) it interrupts and threatens to displace the function of juridical rationality as the site and register of ethics. I argue that these five crucial transformations, which intersect and mutually constitute one another, are underway in neoliberal social rationalities and are profoundly altering how overdeveloped cultures practice, understand, and respond to both social difference and ethics.

THE APORIA OF ETHICS

Foucault thereby conceives the overarching relation of neoliberalism to liberalism not as an instance of a clear historical break, but as the gradual economic and cultural intensifying of these neoliberal concepts as they become materialized more and more fully. Neoliberal practices emerge in cultures that are structured by classical liberalism. This historical overlay, wherein liberalism's central concepts and values continue to circulate "underneath" those of neoliberalism, requires that we learn how to conceptualize these heterogeneous modes of liberalism and neoliberalism alongside one another. To conceptualize, say, subjectivity as if it were operating in a purely liberal or neoliberal mode is to misunderstand both the epistemological genesis of neoliberalism out of liberalism and the materialization of neoliberal practices amid longstanding practices of liberalism. We must learn to analyze the individual threads of this complex fugue, with all their intersections, overlaps, and silences.

Keeping in mind that these metamorphoses are the processes of intensification, not of a clean break and replacement, I offer a heuristic schema to begin tracing the contours and impacts of these emergent formations (see table 1.1). Despite the risk that this kind of schema might flatten the relations, ambiguities, and sheer historical messiness of the discourses that it is charting, I offer it as a heuristic device that distills the dominant categories under investigation. While the first set of concepts (in the lefthand column of the table) is all too familiar to us in the long-standing, dominant liberal iteration of the modern episteme, the second set (in the righthand column) begins to mark the aspects in neoliberalism that are new: the market, not the contract, emerges as the epistemological and material principle of evaluation; entrepreneurialism contests ownership as the barometer of achievement; the individual begins to be reconceived as an interest-driven consumer, rather than a rights-bearing citizen; the subject aims to expand her human capital, rather than protect her precious utility; and economic calculation emerges as a primary mode of rationality, challenging the singularity of juridical authority for evaluative judgments. With the slow shift from the contract to the market as the site of veridiction, the entrepreneurial subject of interests and the economic calculation of enterprise form the new social rationality that is increasingly structuring not just our politics and economics, but our lives.

Consequently, in lived cultures of neoliberalism such as those that are dominating globalized cultures, we encounter all kinds of doublings, displacements, suppressions, repressions, and hybridities among these overlapping but also heterogeneous social rationalities of liberalism and neoliberalism. The question of these crossings shapes my analysis of the politics of social difference and the transformation of ethics in contemporary neoliberal cultures. If, for example, neoliberalism renders us enterprising subjects who endlessly calculate our own interests, how can we make ethical evaluations that extend beyond the economic calculation of our own egoist desires? Without any easy recourse to the liberal mode of ethical evaluation that draws on juridical, transcendental foundations, how can we make evaluations of worth that still carry sufficient psychological cathexes to inform everyday practices of living? And in the register of social difference, how can we make sense of the ongoing xenophobic violence against bodies that are marked as "differ-

TABLE 1.1 Neoliberal Categorical Transformations of Liberalism

	Liberalism	Neoliberalism
Sites of truth	Contract	Market
Truth mechanism	Ownership (protection)	Maximizing interests (expansion)
Social value	Utility	Activity of labor, human capital
Freedom	Rights of man	Subject of interests
Subjectivity	"Citizen"	"Entrepreneur"
Rationality	Juridical	Calculation of enterprise

ent," especially those that are racialized as different, amid the adamant celebration of diversity that reverberates all too loudly in classrooms, in corporate training, and in the onslaught of the advertising machine? How, exactly, has the liberal rhetoric of tolerance and its highly prized veil of neutrality transformed into the impossible demands of colorblindness and multiculturalism?

The spirit of such questions haunts Foucault, even if he never frames them in these early twenty-first century ways. With an eye toward developments in France, Foucault focuses on the historical development of two different forms of neoliberalism, Germany's and the United States's. For each of these, he again uses a longer time frame than most contemporary discussions of neoliberalism, focusing on developments from, roughly, 1930 to 1950, rather than the more typical focus on the early 1970s. With different histories of politics and economics (legacies of Bismarck, Weimar, and Hitler in Germany; the New Deal and Keynesian policies, along with the wartime Beveridge Plan, in the United States), each of these forms of neoliberalism enacted different sets of concerns and fears. In contrasting the two, Foucault positions the United States as the more radical, even calling it "American anarcho-capitalism" (BB, 145) at one point. But it is the lingering socialist concern for *vitalpolitik* in the German ordoliberal organization of society into a *Gesellschaftspolitik* that provides an instructive example of how these heterogeneous forms of liberal and neoliberal freedom and subjectivity are and are not reconciled in cultures where neoliberal practices ascend.

While the American Chicago School neoliberals extend the economic mode of calculative rationality into all parts of life apparently without qualms, the German ordoliberals express a lingering concern with forms of alienation and its consequent concept of authenticity. Forming what Foucault calls "an economic-ethical ambiguity around the notion of enterprise itself" (BB, 241), the ordoliberals continue to use a noneconomic barometer for evaluating their projects. For example, Foucault quotes Rustow as insisting, "We have to organize the economy of the social body according to the rules of the market economy, but the fact remains that we have to satisfy new and heightened needs for integration" (BB, 242). Invoking the Marxist schemas of wholeness and alienation, this persistent concern for integration distinguishes the ordoliberals from the US neoliberals as still involved in questions of morality—questions of what Foucault calls "'warm' moral and cultural values which are presented precisely as antithetical to the 'cold' mechanism of competition" (BB, 242).

But if Foucault locates a lingering concern with extraeconomic modes of evaluation in the German ordoliberals, it does not surface in recognizably ethical terms, as we see in his discussion of the ordoliberal analysis of Nazism. In what Foucault argues is a necessary condition for their entire reversal of the state-market relationship, the ordoliberals analyze Nazism as fundamentally caused by "the anti-liberal variant" (BB, 111) of a statist economy. That is, National Socialism was not a monstrosity of either ethics or racism, but merely an extreme case of the same kind of antiliberal statist economic policies that one can find in "parliamentary England, the Soviet Union and America of the New Deal" (BB, 111). Subsequently, the ordoliberal answer to avoid Nazism is, unsurprisingly, a robust embrace of neoliberal principles, namely, the full reversal of the state-market relation: the market economy should become the internal organizing and regulating principle of the state, rather than vice versa.

Foucault does not remark on the complete omission of racism and anti-Semitism from the ordoliberals' discussion of National Socialism. But his silence signifies. I read it as part of the ongoing attempt across these lectures to reorient the level of our analyses. Precisely by not turning toward the category of racism in the ordoliberals' analysis of Nazism, Foucault maintains his own analyses at the level of the transformations that I am excavating, namely, the transformation at the level of categories. This does not mean that he is unconcerned with problems such as racism—far from it, as his own work and the contemporary scholarship it has generated demonstrate.[19] It does, however, situate such questions at a different level than the sociological and ideological accounts of contemporary theorists working on race and racism in neoliberalism.[20]

Rather than allowing categories such as race to function as given, self-evident categories of identity and politics with clear meanings and histories, Foucault reorients the level of analysis. He pushes us to excavate the transformations in the category and role of social difference itself, as well as modes of social cathexes that animate it, in the neoliberal iteration of the modern episteme. Given that Foucault argues that the question of ethical, noneconomic evaluation no longer functions at all in the American neoliberals, this project of excavating the transformation at the level of categories, rather than as historical or sociological phenomena, is all the more urgent in the US iteration of neoliberalism. But it is also all the more convoluted, since it is largely a process of excavating erasures.

Despite the differences between the two forms of German and American neoliberalism, Foucault argues that they still have the same point of departure: "The idea that the economy is basically a game, that it develops as a game between partners, that the whole of society must be permeated by this economic game" (BB, 201). Neoliberalism intensifies and extends the shift from the contractual, juridical law to the truth-making market as the locus of limits to state power that we already find in liberalism. For liberalism, the possibility that a performative principle of rationality might instantiate sufficient force to grant a social evaluation is but a stray thought in economists' heads: the true mechanism of evaluation remains the juridical authority that enforces contractual rights and duties. For neoliberalism, however, the market becomes the sole site of veridiction, casting these juridical principles in an oddly nostalgic hue. In neoliberalism, the "free space of the market"—that is, the eighteenth-century liberal insistence that the government must not intervene in the processes of the economy—gradually becomes the primary space of reflection, whether social, political, legal, or, eventually, even personal. It thus enacts a new kind of power that results in a substantive transformation of social rationality and subject formation therein.

It is here that Foucault's insistence on the singularity of neoliberalism seems to be most pressing. While locating its genesis internally in liberalism, Foucault nonetheless insists that neoliberalism emerges as a singular social rationality that has not been encountered historically. He insists that neoliberalism outstrips "the three analytical and critical frameworks with which [it] is usually approached" (BB, 130)—namely, that of Adam Smith (liberalism's freedom of the market from political intervention), Marx (ideology and, as I will extend, Althusser's account of interpellation), and Solzhenitsyn ("the concentration camp world and the Gulag" [BB, 151n1]; or what we might now call "conspiracy theory"). Attempting "to grasp it in its singularity" (BB, 130), Foucault focuses on neoliberalism as an epistemological intervention: the transformation that occurs when economic rationality is extended into matters as intimate as the relation between parent and child, as abstract as genetics, as political as education, and as sociobiological as health care and public hygiene (BB, 227–30). These extensions and intensifications initiate a new social rationality that is internalized by subjects and externalized by governmental practices, rendering overdeveloped cultures "not a market society, but an enterprise society" (BB, 147).

The task before us then appears to revolve around the possibility of erecting a new set of categories that can respond to the ethical problems that the material practices of neoliberalism are creating across the world. Attempting to grasp the shifts and transformations enacted in neoliberalism requires us to hold a variety of heterogeneities in tension without reducing them to modern epistemologies of coherence or completeness. While Foucault frames neoliberalism as exacerbating many of the developments already alive in liberalism, the relation between the two is not conceptually or materially symmetrical.

That is, neoliberalism does not, for example, merely intensify liberalism's turn toward the private in order to arrive at its structure of "the subject of interests"; to the contrary, as I will develop, neoliberalism's subject of interests operates in entirely new, different, and foreign registers than any we can find in liberalism. As Foucault tells us in the context of the two kinds of freedom that he finds intrinsic to liberalism itself, "I will try to show in these lectures the connections which succeeded in holding together and conjoining the fundamental axiomatic of the rights of man and the utilitarian calculus of the independence of the governed" (BB, 42–43). While neoliberalism exacerbates the latter "independence of the governed" into a purely isolated "subject of interests," it does not do so by displacing liberalism: a freedom of interests does not displace a freedom of rights; the calculus of utility does not displace the certainty of the juridical. Both sets of concepts and values circulate alongside and on top of each other as neoliberalism emerges and takes hold.

It is precisely because neoliberalism never fully displaces liberal modes of rationality and evaluation that we are most often confused and frustrated when confronted with situations invoking ethical evaluation. As a late iteration of the modern episteme, neoliberalism emerges historically in the same period as poststructuralism. Accordingly, it enacts a similar kind of antifoundationalism that poststructuralists of various stripes have been diagnosing for at least four decades now. Unlike previous struggles with "postmodern nihilism" that beleaguered much of the poststructuralist "linguistic turn" in the 1980s and 1990s, however, the "neoliberal turn" accentuates the absence of ethics materially: the same rationality that produces these fully externalized neoliberal subjects of interests is simultaneously producing historically unforeseen global economic disparities, both between and within nation-states.

The ethical stakes could not be more glaring. And, yet, we—we who are benefiting from neoliberalism in overdeveloped countries—are failing to respond to or even recognize this geopolitical landscape as a problem of ethics. Mainstream political and cultural discourses swirl about in endless questions about the efficacy of one economic policy over another, as glaring ethical problems of the global and local expansion of poverty, intensified environmental disasters, and increased warfare become more and more common. We can only deny or repress or sublimate or ignore or otherwise transform them into psychologically palatable bytes in an effort to preserve our own insulated view of the world.

But it may be precisely at the level of the psychological that the ethical quandaries of neoliberalism confront its aspirations to erase liberalism entirely and become the dominant social rationality. When we finally come face to face with questions of evaluation that are not comfortably submitted to the calculations of enterprise, such as how to respond to the xenophobic and nationalist baiting of Islam as a religion of terrorism or the persistent, if more coded and covert, expressions of racism in US popular culture, we neoliberals often feel like walking contradictions or, even worse, slightly schizophrenic: we long for a moral absolute, while simultaneously refusing any such limitation to our enterprising lives. Responses by the implicitly Marxist leftists of the cultural and intellectual industries seem largely to fail to engage this limited psychological palette of neoliberal culture. In the language of psychoanalysis, they fail to cathect the subject of interests that circulates endlessly, and mostly quite happily, in neoliberal practices. Part of this project is to map out the exact sites of that failure, and I show in the following chapter how ideological analyses, especially as carried forward by Althusser's concept on interpellation, fail to map onto the new epistemological and sociopsychological terrain of neoliberalism.

Rather than frame this failure to respond ethically as the rational impossibility of the postmodern or late-capitalist condition, Foucault's lectures help us to see how this confusion and frustration may be caused by our inability to reflect upon and understand these overlapping, coexisting, and conjoining and yet also disparate and heterogeneous sets of liberal and neoliberal values at work in our current episteme. Quandaries that we name "ethical" bring us face to face with the limits of those values of calculating entrepreneurial success (whether fiscal, sartorial, emotional, or political) that neoliberalism holds so dear. But, at the same time, we have yet to develop the epistemological tools to articulate any other values.

Consequently, we seem to vacillate between falling back into the comfortable habits of moral absolutes (sometimes in the form of religious fundamentalism) and unburdening ourselves of the responsibility altogether through fuller immersion in the enterprising projects of our lives and worlds. But neither of these suffices: moral absolutes, despite our lingering nostalgia, no longer cathect us and fuller immersion in our enterprising lives cannot, finally, suppress the burn of true ethical questions. And so they go unanswered. And, as we are now seeing with an unnerving regularity, the energy of the ethical cannot dissipate: unanswered, it turns violent.

Just as Georges Bataille locates heterogeneity in what psychoanalysis calls the unconscious, so too am I suggesting that our culture's contemporary unconscious, filled with these heterogeneous values and concepts, is deeply unsettled. We cannot turn our backs on the need for ethics. With cruel irony, neoliberalism is sharpening the need for ethics with increasing urgency, while simultaneously undermining its possibility. Neoliberalism is, in precisely this proliferation of ethical injustices that can then find no language of response, nihilist. We must find our ways—as neoliberals, however consciously—to a meaningful language of ethics that is not merely the miming of past generations.

FIGURE 1a.1 Snoopy as Joe Cool. *Peanuts* © 1971. Peanuts Worldwide LLC. Distributed by UNIVERSAL UCLICK. Reprinted with permission. All rights reserved.

INTERLUDE 1

Old School Cool

One of the most memorable of Snoopy's many alter egos, Joe Cool introduces the cool irony of masculine detachment into the *Peanuts* lexicon of political references. While Snoopy showed up on October 4, 1950, only two days after *Peanuts* began as a comic strip, Joe Cool doesn't appear until May 27, 1971. Transformed immediately through the simple donning of shades, Snoopy becomes Joe Cool effortlessly: shades on, strike a pose, and—"Voila!"—coolness abounds.

This effortless sartorial transformation enacts the heart of coolness—in Charles Schulz's beloved *Peanuts* strip and beyond. As the first clip of Joe Cool's appearance shows so (ahem) effortlessly, cool enshrines precisely the shunning of effort. Too cool for school, Joe Cool is a man (a boy? a dog? a fantasy?) of pleasure. As the character develops in song and film, this pleasure assumes two primary registers: the sexual and the rebel.

In the first set of lyrics written by Desirée Goyette and scored by Vince Guaraldi, we find Joe Cool "dressin' up right / Going out to catch a lady to take out tonight."[1] Of course, this really just means putting on those shades—this is 1971, three decades before the ascendancy of any metrosexual guy. And it isn't clear whether any of the ladies actually fall for his act. The first one already has a date and snaps, "I'll catch you later, Jack."[2] And the second, allegedly successful one agrees to the date only to lure him in for a slap, reminding him that he hasn't called her in a year

PEANUTS
HERE'S JOE COOL HANGING AROUND THE STUDENT UNION

HI, JOE.. HOW'D YOU DO IN CHEMISTRY TODAY?

THAT CHEMISTRY IS A DRAG, MAN

JOE COOL CAN'T WORRY ABOUT CHEMISTRY WHEN HE'S BUSY HANGING AROUND THE STUDENT UNION

FIGURE 1a.2 Joe Cool's first appearance in *Peanuts*. *Peanuts* © Peanuts Worldwide LLC. Distributed by UNIVERSAL UCLICK. Reprinted with permission. All rights reserved.

or more. But, of course, Joe Cool is cool, girlfriend or not. Image intact: coolness is all the cool guy needs.

In the second and third (and final) set of lyrics, Charles Schulz carries this rather comically misdirected sexual bravado to its more clownish ends as Joe Cool finds himself kicked out of both school and job. In the 1972 television special, *You're Not Elected, Charlie Brown*, Joe Cool is literally tossed out of school when he cannot do simple addition; in the 1973 television special, *There's No Time for Love, Charlie Brown*, he is apparently fired from his job as a supermarket cashier for puerile antics and disdain for the rules. In both of these instantiations, the clownish character of Joe Cool's coolness comes to the fore: the other children shun him in school; his school notebook binder painfully clamps on his little paw not once, but twice; he squashes the produce in the market; and he cannot bag groceries. But the responses of others seem not to matter. His coolness always saves him, in his own mind, at least. He is, after all, Joe Cool.

The image of coolness that Schulz gives us is thus ambiguous, at best. Always still the charming beagle, Joe Cool offers a glimpse of the pleasures and possibilities of antiestablishment rebellion. When paired with the best-known of Schulz's creations, *A Charlie Brown Christmas*, Joe Cool's inability to function in the institutions of the School and the Marketplace take on anticapitalist hues. First aired in 1965, this classic of children's animation continues to air on network television in the United States at least once every year during the Christmas holiday season, making it the longest-running cartoon special in history. The plot is basic: consumerism and the marketing of Christmas have sucked the real meaning out of the holiday. While Schulz's insistence on leaving a very long quotation from the King James Bible's Gospel of Luke easily leads audiences to read this as a message from the Religious Right, Schulz himself was explicitly against orthodox religion and the 1965 cartoon precedes Ralph Reed by roughly twenty years.[3] It is the anticonsumerism thread that persists in the comic strip, intensified in the 1972 and 1973 appearances of Joe Cool, where he is described as "workin' in the supermarket, just like a mule."[4] Joe Cool is warned to "be careful of the manager, he's dy-na-mite. / Check each item, get those prices right!"[5] It is the shopping carts that finally smash Joe Cool and wheel him out of the job.

But it's all cool. Joe Cool shows us how vapid capitalism and its institutions can become.

Or does he?

The original *Charlie Brown Christmas* included opening and concluding title slides by its corporate sponsor: Coca-Cola.

(And, unsurprisingly, I was unable to secure the rights to that final image.)

CHAPTER TWO

Rethinking Difference

THE LIMITS OF INTERPELLATION

Across the years that I have been working on this project, I have had to deal with that slightly uncomfortable experience of explaining what I am working on. In response to the apparently simple question "what's the book about?" I have found myself giving two different answers. At first, this was just a matter of where I was in the project; but in retrospect, the strikingly different responses illuminate the problematic about neoliberal transformations of social difference and ethics under investigation in this book.

While writing chapters 4 and 5, I would tell people I was writing about contemporary changes in categories and concepts of social difference in the United States; after a bit of explanation, people usually became fairly animated, often regaling me with stories of their own confusion, code-switching, and (albeit unwittingly) latent racism. While writing chapter 6, however, I explained that I was writing about neoliberalism and ethics. To this, I received one clear and common response: "That's an oxymoron!" Unlike with the other response, when I often found myself trying to wriggle gently out of uncomfortable situations after failing to introduce a broader reflection, this response short-circuited the conversation entirely. There was, quite obviously, nothing more to be said. (And I had clearly lost my mind.)

While mainstream US culture seems fairly aware of the schizophrenic state of conversations about diversity, multiculturalism, color-blindness, and good ole fashioned race and racism, we seem to be quite certain that there is nothing at all to be done about advanced capitalism and its total erosion of ethics. "TINA" (There Is No Alternative), the catchphrase from the 1980s, still seems to hold, describing this general consensus that there is no alternative and no viable critique of advanced capitalism; consequently, mainstream US culture seems resigned to the impossibility of any meaningful ethics in these neoliberal times.[1] Only crazy leftists and idealistic academics still ask such questions.

Of course, it was always only crazy leftists and idealist academics who asked these questions. And, according to this mainstream narrative of US culture, it was only ever asked through one rubric: Marxism. Functioning synecdochically as the only attempted critique of capitalism, Marxist critique is readily discounted in the United States by such shibboleths of political history as Perestroika and the fall of the Berlin Wall. Consequently, with this clear evidence of its failure as a viable realpolitik, any critique of capitalism is cast into the naïve hues of nostalgia and romanticism. The dominant cultural narratives thus become those of liberalism's progress, naïve Marxist critique, and capitalism's final victory, rendering the challenge of an ethical critique of neoliberalism affectively as well as conceptually quite difficult. (And yet, something funny *is* going on with our vocabularies of social difference: hmmm. . . .)

This failure of the spirit or language of Marxist critique to cathect mainstream US culture is part of my motivation to try to think beyond Marxist frameworks here. Clearly, there is a rich (and ongoing) history of Marxist critique through which scholars of political economy have realized the limits of classical Marxist analyses and thereby reconceptualized them for the intricacies of globalization, socialism, postsocialism, and neoliberalism. Following Stuart Hall's incisive analysis of the various strands of Marxist critique across the twentieth century in his essay "The Problem of Ideology: Marxism Without Guarantees," published in 1983, I do not call out the entire Marxist apparatus as irrelevant to our analyses of neoliberalism.[2] Not only would this kind of complex analysis of liberalism, Marxism, and neoliberalism be far beyond the scope of my abilities, but I also reiterate again that analyses of neoliberalism in the registers of political economy are both urgent and necessary.

When considering the thorny questions of subject formation, social difference, and ethics in the neoliberal iteration of the modern episteme, however, I want to follow Foucault's insistence that neoliberalism does not function as an ideology. While Foucault's distancing from Marxist apparati is not a new theme in his oeuvre, the impact of it in his analyses of neoliberalism is particularly jarring for contemporary scholarship, as I outlined in chapter 1. Therefore, following Hall, I turn specifically to those accounts of ideology and interpellation by Louis Althusser, especially in his famous essay "Ideology and Ideological State Apparatuses (Notes Towards an Investigation)."

As Hall shows so deftly, we must turn to Althusser for these kinds of questions about "the processes by which new forms of consciousness, new conceptions of the world, arise" or "how social ideas arise."[3] We must turn to Althusser, that is, for cohesive accounts of ideology because "Marx developed no general explanation of how social ideas worked, comparable to his historico-theoretical work on the economic forms and relations of the capitalist mode of production."[4] It is Althusser, as Hall argues so persuasively, who "put on the agenda the whole neglected issue of how ideology becomes internalized, how we come to speak 'spontaneously,' within the limits of the categories of thought which exist outside us and which can more accurately be said to think us."[5] But there is yet another reason to turn to Althusser here: the profound, long-standing, and ongoing impact of his theories of interpellation across the theorizing of gender, sexuality, and race.

QUEER THEORY: THE LONG ARC OF THEORIZING RACE AND GENDER THROUGH INTERPELLATION

With a slightly ironic tone, Stuart Hall concludes his analysis of Althusser with a rather barbed rhetorical question: "If the function of ideology is to 'reproduce' capitalist social relations according to the 'requirements' of the system, how does one account for the subversive ideas or for ideological struggle?"[6] Or, in terms that may be a bit more familiar, if we are all interpellated, how can we resist? I am guessing this is not a new question for most, if not all, readers of this book. I am also guessing we have a similar range of answers, especially if we are at all versed in queer theory: performative repetition, disidentification, or perhaps (still) just "drag." Althusser's theorizing of interpellation, with its underpinnings in ideology and identification, is foundational to queer theory. Moreover and more specifically, it is foundational to two rather different foundational figures of queer theory: Judith Butler (*Gender Trouble*) and José Esteban Muñoz (*Disidentifications*).[7] In each of these theorists, Althusserian interpellation provides the foundational conceptual schema, albeit through diametrically opposed modes of citation, through which they reorient us to queer understandings and practices of gender, sexuality, and race.

This is unnerving not only because it may render the conceptual resources of queer theory woefully limited for the analysis of neoliberal social rationalities, but also because Butler and Muñoz initiate fairly different fields of scholarship, pedagogy, performance, and even activism. Canonized as a founding figure of queer theory per se, Butler and her theories of gender performativity as a mode of interrupting and resisting the heterosexual matrix have impacted so many fields I would not dare to enumerate them. Muñoz, however, is canonized as founding a particular field within queer theory—namely, queer of color critique—through his remarkably innovative work in performance studies with the politico-aesthetic concept of disidentification.[8] This bifurcation, wherein Butler founds the racially unmarked "queer theory" and Muñoz's work is marked by his race, captures part of my concern and is a long-standing fault line within queer theory. But rather than hashing over these problematics internal to queer theory, I raise a loud caution for the field as a whole and turn explicitly to each of these theorists as powerful examples of how we have come to theorize gender and race.

Race and gender operate very differently in the neoliberal episteme. By rooting my analysis of both of them in figures central to queer theory, I take the entanglement of both race and gender with sexuality to be self-evident. More strongly, I take both gender and race to be constituted in and through sexuality. But, as I will elaborate across the remainder of the book, I argue that gender largely carries forward the aestheticizing of social difference inherent in neoliberal social rationalities, while race lingers in deep historical reservoirs that jam the neoliberal machine.

In Butler, the role of Althusser in *Gender Trouble*, published in 1989, is apparently so profound that she does not even recognize the need to cite him: his name is not listed in the index. Her arguments are, however, thoroughly Althusserian, arguing over and over that "gender is performatively produced and compelled by regulative practices of gender coherence,"[9] which sounds remarkably similar to the processes Althusser calls interpellation. To make the matter even worse, her example (arguably the exemplar) of birth as the site of gendering is precisely the same example Althusser describes in "Ideology and Ideological State Apparatuses," published in 1970. Illustrating how interpellation works, he writes:

> Before its birth, the child is therefore always-already a subject, appointed as a subject in and by the specific familial ideological configuration in which it is "expected" once it has been conceived. I hardly need add that this familial ideological configuration is, in its uniqueness, highly structured, and that it is in this . . . structure that the former subject-to-be will have to "find" its place, i.e., "*become*" *the sexual subject* (*boy or girl*) *which it already is in advance.*[10]

I read this omission as largely caused by Butler's focus on sorting out the Lacanian symbolic in this early work of hers. Given the Lacanian scaffolding of Althusser's arguments, this makes sense. I do not, therefore, pretend here to call out some aspect of Butler's thinking that has never been noticed or that somehow renders the work flawed or lacking value. *Gender Trouble* is one of the most influential books of the late twentieth century. I am not attempting to dethrone it. While I do think the profound influence and absence of Althusser in *Gender Trouble* may point to a problematic dominant reading of Foucault that comes out of Butler, I do not pretend to rehearse those arguments here. Rather, I am interested in this project because of the massive circulation and impact of *Gender Trouble* in the late twentieth and early twenty-first centuries in overdeveloped countries. I will return to this at length in chapter 4.

Turning to Muñoz, we find the role of Althusser much more explicit in his *Disidentifications*, published in 1999. Indeed, in the fabulous opening scene with Marga Gomez, Muñoz tells us that she "performs her disidentificatory desire" and thereby calls attention "to the mysterious erotic that interpellated her as a lesbian."[11] He then proceeds to explain his indebtedness to Althusser explicitly through the work of Michel Pêcheux, who developed the concepts of identification, counteridentification, and disidentification directly out of his readings of Althusser. Muñoz thereby defines disidentification as "the third mode of dealing with dominant ideology, one that opts neither to assimilate within such a structure nor strictly opposes it; rather, disidentification is a strategy that works on and against dominant ideology."[12] Tellingly, in the very next paragraph, Muñoz claims a parallel use of disidentification in the work of Judith Butler.

The roots of this term for Muñoz also emerge out of Norma Alarcón's use of it in her important essay "The Theoretical Subjects of *This Bridge Called My Back* and Anglo-American Feminism," published in 1991.[13] Again, in the opening lines of the essay, Alarcón cites Althusser explicitly to describe her analysis of the writers of *Bridge* as "being aware of her displacement across a multiplicity of discourses: feminist/lesbian, national, racial, and socioeconomic."[14] For Alarcón, this holding of multiple positions within one's subjectivity is precisely what Anglo-American feminists cannot conceptualize, wedded as they are to "a modal person" who "proceeds according to the logic of identification."[15] Disidentification, for which she also acknowledges Pêcheux's work, thereby emerges in Alarcón's work out of the multiple voices of *Bridge* and their embodiment of multiple, antagonistic subject positions. Muñoz calls this kind of multiplicity "identities-in-difference [that] emerge from a failed interpellation within the dominant sphere."[16]

The political ethos that animates all three theorists (Butler, Muñoz, and Alarcón) is the project of destabilizing the subject. Across all three, this occurs through both complex theoretical maneuvering and the archiving and reporting of various cultural performances, with a careful eye toward what Muñoz describes as "laboring to enact permanent structural change while at the same time valuing the importance of local or everyday struggles of resistance."[17] These theorists are brilliant, incisive, creative writers to whom I, along with so many, am deeply indebted for opening various possibilities for thinking both normativity and resistance. But the projects of destabilizing a subject with deep interiority and the various characteristics that often find purchase there, such as agential rationality, stem largely from classical liberalism and the general schema of the Enlightenment that critical theory gives us (and clearly influences Butler and Muñoz). That is, while both Butler and Muñoz have had a remarkable impact on our theorizing of gender, race, sexuality, and resistance, the terms of their thinking in these early, groundbreaking texts are distinctly Althusserian. And as such, they may have less traction than we imagined when it comes to understanding and interrupting neoliberal subjects of interest.

THE LIMITS OF INTERPELLATION

To move through the kinds of transformations in subject formation that Foucault excavates and that I argue are well underway in this neoliberal iteration of the modern episteme, I begin to bring the Lacanian scaffolding of Althusser's thinking to the foreground. In an essay written in 1964 simply titled "Freud and Lacan," Althusser elaborates his defense of both Freud and Lacan as critical resources for theorizing the complex processes of social change, especially at the level of the subject.[18] Defending "the scientificity of psycho-analysis" (LP, 129), Althusser focuses on two axes: "the familial ideology" (LP, 129) and Lacan's recasting of Freudian schematics into language. Fused together, he gives us a succinct elaboration of the symbolic, which he notably refers to interchangeably as "the Law of Order" and "the Law of Culture" (LP, 142). With a brief noting of "the imaginary fascination of the ego" (LP, 143) in Freud's accounts of the pre-Oedipal fort/da scene in *Beyond the Pleasure Principle*, Althusser focuses on the symbolic to give an explicitly Lacanian account of interpellation. Calling it "the dialectic of the symbolic Order itself, i.e., . . . the dialectic of human Order, the human norm" (LP, 143), he develops it precisely in the order of what we post-Butlerians call "gender," again offering a reading of infancy that strongly echoes that of *Gender Trouble*.[19]

While this essay is fairly elementary in relation to contemporary Lacanian theorizing, I bring it forward to emphasize the explicitly Lacanian understanding of social authority that structures Althusser's account of interpellation. The Marxist frame of Althusser's work and our uptake of it is explicit. But Althusser's crucial addendum of interpellation to the Marxist account of ideology is explicitly Lacanian, as the final sentence of the essay shows: "This has opened up one of the ways which may perhaps lead us some day to a better understanding of this *structure of misrecognition*, which is of particular concern for all investigations into ideology" (LP, 149). Even more importantly for my argument, however, only two of the three registers of Lacan's heuristic schematic constitute Althusser's reading of Lacan: he emphasizes the symbolic and notes the imaginary, but the real never surfaces in any of Althusser's thinking about interpellation.

This crucial omission has deeply skewed our understandings of race, especially in these neoliberal times.

To elaborate this argument, which absorbs the rest of this book, I begin by arguing that the concept of social authority as a continuous, cohesive, singular function that serves as Althusser's bedrock assumption no longer functions solely in these manners.[20] One of the most jarring of transformations underway in this neoliberal iteration of the modern episteme is the gradual and sporadic eclipse of the symbolic and our social cathexis to it.

In her provocative *Democracy and Other Neoliberal Fantasies*, Jodi Dean argues that neoliberalism, particularly as exacerbated by the techno-frenzy culture that she names "communicative capitalism," evacuates previous social scripts and the identities they spawn. Drawing on Žižek and his reading of Lacan, she shows how neoliberalism effects "the decline of symbolic efficiency,"[21] which in turn renders the traditional mode of subjectivation via interpellation ineffective. Linking it to Michael Hardt and Antonio Negri's account of the crisis of institutions such as the nuclear family, the school, the neighborhood, the church, and so on, Dean emphasizes how this lack of symbolic investiture has multiple, mostly damaging effects. We no longer have any clear models of authority: whether a progress report from the school or a medical diagnosis from the doctor or a piece of advice from the cleric, we immediately seek second, third, even fourth opinions (most often via our favorite screen) and thereby extend our ambivalence about the very possibility of certainty. Stripping modern epistemologies of their barometers of certitude, this eclipse of symbolic force and cultural authority fragments and multiplies both rationalities and subjectivities: identities no longer function with clear and distinct boundaries, roles, meanings, or purposes.

For Dean, this renders individuals even more vulnerable to mechanisms of control and manipulation. As she writes, "Communicative capitalism's circuits of entertainment and consumption supply the ever new experiences and accessories we use to perform this self-fashioning" (DNF, 66–67) that neoliberalism enjoins its subjects to engage. She thus follows out Žižek's reading that, in this failure of the symbolic order to interpellate, we are regulated through another register of the Lacanian schematic, the imaginary. Subjects regulated purely by the imaginary are governed by the endlessly proliferating comparative devices of an ideal ego. This renders us endlessly aspirational as this purely social (not moral or epistemological) apparatus dishes up endless ideals to simulate.

In the neoliberal episteme, this translates into following out one's interests in any of the endless avenues presented to them by their economic and consumer interests, that is, by the market, writ very, very large as the social fabric per se. In the techno-frenzied field of advanced capitalism, these can be dizzying, but this vertigo should only further stimulate the quest for cooler and cooler stuff—and cooler and cooler selves. Enacting a full externalizing of identity, neoliberalism offers what Dean describes as "an immense variety of lifestyles with which I can experiment" (DNF, 66). Subjects of neoliberalism are enticed to engage in the endless and also constantly changing practices of self-fashioning, landing us all in an infinite quest for that perfect self, which turns out to be that perfect look. That the quest is infinite need not make it pernicious—such would only be the response of a symbolically interpellated subject, a subject with clear expectations, roles, and designs. For this imaginary subject of neoliberalism, the proliferation of interests is precisely the play of subjectivity itself. Ateleological to the core, the neoliberal subject of interests is not invested in reaching any resting place of a singular, fixed identity. To be The Perfect Mother or The Perfect Student or The Perfect Worker is the death of subjectivity, the cessation of the freedom of self-fashioning, for the neoliberal subject.

While Dean assumes Žižek's Lacanian registers, her descriptions also elaborate Foucault's analysis of the neoliberal subject as a subject of interests. Driven by external economic incentives, these imaginary identities of neoliberalism are increasingly aestheticized and, consequently, so are the modes of determining worth and meaning: we are what and how we can buy, what and how we can compete, what and how we can look, what and how we can appear. This is the full-blown California cult of self with which, despite his adamant disavowals, Foucault's late writings on the care of the self are so often confused.[22] It is also, as Dean clearly sees, how neoliberalism is the birth-site of biopolitics: despite the illusion of freedom that this enticement to endless self-fashioning offers, these neoliberal imaginary subjects of interests become subject to greater and more diffuse societal controls.

Evacuated of internal controls and boundaries that the prescripted identities of symbolic interpellation secure (for better or worse), this externalized subject of neoliberalism is left utterly vulnerable to the whims of media, styles, fads, and trends: "*I must be fit; I must be stylish; I must realize my dreams. I must because I can—everyone wins. If I don't, not only am I a loser but I am not a person at all; I am not part of everyone*" (DNF, 67). As Dean writes, neoliberal "imaginary identities are incapable of establishing a firm place to stand" (DNF, 67). Consequently, when violence becomes cool or disasters become fascinating, neoliberal subjects have no internal script with which to respond: we lack a vocabulary of evaluation other than that of the enterprising maxim "maximize interests."

Foucault's insistence that neoliberalism does not function as an ideology and his excavation of the neoliberal "subject of interests" exceed the Althusserian conceptual schematic. Living in diffuse states of heightened stimulation, as the work of Jodi Dean shows, neoliberal subjects of interests undergo processes of subject formation that no longer fully succumb to the psychosocial force of Althusserian interpellation. A concept that has dominated post-Hegelian, leftist theory, interpellation has been the primary heuristic for analyzing sociopsychic formation across the last four decades, whether explicitly in Marxist and neo-Marxist analyses or implicitly in feminist and queer analyses. While it has offered many insights about subject formation, the limits and possibilities of social resistance, and (of course) the basic functioning of ideology, interpellation has also failed to grasp many of the messy and irrational aspects of sociopsychic formation. Focused on processes of identification through the force of cultural authority, interpellation constrains analyses of sociopsychic formation to frameworks of hegemony. This has been and still is a valuable and insightful analysis, but we need to sharpen our topography of the neoliberal social landscape to locate the spaces where the Althusserian analysis applies more precisely.

In Foucaultian terms, as Eva Cherniavsky and Falguni Sheth argue, the role and force of sovereign power have been eclipsed and transformed, but have not disappeared from the contemporary episteme. Cast in the terms of the classic liberalism that grounds the Marxist-Althusserian framework, the neoliberal rejection of the state can never be fully complete. Rather, I argue that the role of the state is shifting in this neoliberal episteme to a narrower and more explicitly racializing function that we should aptly call the carceral state. But as a neoliberal social rationality has encroached more and more upon all of our modes of reflection and everyday practices, the role of the state in mediating subjective formation has weakened considerably. This is an example of how neoliberal practices eclipse the role and force of the symbolic and how, consequently, interpellation's lacunae become more and more pronounced. By turning directly to Althusser's classic formulation of the constitutive parts of interpellation, I aim to map precisely how and where interpellation is still fully in force and how and where it is losing traction in sociopsychic formations underway in neoliberal social rationalities. This will, in turn, help to excavate the precise contours of neoliberal racializing schemas.

REREADING ALTHUSSER, AGAIN

In his classic text "Ideology and Ideological State Apparatuses (Notes Towards an Investigation)," Althusser develops an account of social authority that, while explicit in Marxist ideological analyses, is also implicit in the classical liberal contractarian traditions. It is thus still functioning, albeit in a greatly transformed manner, in the neoliberal iteration of the modern episteme. (And in the sociohistorical fugue of my analysis.) Althusser emphasizes several structural factors that enable interpellation to call various subject positions into existence: the fundamental unity of the multiple Ideological State Apparatuses (ISAs) through the unified function as (ruling) ideology;[23] the ways in which, albeit sometimes subtly, ISAs are conditioned by the existence of Repressive State Apparatuses (RSAs), such as the police or the army; the material existence of ISAs in people's everyday practices, which are in turn regulated through rituals; and the explicit, clear moment of recognition in the act of hailing, which Althusser insists is "one and the same thing as ideology" (LP, 118).

The explicit location of ideology in material practices of individuals and, even more so, Althusser's insistence on the multiplicity and plurality of ISAs begin to look like the fragmenting of the social fabric that Jodi Dean diagnoses in neoliberalism. His ongoing insistence on the fundamental unity of these disparate practices, however, focuses his analysis on the dominant (hegemonic) functions of the liberal contractarian aspects of the modern episteme, namely, a social authority that functions through a juridical rationality and an obedient subject who responds with a psychological interiority. Bracketing for the moment the function of the police and army as Repressive State Apparatuses that structure and enforce a neoliberal racializing schema, I argue that Althusserian interpellation misses a great deal of the kinds of "new" sociopsychic formations underway in the neoliberal iteration of the modern episteme.

Practices of neoliberalism, as Jodi Dean's accounts contend, occur at the level of everyday practices. Unlike in Althusser's account, however, the neoliberal subject of interests is no longer the sedimented effect of assuming a socially scripted position: the neoliberal subject of interests is purely the effect of his or her practices, which are driven by his or her calculated interests, which are manipulated and produced by multiple markets. These practices and the fragmented, multiplied, intensified subjectivities they produce have no concern or investment in unity, whether that unity is registered as societal (nation, race, family, class, gender) or individual (secured interiority). To the contrary, any question of social or even personal cohesion is subsumed under the single, pressing question of return on and, even more so, maximizing investment. Whether that investment is monetary, temporal, aesthetic, emotional, or some other kind, the drive of neoliberal subjects is to intensify and maximize, not to unify. There is no unity, even at the most subtly ideological level, endemic to practices of neoliberalism.

The sheer plurality and variety of these normalizing, entrepreneurial, enterprising practices of neoliberalism then bring us to perhaps the most decisive break from these mechanisms of interpellation: the role of rituals to synthesize and unify ideological practices. If there is one way to capture a good deal of the changes in sociality in neoliberalism, this strikes me as it: the attenuation of the role of rituals. While one could imagine arguing that contemporary sociality still partakes in rituals, but with very different kinds of codings, they are not the kinds of rigidly scripted rituals that Althusser relies on to produce the semblance of timelessness to assure either the eschatology or the naturalness of the values sanctified by the rituals.

Take Žižek's favorite example: choosing a ridiculously complex drink at Starbucks, while being soothed by the knowledge that one is "doing one's part" for the environment and the globalized economy.[24] While this practice, which Žižek reads as a quintessentially neoliberal practice, certainly occurs in patterned kinds of behavior that one might call a ritual, it is but a fleeting practice among hundreds of others that might supplant, enhance, confuse, conflict, or simply disregard it at any moment. Keeping up with the changes in Starbucks menu is itself a dizzying practice: this is not the kind of ritual that ideological interpellation enacts. Moreover, a mere five years from now may well bring the intensification and marketing of practices around breathing fresh air or standing up straight or laughing more boisterously, rather than drinking different coffees.

Whatever the new trend, the kinds of practices involved are not the kinds of rituals Althusser has in mind, which are culturally, historically sedimented repetitions such as attending Mass on Sunday, kneeling to pray, obeying the headmaster, getting married with no concept of a divorce (or a prenuptial contract), keeping one job for an entire lifetime, obeying and pleasing one's husband, devoting oneself entirely to parenting, and professing undying loyalty to one's nation, one's race, one's community, one's sports team, and so on. These are the rituals that bind ISAs together: they are the heart and blood of ideology. And, most importantly, they are the rituals that interpellate us into clearly scripted subject positions.[25] But they are no longer the kinds of everyday practices that animate living in these neoliberal times.

Finally, we come to the celebrated moment of that infamous cop: the hailing of interpellation that is the most explicit moment of contact with the Law. In his development of this critical aspect of ideological interpellation, Althusser emphasizes that "the existence of ideology and the hailing or interpellation of individuals as subjects are one and the same thing" (LP, 118). He is most concerned to disabuse us of the temporal succession that the classic story of the cop hailing a person on the street implies. As he says, "For the convenience and clarity of my little theoretical theatre I have had to present things in the form of a sequence, with a before and an after, and thus in the form of a temporal succession" (LP, 118). But this is misleading: "In reality these things happen without any succession" (LP, 118).

The recognition that one is always already hailed is immediate. Even more so, one becomes a subject capable of such recognition precisely through the ideological hailing itself: without hailing, there is no subject.

And yet, we are always already subjects—and thus always already hailed, always already interpellated by ideology. As Althusser puts it, "The category of the subject is the constitutive category of all ideology, whatever its determination (regional or class) and whatever its historical date, . . . [but] the category of the subject is only constitutive of all ideology insofar as all ideology has the function (which defines it) of 'constituting' concrete individuals *as subjects*" (LP, 115–16). Butler's classic work in *Gender Trouble*, as I have already suggested, accentuated and popularized this dynamic considerably.

Once more, however, we find that this aspect of ideology is no longer fully functioning in neoliberalism. In the endless practices of self-fashioning that are driven by the incitement to maximize interests, one is never a concrete, singular individual replete with the interiority assumed by this model of subject formation. Indeed, the concept of "freedom" in neoliberalism has arguably become the ability to change one's self endlessly, even in a single day: one can be the trampy girl in the morning, the good student in the mid-morning, the happy worker at noon, the disgruntled tenant in the afternoon, the dutiful daughter in the early evening, the creative artist in the evening, and the debauched lover of fun in the night (perhaps returning to trampy girl in the morning, but perhaps having a nice latté instead). Yes, this little riff comes from the schedule of a young woman in college, which is a very particular time of a very particularly classed life that US culture encodes as unusually elastic and unstructured, but it nonetheless captures the kind of alterations in self-presentation that neoliberal social rationalities encourage and incite in us. Toss in the frenzies of techno-culture and, as the work of Juana María Rodríguez in *Queer Latinidad* so provocatively shows, a single person can take on countless identities—even of the most radically different kinds—simultaneously in the virtual world.

Our neoliberal ways of living are outstripping our liberal, modern epistemologies. While interpellation certainly involves the phenomenon of being multiply interpellated, the Althusserian schematic does not describe what is occurring in the neoliberal modes of subjectivation. Whereas the Althusserian notion of interpellation allows for self-reflection on the ways that we are always already interpellated and, arguably, thereby allows for some modicum of agency in negotiating (performing, disidentifying with) the given set of social scripts, neoliberal subjects *have no interest* in breaking up, disrupting, or dismantling social scripts of set subject positions: we are not cathected to them. Such scripts and the hegemonic authority they enact (for better and for worse) are of no interest to neoliberal subjects of interests. Indeed, they may not even hold any meaning at all for us. In Jodi Dean's Lacanian-Žižekian formulation, these identities may be better understood as operating in and through the Lacanian imaginary, rather than through symbolic interpellation: neoliberal subjects are quintessentially postmodern subjects of pure surface, evacuated of the heavy baggage of identities.

FROM THE RACIAL CONTRACT TO THE CARCERAL STATE

Having located the lacunae of interpellation as a heuristic device for subjective formations underway in the neoliberal episteme, I now turn to the precise site of its ongoing relevance: the carceral state. Clearly a racializing institution, the carceral state in its emergence in the neoliberal episteme indicates one of the fundamental limits to the neoliberal transformation of liberal values. Arguably functioning at the very heart of the neoliberal episteme and most certainly at the heart of my sociohistorical fugue, the carceral state exposes the one persistent historical pattern that has deep roots in cultures of liberalism: racialization.

True to Foucault's account of neoliberalism as emergent out of theories, concepts, values, and practices of classical liberalism, the question of the state (its role, its size, the modes of its governance) in the neoliberal iteration of the modern episteme is extremely thorny.[26] Without pretending to do justice to those debates, I argue that the explosion of incarceration rates in the US since the 1970s shows the ongoing relevance—and limits—of Althusserian interpellation for our concepts of race. That is, I am more interested in what the emergence of the carceral state means for processes and concepts of race than in what it means for transformations in the functioning of the state. (Accordingly, I continue my discussion of the racializing project of the prison industrial complex in chapter 5.)

The carceral state, as I am calling it, provides an urgent example of how neoliberal social rationalities and formations emerge out of, intertwine and overlap with, and sometimes intensify classically liberal social rationalities and formations. Reading it as a racializing institution then beckons for new concepts of race to capture its complex (and new) processes. Given the horrific rates of incarceration for people of color in the United States and the compounding epidemic of state-sanctioned violence and killing of people of color that the #BlackLivesMatter movement is finally exposing, the carceral state as a racializing institution particularly sharpens the need for new concepts of race that can move beyond the classically liberal reliance on inclusion and a broadening of the social contract as sufficient to ameliorate long-standing historical racial inequality.[27]

In Althusser's account, the Repressive State Apparatuses (RSAs) crucially enforce a unity upon the plural, material instantiations of ideology. While I have argued that this kind of unified sociality is no longer cathecting neoliberal subjects of interests, the role of state force nonetheless continues to regulate—indeed, to criminalize, imprison, and kill—a racially selected portion of the US population. Althusser's account of the RSAs thereby brings us to some of the thorniest issues confronting analyses of neoliberalism.

First of all, it forces the issue of the neoliberal state, which sounds oxymoronic. The break from the state is the animating point of departure for neoliberalism as an economic policy: both German and US forms of neoliberalism argue explicitly against Bismarckian and Keynesian welfare policy, respectively. The state is, from the beginning, anathema to neoliberal theories and policies. But that rejection of the state, which can never be complete, focuses primarily on the state's interactions with the economy, granting vast latitude to other functions of the state, especially the repressive functions of the police and the army.[28]

In the US iteration of the neoliberal episteme, RSAs no longer unify interpellation for all citizen-subjects. Intensifying for particular parts of the population, they transform from a general to a selective operation of repression that enacts long-standing schemas of xenophobia, especially racism, while enabling circuits for neoliberal subjects to maximize their interests. To put it too bluntly, who gets to maximize their interests and who gets imprisoned or enlisted in or killed by the military and police becomes an enactment of these long-standing historical schemas of racialization and xenophobia. The persistent role of the RSAs in the neoliberal episteme thereby forces a second difficulty: the persistence of racism, despite the neoliberal celebrations of diversity and the insistent evidence of a postracist era in phenomena such as the black middle class.

The classically liberal answer to this alleged problem of racism is to frame it as an historical accident of exclusion. The corrective, accordingly, involves the gradual extension of the social contract and its benevolent bequest of rights upon more and more disenfranchised minoritarian populations, often conceived as "getting in line" in a stunning teleology.[29] The carceral state refuses such iterations of the benevolent social contract, halting this progress narrative in its tracks. As Michelle Alexander's (among many others') work shows, the state apparatuses of the police and the army have expanded to historically unforeseen proportions in this neoliberal episteme and are directly enforcing and enacting racist demarcations upon select populations: the prison and the army have become explicitly racializing institutions.[30] Just consider the long litany of now-named laws, such as "Stand Your Ground" or "Stop and Frisk," that have direct, explicitly racist effects. Or consider the astoundingly global exposure of police brutality against people of color in the United States by the #BlackLivesMatter movement in the fall of 2014. It would appear to be a foregone conclusion that Althusser's RSAs are fully in effect, functioning as repressive structures to enforce an ideology of racism.

I caution, however, that this is only viable as a partial explanation, albeit a very important one, especially given the flows of capital. The focus on these actions of the police and military often problematically feeds the kind of simplified and flattened ideological reading of neoliberalism that posits the carceral state as doing the dirty work of the elite class, albeit with varying allegations of intentionality and in various guises, including such things as the defunding of inner-city schools that then funnel those populations into the military and prison.[31] Given the neoliberal mantras of "diversity" and the "historically accidental" character of racism, however, this kind of analysis finds very little, if any, traction with neoliberal subjects of interests who are adamantly postrace and, more broadly, postxenophobia. Neoliberal subjects of interests do not cathect with the materially brutal reality of the carceral state as anything other than the fodder of ideological warfare—and the cynicism it breeds. Given that the state apparatuses of the police and the army do not directly interpellate and repress the entire polis, we must read them beyond (if alongside) the Althusserian schematic of ideology, interpellation, and RSAs. In the neoliberal carceral state, the police, military, and other extrajudicial security forces function, rather, as limits to the maximizing efforts of proper neoliberal subjects of interests—limits that are, crucially, racializing.

The #BlackLivesMatter movement, which is emerging in the United States and globally literally as I send this book to the final stages of production, is dramatically exposing the violence of these racializing limits. The potential of this movement is astounding, so I cannot possibly anticipate how it might unfold beyond December 2014. For the analysis of neoliberal racism I am developing, however, the demands of the movement will be sadly limited if they are framed solely in juridical terms. I understand the carceral state to include the rule of law, which is how the failure to indict the "cops" (whether employed by the state or privatized security firms) who killed Trayvon Martin, Michael Brown, John Crawford, Eric Garner, and countless others is unsurprising. As Lisa Marie Cacho argues, "legal recognition is not and cannot be a viable solution for racialized exploitation, violence, and poverty."[32] If this movement reaches beyond the arc of legal remediation, which is so often the scene of ideological embattlement, it could ignite new forms of antiracism sufficient to the neoliberal contortions of race and racism. If, that is, this movement reaches beyond the purview of the carceral state to incite awareness of—and caring about—the insidious forms of racism that live in the crooks and crannies of our everyday lives, then it may incite an antiracist ethics.

My concern is, therefore, to track how the carceral state's racializing limits to neoliberal subjects of interests instantiate and depend upon a transformation of social cathexes and social difference. Before turning directly to that in the following chapter, I return briefly to Foucault's provocation about a split subjectivity at the heart of liberalism.

Recall that Foucault sketches, through the texts of Hume, Locke, and various eighteenth-century economists, how the social contract tradition of liberalism posits both the subject of rights and a subject of interests. While the subject of rights anchors the rich tradition of the citizen and his (always still his) obligations and sacrifices to the state, the subject of interests circulates much more quietly as the egoist interest (*homo economicus*) that the market serves, with an intriguingly invisible and unknowable rationality. Extending Charles Mills's historical evidence that the social contract is always already a racial contract, I argue that this exalting of the citizen over *homo economicus* is also always already a racializing schema.

By locating the state and its regulation of citizenship as the primary, if not only, site of political intervention, the contractarian tradition effectively erases the role of *homo economicus* from any kind of historical exclusions—whether racialized, classed, gendered, sexualized, abled, nationalized, etc. The contractarian tradition and its exaltation of citizenship as the singular category for redress thereby set *homo economicus* free from any role whatsoever in such kinds of historical, patterned prejudices and disparities. And this is, of course, precisely what neoliberalism intensifies and exacerbates, setting *homo economicus* loose to pursue its interests ad infinitum, without any limit from the state on matters of citizenship or exclusions whatsoever. *Homo economicus* finds its true freedom in the unfettered, gloriously neutral plane of the neoliberal market, intensified to the place of truth in the neoliberal episteme.

When Foucault locates this kind of subject of interests at the heart of liberalism, he at least sets a different stage than the one we have inherited from the state-centric, law-abiding one of the social contract tradition. If *homo economicus* has always already been running alongside the subject of rights, mostly underneath and preferably invisibly, then perhaps it has not been utterly uninvolved in the historically sedimented patterns of xenophobia that the liberal social contract—especially in contemporary, neoliberal iterations—prefers to refer to as unfortunate exclusions. For example, as the work of Naomi Zack shows, chattel slavery enacted a monetization of race by delineating clearly between those bodies who extrapolate labor into commerce and those bodies who are the commerce—that is, between those who breed other bodies for profit and those whose bodies are bred.[33] Or, in the language of neoliberalism, those who are entrepreneurs and those who are *not*.

In this light, race has always served as a systematic, generalizable schematic to distinguish between those who can and those who cannot pursue the egoist interests of *homo economicus*. While the subsumption of *homo economicus* into the subject of rights deferred our attention onto the sacrificial logic of obligation and responsibility, this return to the disavowed part of liberalism's split subjectivity helps us to see how the primary question of cathexis to the social contract has always already been racialized. Not only is the cruelty of the racial contract historically noxious and destructive to racialized bodies, but access to becoming a *proper* entrepreneur is also barred from racialized bodies.[34] Despite Milton Friedman's protestations, the market has never been neutral.

As practices of neoliberalism then begin to intensify *homo economicus* as the primary mode of subjectivation, these racialized histories still haunt the socially stratified enterprising activities of various, even conflicting stripes. For a quick example, popular, mainstream, white culture in the United States fetishizes black "gangsta" culture precisely as the victory of this enterprising impulse. Various modes of media screens allegedly celebrate the ostentatious displays of wealth by black stars of the music industry. But they do so only as an aberration that is an exception to the invisible and unspoken rule of proper enterprise. The carceral state then clearly enforces these limits and confines this subculture, policing the black instantiation of enterprise specifically as aberrant. Framed as a protection of the social sphere (that is, the social contract), the racializing of the market—that sacredly neutral social rationality—never comes to the fore. Rather, the carceral state appears to function as a disconnected, wholly external limit to the unlimited practices of neoliberalism: white bourgeois kids are totally cool for listening to and even parodying gangsta hip-hop in the suburbs, but they are not incarcerated for smoking the same weed.

RETHINKING RACE

If we are to understand these dynamics, we must push beyond interpellation as our analytic device for processes of subject formation and, especially, for racialization and racism. In the Lacanian terms that undergird Althusser's account, the reduction of social and subject formations to the concepts of ideology and interpellation restricts our thinking to the registers of the symbolic and the imaginary: symbolic authority (master, phallic signifiers, as they are known) structure an imaginary social field that is configured through dyadic, comparative relations, endlessly pursuing the ideal ego put forward by the symbolic function. But in a social field that lacks investment in and cathexis to a singular, unified symbolic, ideology becomes a purely imaginary formation wherein social controls cathect subjects through the endlessly comparative process of idealization, not authority. We are consumed with purely imaginary pursuits, that is, with endless comparative pursuits of phantom-like ideals that ricochet about the social field of ego-projections, fears, and ambitions. It's like a carnival funhouse, full of contorted mirrors and their disorienting images, projections, and spatiotemporal confusions.

If we continue to read processes of racialization and racism as ideological formations, we constrain ourselves to this space of the imaginary, which is largely dyadic. Lacan's originary accounts of the imaginary (for example, in the 1949 account of the mirror stage and the account of the inverted bouquet from seminar I in 1953–54)[35] locate it in the dyadic space of the mother and child, which is then extended through language into the ontology of other and self. In that (early) developmental account, misrecognition and alienation incite the incipient ego to develop as a "fortress" to guard against the aggressive imago, which is (mis)perceived as the source of pain and trauma. Animated by a fundamental narcissism, the imaginary ego is filled with aggression and competition, with illusions of wholeness ensuring an endless repetition of dyadic battles. (Ripe material for the neoliberal market, needless to say.)

This foundational dyadic formation morphs and constrains the ideological concepts of both race and racism in various ways: for example, (1) race becomes the category that mediates the dyadic self and other conflict—that is, it becomes the conceptual placeholder for Other-ness, which is always framed in an aggressive, narcissistically cathected struggle; (2) racism functions strictly in a dyadic (black and white) manner; (3) race gets framed as a social construction of the same sort we have located in the concept of gender (a deeply problematic move that I elaborate in chapter 4); and (4) as a social construction, race should come undone through ideological or political manipulation (landing us in the contemporary, ridiculous, and pernicious claims of a postracial era).

This ideological understanding of processes of racialization and racism has informed US concepts of race and racism since at least the Civil Rights Movement. Filled with identitarian politics, racialized (which means nonwhite in the United States) subjects have been taught, encouraged, prodded, and otherwise cajoled into becoming distinct, legible, celebratory identities that are readily recognized by mainstream US culture: the happy, well-adapted, healthy, upwardly mobile racialized subject who is "lifting up the race" becomes the damning metric for racialized subjects in the post–Civil Rights United States. As Antonio Viego explains, ethnic-racialized subjects must undertake this kind of healthy identity formation "in order to be considered a socially and culturally intelligible citizen-subject and . . . failing to do so would condemn him to radical subjective illegibility."[36]

To become a distinct, legible identity as a racialized subject requires a kind of pretense of wholeness, completion, and cohesion that necessarily disavows the messy, irrational, chaotic processes of subject formation. Moreover, this pursuit occurs simultaneously at the level of both the individual and the community, since the legible racialized subject is always already the tokenized representative of the race. In the ideological reading of processes of racialization, the command to become that ideal-racialized subject is always already to become the spokesperson for the entire race. As an ideal ego, the aspiration always fails, leaving the racialized subject the site of pathology, the subject in need of compensatory strengthening of the ego to adapt better to his or her culture—his or her *racist* culture. Who can bear that weight? And what kind of politics can we find here but the most conciliatory assimilation?

The turn away from trauma as a profound site of racialization in the United States warps our understandings of race and racism. It warps our theories, our politics, our abilities to reflect upon these complex, longstanding, sociopsychic dynamics. It warps our lives. As Viego incites us, we must theorize this loss and trauma "at the psychic, political, juridical, and economic levels."[37] We must do so to avoid providing, as Viego warns, "precisely the image of ethnic-racialized subjectivity as whole, complete, and transparent, an image upon which racist discourse thrives."[38] But we must also do so to find our ways through the madness that neoliberal forms of racism are becoming.

We must find a way to speak about race and racism that cuts against these ideological frameworks. While there is, of course, much sociologically explanatory power in each of the claims I enumerated above, they are also easily manipulated into ideological disagreements and their inevitable cynicism. In attempting to jar us from that register, I conclude with a powerful thread we find in the authors of *This Bridge Called My Back*. For example, listen to the visceral, embodied language of Andrea Canaan: "Racial memory coursed through my veins. Memories of being snatched away by friend and stranger, stuffed into vessels that traversed vast spaces of water, chained, whipped, branded, hunted and sold by overlapping generational systems of degradation."[39] Memories coursing through veins are not subject to ideological manipulation. "Sharing a common disaster," as Stuart Hall defined racism, is not subject to ideological manipulation.[40]

The call to embodied memory is thereby the line I want to cultivate. To do so, I continue to develop the Lacanian lexicon, moving toward a reading of race in the register Althusser omitted from his analysis: the real. Cast far beyond subjectivity as reduced to identity markers, the real allows us to think race and racism as powerful forces that refuse the reduction to sociological categories of identity—or remedies cast purely in their terms. If we are to think about ethics in these neoliberal times, we must create a meaningful way of talking about race and racism that cathects us to the long violent history of racism. To foreshadow arguments to come and riff on Hortense Spillers, we must find a language to talk about the censored chapter of our American grammar.

FIGURE 2a.1 John Lennon. © Bob Gruen / www.bobgruen.com.

INTERLUDE 2

Instant Cool!

John Lennon is undoubtedly one of the coolest white dudes ever known. And "Instant Karma!" encapsulates that coolness with remarkable historical clarity. Written in January 1970, evidently at breakneck speed, the song quickly became a kind of anthem for social justice movements and general antiestablishment resistance politics.[1] Lennon bestowed many such political gems upon us: "Give Peace a Chance," released in March 1969, and "Power to the People," released in December 1971, both easily come to mind as overtly politicized anthems aiming to galvanize a movement. But the lyrics of "Instant Karma!" capture more than the typical Lennon-esque cosmic plea for universal love. While the passing of that kind of plea from "cool" to "quaint" speaks to the aestheticizing, depoliticizing, and dehistoricizing slide of coolness that frames my work here, the lyrics of "Instant Karma!" directly mark the kind of cross-cultural, cross-racial politics that was just emerging in the early 1970s and that set the groundwork for the grand march of multiculturalism in the 1980s.[2] In 1970, the fans of John Lennon—living in northern and western Europe, North America, and Japan—did not know what "karma" was.

Of course, we all know what "karma" means now, more or less. And Lennon's claim of its happening instantaneously still holds immense appeal, even if the ethos and politics of the song are woefully outdated. It isn't the karma that we are concerned about. It is what the karma promises to deliver to us, instantaneously, that frames one of neoliberalism's most powerful fantasies: instant wealth!

CHAPTER THREE

From Instant Karma to Instant Wealth

THE FANTASIES AND CATHEXES OF THESE NEOLIBERAL TIMES

AIN'T NO USE: INSTANT WEALTH AND THE FRAYING OF THE AMERICAN DREAM

Why work hard when you could just, all at once, instantly become wealthy?! Why wake up early, punch the clock, work all day, punch the clock, unwind all evening, and then punch the alarm clock to do it all over again? Why spend the majority of your life toiling away just to pay the bills if you could, simply and magically, instantly become wealthy?

I am by no means an expert on and am, in fact, barely a consumer of popular culture in the United States. By the time I notice a pattern in popular culture, it is safe to assume it has become passé. So, please indulge this beginning with the banal and passé: the fantasy of instant wealth has become a regular mantra in cultures under the sway of neoliberal social rationalities. It seems clear, as we enter the mid-2010s, that US popular culture has been creating and widely disseminating the dream of instant wealth as an escapist fantasy of pure wish fulfillment for over two decades. Unlike the exception that has always haunted—and thereby also proved—the rule of liberalism and its mandate of the Protestant Work Ethic, the fantasy of instant wealth has transformed in neoliberal social practices into a widely circulated *possibility*. No longer just those crazy gold diggers headin' west, we neoliberals seem to believe that it is possible to become, all at once and with no effort, instantly wealthy. Or, at least, we like to watch and read and talk about this narrative a great deal: we enjoy the fantasy.

As with any widespread cultural phenomenon, there are many ways to interpret this ascendancy of instantaneous wealth as a possibility that various populations seem to believe is a viable moment in their individual lives. Read ideologically, for example, it can be understood as the kind of pernicious duping of the downwardly mobile middle class and working poor that politico-economic systems of neoliberalism wreak. This certainly offers insight into one aspect of the sociopsychic and material effects of the intensifying income disparities caused by neoliberal economic and political reforms. But it does not account for how and why people living in cultures where neoliberal social rationalities are circulating find this particular fantasy so alluring. The explanation that we are just grossly duped by hegemonic structures leaves subjectivity rather infantile, constantly tricked and confused into wanting things that the authorities make us think we want.

If Jodi Dean's extension of Foucault's analysis captures some crucial aspect of the transformations underway, then we need an analysis of this fantasy that does not position us as infantile subjects of desire.[1] Pursuing our interests kinetically, we need an explanation that does not fall back into the orders of the symbolic. We need an explanation of how and why we are so cathected to the fantasy of instant wealth. But, to foreshadow the Lacanian lexicon in which I undertake these analyses, we need to examine how this distinctively neoliberal fantasy functions in the register of the drive, rather than desire, where classically liberal fantasies cathect subjects with deep interiority.

Eerily, if also unsurprisingly, this fantasy of instant wealth manifests differently according to racialized dynamics that are very similar to the social effects of utility in cultures of classical liberalism (which I examined in *Queering Freedom*). The lure of the ostentatious, utterly over-the-top wealth of rap, hip-hop, and sports stars speaks differently—that is, receives and generates different cultural representations—than the ostentatious, utterly over-the-top wealth of college-educated, geek entrepreneurs or savvy investors. The life story of Mark Zuckerberg spun by the media is, for example, quite different from the kind of story of aberration that attaches to figures such as Snoop Dogg or 50 Cent. These differences matter, particularly as the differing kinds of displays of this wealth belie the persistence of long-standing racialized schemas, while simultaneously instantiating new ways to modulate them. But it is the formal sameness of the fantasy itself that I want to examine before turning to what it tells us about persistent racism in new, neoliberal racializing schemas.

I argue the fantasy of instant wealth offers a cultural representation of the neoliberal subject of interests as inhabiting a Lacanian circuit of the drives, wherein instant gratification, not the delayed anticipation of desire, animates activities. We love the fantasy of instant wealth because it is the direct effect of pleasurable activity, not the hard-earned, well-deserved satisfaction of good, honest labor and orthodox education: these neoliberal icons are so fabulous because they get instantly wealthy by simply doing what they love, by simply having fun, by simply *enjoying* themselves—over and over and over. As an instance of the shift from desire to the drive, from the subject of rights to the pursuer of interests, the fantasy of instant wealth simply eschews any social cathexis to utility, that sacrosanct value of liberalism. Again, in the Lacanian terms that I develop in this chapter, this precious *objet a* (utility) of liberalism's fantasy of neutrality loses its mooring in this dream of instant wealth and the desiring subject itself begins to fade from the neoliberal iteration of the modern episteme.

Once more performing what Husserlian phenomenologists might call an eidetic reduction, I bracket the racialized manifestations of this fantasy of instant wealth in this chapter to focus on its formal structure. First, I develop Jodi Dean's provocation that subjective formation in neoliberalism is structured by a shift from desire to the drive, emphasizing particularly how this manifests in a systemic move toward formalizing social difference itself. I then remain in a Lacanian analytic and frame liberalism through the psychoanalytic concept of a fantasy, arguing that cultures of liberalism are structured by the doubled fantasies of tolerance and neutrality.[2] I then return to this neoliberal fantasy of instant wealth to show how the neoliberal waning of the social cathexis to utility reverberates in alterations in the social cathexis to xenophobia, especially racism, and its structuring of social difference; accordingly, the doubled fantasies of neutrality and tolerance are also undergoing profound transformations. I conclude the chapter with a discussion of the implications of these transformations for meanings, modes, and cathexes to normativity in the neoliberal social rationality of calculation, especially in the exemplar of statistics, and the transformation of concepts of social difference into units of fungibility. While this is also not a particularly cool chapter, it is only after clearing this ground that I can begin turning toward rethinking race as the real.

CIRCUIT OF THE DRIVE AND FANTASY

Given Foucault's analysis of the overlaying and (at least) partial displacement of liberal modes of subjectivity and rationality by neoliberalism, neoliberal subjects do not lament the loss of an internal, juridically structured script. While it may be true that those modes of liberalism are not wholly displaced, while it may be true that we do still have some (albeit largely habitual and often desperate) recourse to transcendental foundations and juridical structures, the effect—especially the social cathexes—of such recourse is considerably weaker. Foucault's insistence that neoliberalism does not function as an ideology and his excavation of this "subject of interests" thereby give us a provocative way to approach this new social landscape, where we live in states of heightened stimulation that no longer fully succumb to the psychosocial force of Althusserian interpellation, the dominant lens through which post-Hegelian social theorists have understood subject formation, difference, and ethics.

The Lacanian schemas of the drive thus further enhance Foucault's analysis of these new social formations. Unlike ideological critiques of advanced capitalism, a Lacanian analysis of neoliberalism that derives from "the later Lacan" of the drive and the real avoids the naïve critique of consumerism as a classic instance of "chasing the phallus." We do not have to read the endless quest for cooler and newer stuff as a Marxist affirmation of alienation or as, in Freudo-Lacanian terms, an endless pursuit of fetishes to hide over the fundamental lack that marks all subjects in a phallocentric symbolic. The reading of neoliberal enterprising practices as enacting the circuit of the drive shows us how these practices of consumerism are, in and of themselves, quite satisfying. Practices of self-fashioning become practices of freedom in neoliberalism. The infinity of the endless quest for cooler and cooler stuff—and cooler and cooler selves—is precisely what sets subjectivity into play. Only a symbolically interpellated subject, still bound to the logic of wholeness, would find this infinity pernicious. To the contrary, for the neoliberal subject of interests, the endless proliferation of interests is precisely the play of subjectivity: the more you can intensify your interests, the more expansive, enterprising, and interesting you are. And the more you can stuff your mouth![3]

As this endless calculation of interests becomes an obsessive social rationality, it aims to absorb all aspects of living into a flattened horizon of endless accumulating and enhancing of interests. It thereby comes to function as a circuit of interests that, as the heuristic of Lacan's circuit of the drive accentuates, floats freely across the surface of relations without any social, historical, or ethical anchor. Whether our interests bolster a democratic or fascist state, whether they render us vulnerable or secure, whether they sustain social relations or enhance an isolated egoism is all beyond the purview of our pursuits. We are interest-seeking beings, purely and solely. And because we are such, the Law as a grand interdiction that regulates the dual functions of prohibition and transgression fails to engage us. To lament this loss is understandable, perhaps even necessary as a crucial memorial to the historical structures under erasure. But it is ultimately insufficient: nostalgia is just another quaint accessory, transformed into the coolness of "retro" through the neoliberal evacuating of historical signification.

As I discussed in chapter 2, Jodi Dean therefore argues that neoliberal subjects of interests respond primarily to the Lacanian register of the imaginary, wherein social controls cathect subjects through the endlessly comparative process of idealization, not authority. We are constantly comparing ourselves to ideal egos, aspiring to be more and more like them—only to find that this process repeats itself endlessly. For Dean, this initiates astute readings of how easily and subtly neoliberal subjects are thereby manipulated politically. Wholly externalized, we neoliberals are at the mercy of whatever political winds are blowing. Dean's extension of a Žižekian articulation of this in Lacanian registers emphasizes this move from the symbolic to the imaginary as the fundamental shift in political dynamics. I do not disagree with Dean's analysis, but I am interested in a different social register and, accordingly, a different psychosocial dynamic, namely, the ethical and our processes of cathexes, especially to social difference. Therefore, I take up her provocation that neoliberal subjects inhabit the Lacanian circuit of the drive to examine how this intersects with the fraying of two mutually constitutive ideals of liberalism: neutrality and tolerance.

To do so, I stay in a Lacanian mode of analysis and frame these two ideals as core, constitutive fantasies of classically liberal cultures. By reading the neoliberal social rationality as an eclipse of symbolic authority, I do not want to go so far as to claim that there are no longer any shared cultural scripts or narratives that bind subjectivities to one another, to one's self, and to a (variegated) social fabric. The claim that the neoliberal social rationality, especially depicted as enacting the circuit of the drive, erodes symbolic investiture does not go so far as to suggest that we are no longer partaking of socially shared and scripted narratives. As a culture filled with endless subcultures, we certainly continue to have common cultural referents that bind and unbind, include and exclude, and generally cathect us to specific objects, experiences, and bodies. But in my insistence that this is not happening according to logics of interpellation, I must find some way of explaining these dynamics without recourse to the kind of juridical law that unifies and formalizes authority in symbolic interpellation. Therefore, I turn now to the structures of fantasy to begin cultivating ways to understand this neoliberal kind of social cohesion and the subjectivity it spawns.

By reading neoliberal subjects as existing in the circuit of the drive, we first need to understand how neoliberal practices and values supplant older teleological stories of pleasure as satisfaction. One of the most striking features of the drive, in Lacan's texts, is its circuitous, adamantly ateleological structure. The drive, unlike desire and demand, with which it is closely paired in Lacan's etiologies, does not aim at any object of satisfaction. Structurally ateleological, its circuitous form enlivens repetition, rather than arrival, as the form of pleasure: at a physiological level that risks literalizing, it is the circular structure of the mouth, the ear, and the anus that renders them physical sites of intensified stimulation and thereby exemplars of the circuit of the drive.[4] Repetition in Lacan's account of the drive connects it back to Freud's theories of the death drive, which is always distinguished as "pure repetition."[5]

As a closed circuit, however, the drive begs the question of its relation to social context. First of all, as Dylan Evans emphasizes, the specific kind of cathexis animating the drive is, at the level of the individual, extremely variable and contingent on the life history of the subject—so much so that it might be rendered impervious to social forces and formations. Whether one is orally, scopically, or anally cathected may, etiologically, be mostly determined by one's individual experiences in the very early stages of life. When I follow the suggestion that neoliberal cultures are functioning at the level of the drive, however, I am not attempting this kind of etiological analysis; I am not, that is, attempting a kind of pseudo-Hegelian diagnosis of the grand development—and, inevitably imported into such accounts, lamentable regression or fixation—of culture as read on the model of individual development. Nor am I laying claim to the Freudian schema that ontogeny recapitulates phylogeny at the level of individual and cultural development. Rather, I am using Lacanian formulations as generative heuristic devices: what kinds of possible readings emerge out of this framing of a neoliberal culture as living in the circuit of the drive?

From this angle, it is less the variability of specific cause, content, or kind of drive than it is the formal properties of the drive as a closed circuit of endless repetition that generates insights into how neoliberal social subjectivity functions. As a closed circuit, the drive can never be synthesized into any greater whole; for example, as a sexualized experience, the circuit of the drive renders sexuality as partial, never harmonized into any whole—whether of identity, self, relationship, cultural or religious ideal, and so on.[6] As a closed circuit, the drive is not structurally connected with any symbolic investiture of personhood or transcendent cultural ideals. This does not mean, however, that the drive is not functioning within a social context. In an effort to elaborate how sociopsychic cathexes alter amid the historical overlaying of neoliberalism across liberalism, I develop the heuristic of a Lacanian account of how drives intersect with, diverge from, and resist the form and formation of fantasy.

My use of fantasy, accordingly, draws on the psychoanalytic development of it as a socially articulated framework that conditions our individual making of meaning. Unlike pedestrian connotations, wherein fantasy connotes those aspects of one's internal psychic life that are either unhinged from ("escapist") or compensating for ("wish fulfillment") the strictures of "reality," my psychoanalytic approach uses fantasy to connote a socially articulated set of values or ideals that do not function in fully conscious, rational, or linear manners. Unlike the obfuscations that concepts of hegemony and ideology claim to explain, however, fantasies cannot be properly located in any specific site or structure. While still allowing the differentiation of individual from social fantasies, the psychoanalytic concept of a social or cultural fantasy introduces a socially structured epistemology that does not rely on the central roles of authority and identification that render ideological interpellation insufficient to examine cultures of neoliberalism.

For psychoanalysis, fantasy operates through the cathexes it offers with particular values, hopes, and aspirations. Whether one's individual fantasy clashes or aligns with the constitutive fantasies of one's culture determines the value of that individual fantasy. If the fantasies align, they are seen as core, shared values of a society, scaled to whatever size (family, neighborhood, corporation, city, region, nation). If they clash, the individual's fantasy will be maligned as "escapist" or even "deranged," depending on the magnitude of the threat to the culturally cathected fantasy. (For example, in racialized terms, unaligned fantasies about race in the United States can range from "idealist" to "bigot.")

By using the psychoanalytic structure and concept of fantasy to read the emergent social rationalities of neoliberalism, I can develop a psychosocial taxonomy of the transformations in social cathexes underway in cultures of neoliberalism. As I have already developed, I situate neoliberalism as part of a fugue, wherein it layers upon and intensifies particular aspects of liberalism. The psychoanalytic framework of fantasy allows us to see how social cathexes to the shared, regulative values of classical liberalism—namely, tolerance and neutrality—are transforming in the neoliberal embrace of entrepreneurialism and diversity.

In order to analyze neoliberalism in this manner, I first examine how these twinned fantasies of classical liberalism (tolerance and neutrality) serve as a necessary condition for an individual to make meaning of his or her experience, both immediately and reflectively. Unlike the kind of cultural authority schematized in ideological interpellation, the fantasy serves as the interpretive background that remains unsaid.[7] It does not require constant repetition to enact its values; au contraire, it functions most forcefully when unspoken, fading into the naturalized glow of the communally assumed, unnoted because so fundamental. The structure of this kind of core fantasy helps us to see how the most forceful of a culture's values are (as Nietzsche indicated so long ago) those that remain unsaid—until punctured or challenged or exposed.[8]

It will finally be those moments of and dynamics involved in puncturing, challenging, and exposing that show us what is happening in the shifting social cathexes and evaluations underway in neoliberalism. In Lacanian terms, the kinds of intensifications underway in neoliberal practices expose the *objet a* of the fantasies of liberalism, thereby bringing them out of the background and transforming their functions.

THE DOUBLE FANTASY OF LIBERALISM: NEUTRALITY AND TOLERANCE

In Lacan's schema of fantasy, the cause of desire (*objet a*) subtends fantasy precisely by never coming into full or explicit view as a part of that fantasy. Unlike the phallus that exerts its power through its invisibility, the *objet a* must remain always fully "off-screen."[9] Think, for example, of the ways that a certain look, a tone of voice, an eroticized body part, a particular gesture or—especially in neoliberalism—a distinctive sartorial flair incite desire: utterly formal, these *objet a* expose the essentially impersonal character of desire. It is this utterly formal character that makes the function of fantasy particularly generative for grasping the social cathexes operating in neoliberal social spaces, although the shift from the scene of desire to the circuit of the drive considerably alters the structure of the fantasy and its cathexes with the social body, as I will show.

Reading liberalism in the schema of fantasy, I begin with what is, by now, an obvious set of claims from all ideological quarters. Whether celebrating, defending, critiquing, or protesting against liberalism, all share a common set of assumptions: liberalism sets itself apart from both autocratic and oligarchic regimes through the distinctive claim to both neutrality and tolerance. From classic theorists of liberalism to its various modern instantiations, the grand claim to neutrality as a political and economic system, most often spoken through such quintessentially neutral values as equality and rights, grounds liberalism's claim to be the best possible kind of politico-economic system.[10] Simultaneously and especially, although not exclusively, in the United States, liberalism also prides itself as upholding the virtually sacred value of tolerance, framing itself as the political system that can accommodate all kinds of social difference.

Over the last three decades, the scholarship on classical liberalism has disabused any simple faith in these claims. For example, as the work of Charles Mills shows, the contemporaneous projects of colonial violence and its institutionalizing of slavery are not merely historical coincidences to the rise of liberalism; to the contrary, the violence used to conquer nonwhite races and thus render them socially inferior found direct purchase in the conceptual framework of classical liberalism.[11] The twinned values of neutrality and tolerance carry a long history of obfuscating persistent and systemic violence committed through the disavowals that they perform. By framing these twinned values—neutrality and tolerance—as the doubled fantasy of liberalism, I can examine the structure of these distinct, although mutually constituting disavowals. It is the processes of these distinctive disavowals that neoliberalism as a social rationality is disrupting, thus precipitating profound transformations in both cathexes to social difference and the precipitated modes of evaluation known as "ethics."

The framework of a Lacanian fantasy thus not only amplifies the fantasmatic (and thus forever vulnerable) character of liberalism's longstanding, historical claims to racial and cultural superiority, but also helps us to see more precisely how the crucial fealties to the universality of neutrality and tolerance occur in a sociopsychic register. The important scholarship initiated by Pateman and Mills aims to disrupt liberalism by exposing the horrible ruse of liberalism's mythical status as neutral and tolerant. But such a direct, largely abstract exposure of these systemic histories of xenophobia does not seem to disrupt the liberal fantasy of superiority. Because the fantasy works precisely through the languages of neutrality, it always already has a defense against these charges in place.[12] The scholarship of historical exposure thereby offers crucial evidence for the systemic xenophobia, but falls short of interrupting the power of these twinned values (neutrality and tolerance) as doubled social fantasies with intense social cathexes. Exposing these as myths, as fictions, as untrue to historical facts does not dislodge the profound cathexes they enact. Ironically, perhaps, it is the social rationality of neoliberalism that performs this sociopsychic labor: it transforms and dislodges the longstanding social cathexes to both neutrality and tolerance.

Following out the Lacanian schema of fantasy, then, I position neutrality and tolerance in relation to their respective *objet a*, namely, utility and xenophobia. In what follows, I will argue first for how these are the constituting and forever "off-screen" *objet a* of the two fantasies, respectively. Given the preponderance of scholarship on liberalism and race and racism, particularly the focus on the vexed value of tolerance, I will only sketch how the fantasy of tolerance cathects through the *objet a* of xenophobia briefly and then turn to the fantasy of neutrality's cathexis with the *objet a* of utility at greater length. While scholars such as Jodi Melamed have begun to turn directly to how the concept of race is transforming in neoliberalism, I argue that we must also attend to the transformations in the mechanics that allow for the social value of paid over unpaid labor in neoliberalism if we are to understand how the dynamics and concepts of social difference are altering in neoliberalism.[13] While my work here on the fantasy of tolerance will become germane to and continue to expand in chapter 5 and its focus on race, I argue that the transformations in the pairing of neutrality and utility are actually at the core of the alterations we are currently undergoing: when we no longer cathect with utility, our cathexes to the standard liberal concepts of social difference begin to fray, coming undone in unprecedented and sometimes frighteningly unstructured way.

To help keep these various structures and categories clear, I once more offer a table (see table 3.1), which will expand, as a heuristic.

As Wendy Brown has so forcefully argued in *Regulating Aversion*, at the heart of tolerance lies repugnance. The very meaning of tolerance implies

TABLE 3.1 The Structure of Liberalism's Core Fantasies

	Subjective formation	Fantasies	Register	*Objet a*
Liberalism	Desire	Tolerance Neutrality	Moral Epistemo-logical	Utility as politico-economic metric Xenophobia

the overcoming of disgust, the effort and toil to forgo one's visceral revulsion in the name of some higher moral ground. Like its cousin, altruism, tolerance finds purchase in classical liberalism's command to cloak all claims to superiority in the language of moral sentiments. The crucial embrace of tolerance as a distinctive, core, unassailable value of classical liberalism thereby grants an esoteric vocabulary to the shared but unspoken assumption of cultural superiority.

In the language of a Lacanian fantasy, liberalism animates the fantasy of tolerance as the hallmark of its moral superiority only on the condition of its ongoing cathexes to xenophobia, which is crucially circulating, as the constitutive *objet a*, "off-screen." That is, according to the structure of fantasy, while it must exalt the value of tolerance as the foundation to its moral superiority, liberalism can only subtend this fantasy through its grounding cathexis with its *objet a*, namely, xenophobia. The historically repeated and ongoing coincidence of this exaltation of tolerance and systemic, xenophobic state violence is not a mere ideological contradiction or slippage. It actually animates the fantasy: xenophobia cathects the fantasy of tolerance. Taking the United States as an example, whether eighteenth-century settler colonialism, nineteenth-century chattel slavery, or twentieth-century neocolonialism and racism, it is only insofar as cultures of classical liberalism encounter(ed) social difference as threatening and fearful that the fantasies of tolerance as moral superiority were put into play. But as fantasies, this originating cathexis can never surface, can never come fully on-screen, can never be fully admitted or viewed, lest the fantasy come apart.[14]

While the fantasy of tolerance serves as a moral screen to the systemic xenophobia of liberalism, the fantasy of neutrality functions as its epistemological counterpart. Not a readily recognizable moral claim, neutrality serves as the bedrock epistemological condition of possibility for the objectivity that grounds virtually the entire system of liberalism. It is what allows liberalism to deflect any charges of bias back onto the minoritarian plaintiffs. Neutrality defines the exalted realm of judgment to which reason, when purified of all subjective bias, ascends. Accordingly, given the enormous difficulties of securing entrance to this sacred realm of neutrality, the purification rites fall primarily to one institution: the law.

Through its labyrinthine logic of precedents, the legal institution of liberalism becomes both the protector and the arbiter of neutrality.

Assuming neutrality as the point of departure secured through the historical heft of precedents, the default view of the law is to place the burden of proving the neutrality of any and all claims before it, especially those on behalf of "difference." As the work of critical race theory, particularly the theory of intersectionality that it helped to spawn, has showed for so long, this systemic assumption of neutrality makes the law a very difficult, if not impossible, site at which to secure judgments in favor of social differences, particularly as they are materialized in pluralized, "intersecting" ways. That is, this systemic assumption of neutrality makes the law an impossible site at which to secure judgments that affirm and enable minoritarian claims for differential treatment before the law.[15]

The default of the law, working in and through neutrality, is to mitigate against such differential treatment—to protect "citizens" as neutral bearers of legal rights. Differential treatment is thereby always already positioned as a flaw that must be corrected by the law, most often by pitting one faculty of the law against another—for example, exerting legal judgments against biased acts of the police (in its many guises).[16] But this apparently endless self-correction by the law is framed not as a problem of the law's fundamental assumptions, but rather as a flaw of human nature and its inability to act consistently with pure rationality. Neutrality is the secured, if precarious, realm of the legal system, but it is always an aspirational state of reason for human actors.

Framing neutrality as a core, constitutive fantasy of liberalism opens a more general perspective on its function in cultures of liberalism.[17] First of all, while the law remains, undoubtedly, one of the most intensified sites at which the ongoing tensions between neutrality and difference are negotiated, it does not (thankfully!) saturate our lives in cultures of liberalism and neoliberalism. Taking into account the racialized, sexualized, and classed stratifications of the social fabric, I still contend that none of us lives in constant interface with the myriad forms of the law, despite its best, disciplinary efforts. Secondly, the critical legal interventions regarding social differences such as race and sexuality all too often land in a gridlock that is enabled by this apparently impervious epistemology of and fealty to neutrality. This gridlock gets chalked up all too easily as ideological and thus as a matter of politics. By insisting that neoliberalism is transforming our processes of subject formation, concepts of social difference, and modes of evaluation, I also insist that we must develop critical interventions that do not draw on the epistemologies of the law or ideology. We need as many epistemologies as possible to grasp the often dizzying changes before us; the efforts offered here are but one of many possibilities.

Casting neutrality as a core fantasy of liberalism, then, I contend that it is cathected by the *objet a* of utility. This fantasy operates quite differently, however, from the explicit disavowal that cathects tolerance to xenophobia. First of all, utility is itself a dominant value of classical liberalism, extolled by John Locke and glorified in the United States as the Protestant Work Ethic. Rather than an ugly secret that fuels an esteemed moral value, utility is itself directly a value that liberalism champions. As my own prior work on utility has showed, Locke insists on an ontology of labor that valorizes utility as he simultaneously brandishes it as a metric to justify the colonial possession of lands from Native Americans.[18] But unlike tolerance, which is explicitly embraced as a moral value of liberalism, utility is not an explicitly moral value. Rather, it is framed as a crucial quality that plays a central role in distinguishing between those who do and those who do not merit the benefits of the social contract. Not explicitly and directly a moral value, utility functions as a foundational metric of social value in liberalism. This crucial role is what the transformations underway in cultures of neoliberalism are exposing and fraying.

By framing it as the constitutive *objet a* of the fantasy of neutrality, we can see how this social value of utility circulates strictly "off-screen." Utility must not surface as having any direct or causal relation to neutrality as a core value of liberalism. Secured by its esoteric purity, neutrality commands assent as an aspirational, regulative ideal—or so it claims. But in reading utility as the cathexis that animates the fantasy of neutrality, we locate a sociopsychic register through which to query—and perhaps interrupt—this unreflective fealty to neutrality.

Siphoned off from any connection to neutrality, utility functions as an implicit, assumed value in liberalism, demanding its own direct fealty and cathexis. But the command seems to be lessening, as social authority more broadly is shifting and waning. While neutrality commands a kind of epistemological assent that, sanctified in the hallowed sphere of the law, simply seems beyond question, utility inhabits a much grittier, nastier social location. Caught up in racializing, sexualizing schemas, utility has never been pure or free from ideological warfare. As a groundless ground, the social cathexis with utility has always been political rather than moral, despite repeated attempts (often through Protestantism) to make it into a clear moral value commanding assent.

By framing it as the *objet a* that cathects us to neutrality, we can see more clearly how utility functions, namely, as a metric that, providing a clear and objective barometer to meritocracy, allows neutrality to circulate as a core value of liberalism. Utility does "the dirty work" of socioeconomic adjudication that neutrality eschews—indeed, that it disavows. Whether and how some bodies are judged as "different" while others are judged as "without difference" turn on this metric of utility. This deflection of the act of judging onto utility protects neutrality from any charge of bias: meritocracy, as determined by the scalar judgment of utility, is a purely economic calculation that does not infringe upon the sacred value of neutrality.

But its scalar distinctions have historically been taken up as binary judgments, demarcating clearly between those who are useful and those who are not. That is, the scalar economic distinctions of various degrees of utility have consistently been transformed into a binary judgment that subtends the moralism of meritocracy, while cloaking and grounding its systemic xenophobia (mostly as racist, but also as sexist, heterosexist, nationalist, ablest, ageist, and so on). This systemic xenophobia has rendered the social cathexis to utility always partial, embraced by those deemed useful and rightfully viewed with skepticism and suspicion by those alleged as unuseful. As the precarity of labor grows more intense, however, broadened beyond the racial and national schemas of liberalism through neoliberal practices, loyalty to the social metric of utility is fading across the social landscape. Reading it as the necessarily "off-screen" cause of the fantasy of neutrality, we see that the stakes of this social cathexis to utility are quite high—and also rather precarious.

The doubled fantasies of liberalism—tolerance and neutrality—thereby function differently. In the moral fantasy of tolerance, the *objet a* of xenophobia cathects the fantasy precisely through its disavowal—it is the dirty little secret that cannot surface without puncturing the fantasy. In the epistemological fantasy of neutrality, the *objet a* of utility cathects the fantasy by performing the labor of judgment that the fantasy necessarily disavows. While this disavowal is also required by the fantasy, the status of utility as an effective politico-economic barometer is vulnerable to sociopsychic refusal. Therefore, while the exposure of xenophobia may puncture the fantasy of tolerance, the force of liberalism as an ideology will likely quell any such challenge. (Remember, alignment with core, constitutive fantasies of the dominant culture determines the status of one's own "realities": the claim of xenophobia against liberalism can easily be dismissed as "deranged" or, more likely in the contemporary United States, as "playing the race card.") To the contrary, the role of utility in the fantasy of neutrality relies on an ongoing social cathexis with it as a meaningful social metric. In neoliberalism, this role is fraying both materially and epistemologically and the core fantasy of neutrality is subsequently in danger.

INSTANT WEALTH AND FUNGIBLE DIFFERENCE

I return, finally, to the fantasy that has gained such social traction and cathexis in these neoliberal times: the fantasy of instant wealth. While the long historical view offered by Foucault cautions against proclaiming it a core, constitutive fantasy (it is too early to say), it is nevertheless enacting crucial sociopsychic transformations. Exemplifying the shift from desire to the drive, from the subject of rights to the subject of interests, the fantasy of instant wealth eschews any social cathexis to utility. Utility simply has no place in this fantasy. This precious *objet a* of liberalism's core fantasy of neutrality thereby loses its mooring in this fantasy of instant wealth and the desiring subject itself begins to fade from the neoliberal episteme.

Trying to ferret out the transformation of liberal values underway in the neoliberal episteme, I want to push even further on what this specific fading entails and how it is happening. I contend that, as a shift from desire to the drive, it also displays a systemic move toward formalizing social difference itself. If this is so, then we begin to see how the waning of the social cathexis to utility reverberates in alterations in the social cathexis to xenophobia and its structuring of social difference, especially race; accordingly, the doubled core fantasies of neutrality and tolerance are also shifting ground and perhaps coming apart.

Before turning back to Foucault to analyze the shifts in norms and their metrics, I offer an expansion of the previous table to help track the changes I am excavating (see table 3.2).

TABLE 3.2 The Structure of Liberalism's and Neoliberalism's Core Fantasies

	Subjective formation	Fantasies	Register	*Objet a*
Liberalism	Desire	Tolerance Neutrality	Moral Epistemo-logical	Utility as politico-economic metric Xenophobia
Neoliberalism	Drive	Instant wealth	Aesthetic (pleasure)	Histories of liberalism

To get at the reverberation from the waning of the social cathexis to utility in the social cathexis to xenophobia and its structuring of social difference, I return to Foucault and his broad work on the various historical iterations of norms. As I have showed in the previous two chapters, one of the critical transformations at work in the neoliberal episteme is the move away from contractual logic and its juridical rationality toward a logic of the market and its calculative rationality. Framing this as a process of intensification, I can now suggest that it can also be understood as shifts in cathexes from the contract to the market.

Recall that, as a site of veridiction, the market instantiates a calculative rationality as the most effective mode of thinking for the entrepreneurial subject of interests: as the circuit of the drive, the maximizing of interests becomes the site of cathexis, regardless of any social instantiation. In contrast, the juridical rationality of the contract primarily derives its social force from its authority: as a scene of desire, the subject, replete with deep internal reservoirs of moralizing emotions to be interpellated and structured into identifications by the symbolic, is the site of cathexis. This shift in the site of cathexis—from the subject to interests—sharpens our understanding of what is happening in the shift from a scene of desire to the circuit of the drive. In the erosion of symbolic investiture underway in neoliberalism, the social cathexes that animate the doubled core fantasies of liberalism begin to wane. But this is not merely a matter of newfound apathy toward authority: it is a shift in the social ontology away from the subject of desire and toward the circuit of the drive.

Given the long history of racialized and sexualized injustices—both explicit and disavowed (deflected onto the work of utility)—enacted through the juridical contract, the erosion of the symbolic and its interpellative force in the neoliberal episteme may appear to hold great promise of a better, less racist and sexist future. But such would only be the hopes of a symbolically interpellated subject cathected by such a desire, structured by lack, and forever anticipating a future that never quite arrives. From such a perspective, it might also appear that the social rationalities and practices of neoliberalism simply eschew all normalization, rooted as we are in conceptualizing norms vis-à-vis authority.

By developing the transformations in the dominant metrics of social value at work in the neoliberal episteme, I sharpen our understandings of exactly how the social cathexis to utility is waning—a process that is the effect not only of ideological disenchantment, but also of shifting material practices of labor and its social value. We will thereby gain a more precise schematic of how the cultural embrace of the neoliberal market's calculative rationality registers in our concepts and enactments of social difference: when the liberal social metric of utility transforms into the neoliberal social metric of statistics, liberalism's disavowed xenophobia also destabilizes.

As I have showed, when Foucault argues that, in the middle of the eighteenth century, the market displaces the role of the law as a juridical structure to limit the power of the state, this results in a fundamental split in the modes of rationality dominant in practices of liberalism, namely, the split between the juridical and calculative modes. As we begin to see the erosion of juridical authority in the neoliberal episteme, we also find the lapsing of modernity's epistemology of certitude and a slide toward the neoliberal epistemology of calculating success—or the ascendancy of what I am calling ratio-calculative normativity, which is modulated through exactitude. As the neoliberal iteration of the modern episteme emerges alongside and "on top of" the older one of classical liberalism, juridical appeals to transcendental principles, such as those we find in contractual logic, are gradually displaced as possible modes of evaluative discernment: the calculation of interest, the barometer of acceptable profit and loss, becomes the acceptable mode of evaluation. These transformations in the very mechanisms of judgment both register in and are shaped by a transformation in the signifiers of social difference—and, eventually, in the ethical values—that they do or do not hold.

The exact contours of this shift from juridical to calculative normativity thus merit much investigation. In *Sleights of the Norm*, Mary Beth Mader has argued that the statistical conception of the norm is central to Foucault's account of biopower. While most readings of Foucault have conceptualized biopower's normalization as the gradual process of the homogenizing of cultural forms and values around particular nodes (medical, legal, familial, sexual, and so on), Mader intervenes with an incisive account of the epistemology of biopower's norms as driven by the ascendancy of a numerical standardization of objects. Arguing explicitly against the understanding of Foucault's norm as a custom or tradition, Mader dislodges the (disturbingly Althusserian-Butlerian) readings of it as a genealogy, history, or ancestry. To the contrary, Mader's meticulous analysis shows how Foucault's understanding of a norm turns on the immanently self-referential work of a statistical norm. This entails several crucial shifts, all of which express critical kinds of transformations underway in the neoliberal episteme: the elision of qualitative and quantitative judgment; the slide from binary to continuous, scalar modes of power; and the obfuscation of social exclusion or inclusion via the mathematical continuity inherent in the quantifying methods of gradation endemic to statistical analyses.

If we understand normalizing rationalities of the neoliberal episteme to function fundamentally through statistics, then Mader's analysis explains how this entails a numerical standardization of objects. The norm as number—and especially as ratio—is necessarily abstracted from the object to which it purportedly refers. As Mader shows, for example, in a prolonged discussion of suicide rates, "The expression *suicide rate* no longer refers to any person or persons but to a relation between numbers or quantities alone."[19] She goes on to show how "the move from individual to rate, by way of the group, amounts to a radical shift of ontological register" (SR, 56). That the example here is suicide, not merely height or weight, only makes her work all the more poignant and disturbing: this abstraction of life may be endemic to the neoliberal episteme.

But as Mader pushes even further, suicide is not a kind of limit-case: it is exemplary. Because the reduction of the life-to-death transition to "the mathematical continuity of the number line, or an assumption of continuous quantity" (SR, 58), may still strike us as somehow perverse, this exemplarity is worth heeding. But make no mistake—this ontological elision from individual to group to number (and back again) is the crucially new social metric of the neoliberal episteme and its transformations of our social rationalities and practices. In our blind love of statistical norms, we enter "a *multi*dimensional space of comparison" (SR, 59), extending far beyond the binary, two-dimensional tables (say, of simple normal and abnormal or inclusion and exclusion) that we might continue to inhabit anachronistically.[20] The mean becomes the mediator of social relations: the epistemology of mathematical objects becomes the new social metric. Normalizing panopticism in neoliberalism is, to use Mader's terms, "not architectural but statistical" (SR, 65).

Mader's focus on statistical norms and their abstraction from referential objects, compounded by their immanent self-referentiality, articulates precisely the kind of transformation underway in neoliberal processes of subject formation and concepts of social difference. Abstracted from referentiality altogether, the numerical epistemology of the statistic exemplifies the kind of formalized ratio-calculative normativity that Foucault locates in neoliberal theorists.[21] We thereby begin to grasp the profound alteration in social metrics from liberalism's fraught ideology of utility to neoliberalism's exuberant embrace of numerically abstract statistics. No longer caught in the snares of an ideologically embattled and epistemologically fuzzy metric of utility, the neoliberal subject of interests thrives in the endless calculations of maximizing and enhancing afforded by this numerical metric of social comparability. It enables neoliberal subjects of interests to determine social values through the single barometer of economic calculation, extracted from any historico-social context. That is, the numerical metric of social comparability allows the flattening of the variegated phenomena of social difference to a singular characteristic and register: fungibility. And this is where the reverberations from this fraying of social cathexis to utility begin to surface in its twinned *objet a*, xenophobia.

To be fungible is to have all character and content hollowed out. It is a relationship of equity that requires purely formal semblance. In economic terms, fungibility refers to those goods and products on the market that are substitutable for one another. For example, a bushel of wheat from Kazakhstan is fungible with a bushel of wheat from Kansas, assuming the quality and grade of wheat is the same. Fungibility undergirds the monetary system, since it is the formal quality of bank notes that allows them to be fully substitutable. This is different from exchangeable goods, which must be related to a common standard (such as money) in order to judge their differing or similar values. This central role of fungibility and not exchangeability in neoliberalism is thus one more reason to take our distance from Marxist analyses, with its focus on exchange, production, and consumption.

While this may all make sense at the level of economics, the problematic neoliberal twist is translating it from a dynamic of capital to a dynamic of "human capital": this is arguably the site at which the neoliberal episteme appears to become ethically bankrupt. As the extensive work on the globalized disparities of wealth and poverty shows, the fungibility of human capital is rendering human labor precarious. Just as factory workers in the industrial revolution were expendable, so too has a great deal of contemporary labor become formally interchangeable: assembling technological gadgets can happen here or there (or, in the veiled nationalist language of the US market, "here or offshore"); but increasingly, so can more highly specialized activities, such as medical diagnoses, engineering solutions, and even market analyses.

As the work of Aihwa Ong in *Neoliberalism as Exception* shows, the fungibility of human labor at all stratifications of socioeconomic class—from factories in Malaysia and Indonesia to "cyber heroes" of Silicon Valley—is quickly rendering all human labor both migrant and precarious. Even the human voice is fungible, as the training of telemarketers in Mumbai to mimic the "flat accent" of the Midwestern American renders their human capital fully fungible with any other "unaccented" voice in the United States. In the contemporary globalized labor market, saturated as it is by these neoliberal principles, the aim increasingly seems to be to secure a nonfungible skill: to do so, however, is no mean trick, since one must carefully balance the heightened specialization of such a nonfungible skill and its marketability. The market, after all, tells the truth—and it is increasingly transforming even the most highly specialized skills into fungible units. The exit from this intensifying of planned obsolescence is clear: enterprising innovation. (Just recall the immediate canonization of Steve Jobs.)

This move toward fungibility, away from exchangeability, as the market's barometer transforms the category of social difference in significant and startling ways. Accordingly, it also transforms liberalism's constitutive disavowal of xenophobia in significant and startling ways. When the market outstrips the contract in neoliberalism, its activity and production of social metrics must be constantly stimulated. Foucault emphasizes that, in the distancing from both Adam Smith and Marx (BB, 130), neoliberals do not claim that competition is a natural human state; rather, it is constantly stimulated by the activity of the market as the site of veridiction (BB, 118–21, 130). In order to achieve this constant stimulation of competition, the neoliberals (especially the ordoliberals in Germany) focus on "the formal properties of the competitive structure that assured, and could assure, economic regulation through the price mechanism" (BB, 131). As Ladelle McWhorter notes in her essay "Queer Economies," Foucault specifies: "Competition is a principle of formalization."[22]

Arguing explicitly against a welfare economy, the ordoliberals insisted that the fundamental objective of such policies to create and sustain the equalization of consumption across society was, actually, the death of economic growth. They argued that this crucial price mechanism, which generates the truths of the market, must "not [be] obtained through phenomena of equalization but through *a game of differentiations*" (BB, 142, my emphasis). Inequality is essential to stimulating market competition and, as such, is experienced by all members of the society. It is not that from which government ought to protect us. To the contrary, if the neoliberal aim of rendering the market the site of veridiction—across all aspects of society—is to be achieved, then inequality must be intensified and multiplied until the social fabric becomes a conglomeration of diffuse, fungible differences.

Social difference is thus not so much commodified, as bell hooks's analysis from the 1990s argues;[23] nor is it simply to be erased in the name of globalized homogeneity, as early critics of neoliberalism have argued. Rather, difference must be intensified, multiplied, and fractured in the ongoing stimulation of competition: "The society regulated by reference to the market that the neoliberals are thinking about is a society in which

TABLE 3.3 Neoliberal Transformations of Liberalism

	Liberalism	Neoliberalism
Fantasy(ies)	Tolerance, neutrality	Instant wealth
Subjective formation	Desire	Drive
Site of truth	Contract	Market
Social value	Utility	Maximizing interests
Rationality	Juridical	Calculation
Metric	Certitude	Exactitude
Normativity	Binary	Scalar
Social difference	Xenophobia	Fungibility

the regulatory principle should not be so much the exchange of commodities as the mechanisms of competition" (BB, 147). We are far beyond the politics of multiculturalism: diversity is the explicit aim of neoliberalism, as so many have argued. But it is the explicit aim not as a tool of ideological obfuscation, but as a direct manifestation of the neoliberal social rationality in practice. Insofar as diversity follows out the logic of fungibility that the market demands, these celebrated differences are purely formal—they must be hollow, stripped of any historical residues, especially if those residues bring with them the ethical conflict of xenophobia. If we are to incite an antiracist praxis, such as those #BlackLivesMatter are attempting, we must ignite this agonistic history.

Following the schema of the table from chapter 1, the Lacanian analyses I have offered here result in a considerable expansion (see table 3.3). As I turn directly to the transformation of categories of social difference in the following two chapters, we will see how the affect of coolness captures so many of these cultural shifts underway in neoliberal social rationalities and practices. The transformation of coolness, with its roots deep in black culture, from an ethics of resistance and survival into a formally empty, aestheticized posture of the neoliberal episteme captures many of the ways we neoliberals understand and relate to social difference. Coolness perfectly expresses the neoliberal transformation of social difference from a historical repository of xenophobia to a fungible unit of rational calculation: coolness expresses difference-as-fungible.

FIGURE 3a.1 David Beckham in 2002. © Reuters / Corbis.

INTERLUDE 3

Neoliberal Cool

David Beckham, Brad Pitt, Sam Romano. *Fight Club, American Psycho, Spiderman.* Such were the icons of metrosexuality in its heyday, the early 2000s. "You see," as Mark Simpson put it in his official introduction of the term in 2002 on Salon.com, "'Becks' is almost as famous for wearing sarongs and pink nail polish and panties belonging to his wife, Victoria (aka Posh from the Spice Girls), having a different, tricky haircut every week and posing naked and oiled up on the cover of *Esquire*, as he is for his impressive ball skills.[1] He may or may not be the best footballer in the world, but he's definitely an international-standard narcissist."[2] And so the image of the metrosexual, one of the most purely imagistic of cultural images, was named.

As Simpson goes on to explain, this cultural emergence of the metrosexual marks the birth of a new man—a new straight white man. With uncomfortable dances around the questions of sexuality and a total avoidance of questions of race, Simpson emphasizes the central role of the image to metrosexuality: this new kind of man is mostly "interested in his image—that's to say, [he is] interested in being looked at (because that's the only way you can be certain you actually exist)" (MM). As such, the metrosexual is "an advertiser's walking wet dream" (MM). He's a consuming machine: "A young man with money to spend, living in or within easy reach of a metropolis—because that's where all the best shops, clubs, gyms and hairdressers are" (MM). The metrosexual loves to shop and to spend and to consume—in the endless intensifying of his image. Narcissism unbound.

"Your products are encroaching on my products."

FIGURE 3a.2 A couple discusses bathroom counter space. Cartoon by Liza Donnelly in the *New Yorker*, July 8, 2013. Courtesy of Condé Nast.

Flash ten years forward to 2012: *Salon.com* announces the death of metrosexuality. Sort of. In an article laced with jabs at academic proclamations based on insufficient evidence, Michael Todd reports that academics and *Cosmopolitan* magazine are announcing the passing of metrosexuality.[3] It has passed precisely because it has become passé. That is, it has been absorbed into mainstream popular culture: there is no need to call out and name that which is normal.

And so what has replaced the metrosexual as the avant garde of straight white masculinity?

FIGURE 3a.3 A hipster. Courtesy of quattrostagioni / Flickr.

The hipster. Less well groomed, more androgynous, and downwardly economically mobile (despite expensive coffee, cigarette, and social media habits), the hipster seems to be the latest iteration of cool. But is it, too, already dead? According to Keith Bowers, writing in March 2012 on the *SF Weekly.com* blog, "The hipster aesthetic and lifestyle [are] firmly implanted in the U.S. mainstream. We've known for a while that the whole package—the fixie bike, the skinny jean, the knit cap or cheap-ass short-brim, the 'ironic' facial hair, the black-frame glasses, the PBR—make about as much of a statement as a set of new tires from Costco."[4] Bowers particularly laments the new YouTube channel "American Hipster" as ringing out the death knell for hipsterdom, handing the image fully over to the marketplace.

The hipster is neoliberal cool.

CHAPTER FOUR

"How Cool Is That?"

GENDER AND THE NEOLIBERAL IMAGINARY

Coolness has had remarkable longevity. Emergent in post–World War II black subcultures of jazz and blues, the aesthetics of cool morphed through white working-class icons such as James Dean and Marlon Brando until it was slowly absorbed into the transgressive white youth culture of the 1960s. Mainstream and popular culture in the United States never looked back: we have been speaking the language of cool ever since. Given the global reach of the US culture industry, this aesthetics has transformed geopolitically in considerable and interesting ways: cool is remarkably elastic. But the fundamental pose has not changed, namely, a controlled detachment that enshrines irony and a muted claim to nonconformity as highly valued, preferred social postures.

The stance of countercultural resistance has thus become endemically ambiguous in the white mainstream language of cool. On the one hand, the legacy of the James Dean–Marlon Brando icon imbues cool with the perennial rebellion of masculinist adolescence.[1] But, on the other hand, this folds all too neatly into the teleology of responsible male adulthood, thereby casting cool forever as an affect of adolescence that "real" adults outgrow, even if indulging periodically in culturally programmed midlife crises or the vicarious pleasures of parenthood. This barometer of masculinized adulthood thereby modulates racialization: white culture is only cool as an adolescent, but black culture is forever cool—forever, that is, a teenager in need of authoritarian controls.

The work of bell hooks underscores this racialization as one of the primary, long-standing co-optations of black culture. Focusing on the "fake cool pose" of hip-hop and gangsta culture, hooks positions contemporary black expressions of cool as part of the broader commodification of coolness.[2] For hooks, this "black-face" degradation of cool disengages one of the most powerful modes of social resistance in black cultural history. The founding fathers of cool, ranging from Louis Armstrong to B. B. King and Malcolm X, developed cool as a way to reclaim social life, heal the deep psychic wounds of chattel slavery and its permanent devaluation of black labor, cultivate one's own sense of meaning in the world, and survive. But the gangsta culture of hip-hop and contemporary black aesthetics sells out these deep historical roots of resistance to a posture of cool that is identified with "the white man, with all the perks and goodies that come with patriarchal dominator culture."[3] She emphasizes, in strikingly economic (if perhaps latently Marxian) terms, that this sellout of cool in black culture always comes with the change from the desire for meaningful labor to the desire for wealth and fame. Rebecca Walker follows this line of thinking to collect an entire anthology of black writers exhuming the deep historical reservoirs of black cool. This effort explicitly involves wresting the meanings of cool from the ironic detachment sold by consumerist culture to all shades of alleged subcultures, including contemporary black aesthetics.

Tom Frank argues this is no accident. Marshaling evidence from various archives of marketing theories and the advertising industry, Frank argues that the US marketing machine took full flight in the 1960s largely through the explicit co-optation of cool. Focusing on the industries of advertising and menswear, Frank shows how, "in 1967 and 1968, . . . executives seized upon the counterculture as the preeminent symbol of the revolution in which they were engaged, embellishing both their trade literature and their products with images of rebellious, individualistic youth."[4] Frank draws loosely on Norman Mailer's development of the Hipster, in his essay "The White Negro," as "an 'American existentialist' whose tastes for jazz, sex, drugs, and the slang and mores of black society constituted the best means of resisting the encroachments of Cold War oppression" (CC, 12).

But Frank's project is to investigate the production of this "hip" aesthetic in theories of business and marketing, not to investigate the racialized aspects of this transformation. Labeling this movement as the emergence of "hip consumerism," Frank explains: "What happened in the sixties is that hip became central to the way American capitalism understood itself and explained itself to the public" (CC, 26). Transgression and nonconformity became staples of, rather than threats to, the marketing machine. Framed by the aesthetics of cool and hip, the repeatedly reinvented "counterculture" becomes "an enduring commercial myth" (CC, 32) that fuels the illusion of social resistance, while materially, economically, and psychologically co-opting any last remnant of radical critique.

While I am sympathetic to Frank's arguments, especially about the marketing of transgression and nonconformity as central neoliberal mechanisms, an implicitly Marxian version of ideological critique still structures his general argument of co-optation, especially in implicitly granting intentionality to the theorists of various business and marketing practices.[5] Consequently, the sidestepping of race and gender, which is particularly worrisome because of the long tradition of Marxists' fraught erasures of these categories, misses entirely the critical transformation in the concept of and cathexis to social difference in the neoliberal episteme.

When Joe Cool appears in the *Peanuts* strip and grants a subcultural plotline to the iconic cartoon, Marxist analyses can certainly run the gauntlet and read Schulz as smuggling a working-class critique of capitalism into the all-American narrative of Charlie Brown's angst. But they cannot make any sense of why Coca-Cola would then become the pronounced sponsor of the classic *A Charlie Brown Christmas* television special. In the same vein, a Frank-inspired understanding of marketing as co-opting the cool of youth culture in the 1960s makes some good sense of how, especially in the wake of his assassination and James Deanian tragic death, John Lennon's cultural transgressions become o so cool. But such a loosely Marxist analysis fails even to broach how the racialization of Yoko Ono persists as the hypersexualized, perverting scapegoat for the downfall of the Beatles and Lennon's white, working-class ethos.

The changing meanings of cool run much deeper. The widespread embrace of cool stretches much further than the genius of marketing pamphlets and advertising machines aimed at menswear. The transformation of coolness, with its deep roots in black culture, from an ethos of resistance and survival into a widespread cultural posture of ironic detachment that is formally emptied of any historical or political content captures the transformations in social difference underway in the neoliberal episteme. Coolness perfectly expresses the neoliberal transformation of social difference from a historical repository of xenophobia to a fungible unit of rational calculation: coolness expresses difference-as-fungible. It erases the deep historical roots in black culture, just as hooks argues, but it does so in ways that exceed the explanatory parameters of commodification, where a standard of evaluation (albeit money or consumerism) still holds a singular power over the social field.

Given its purely formal character, difference-as-fungible finds its most meaningful expression in the social metric of numerical statistics. Epistemologically, difference-as-fungible assumes a pure formalism and thereby initiates an aesthetic mode of judgment that cannot become a source of conflict. Social difference-as-fungible becomes merely a particularly intensified zone through which interests can be magnified or minimized, depending on one's preferences. But to prefer is to make an aesthetic judgment—to state one's tastes, one's likes and dislikes, one's proclivities. It is not an ethical judgment about the ontological value of anything.

Under classical liberalism's relation to capitalism, the comparative values of such exchangeable preferences would be solved by the purely formal monetary standard—and the market would provide the commodification of difference a kind of redemptive excuse. But the neoliberal social rationality does not function in that ontology or epistemology: the neoliberal move toward the fungibility of differences heightens and intensifies this purely aesthetic dimension of difference itself. The purely formal character of the differences emphasizes the innocuous character of these fleeting, ephemeral partialities: whether one is "better" than another depends on which interests are being served, in which market, for what infinite permutations of delight.

Coolness allows difference to proliferate and intensify in a purely formal and thus purely superficial manner. It initiates us into the strange social epistemic space of endless, scalar comparison as the barometer of subjectivity. Unhinged from any historical or ethical barometer, social difference-as-fungibility cannot be a source of conflict. And this is precisely how it becomes one of the most insidious transformations of our neoliberal social worlds.

Unsurprisingly, social media enacts this cool fungibility remarkably. The formal similitude of cyber platforms is a vehicle for, not an impediment to, the endless proliferation of "different" poses, snapshots, images, tweets, and witticisms that can then be evaluated on the basis of that treasured statistic: the number of hits determines just how cool one really is. While coolness was once the hallmark of black masculine culture and still carries masculinist social structures, we neoliberals *all* want to be cool: we all want to float across the endless stream of verisimilitude in free, intensified, and stimulating forms, becoming ever so interesting—and ever so cool.

The cathexis to this register of cool thereby animates the neoliberal social rationality. While the Lacanian register of the imaginary, especially when paired with the circuit of the drive, captures the crucially comparative and endlessly looping aspect of this kind of subjective development, it cannot account for the multidimensional, scalar kind of judgment that (allegedly) unmoors social difference from histories of bigotry and xenophobia. Lacan's orientation in his originary accounts of the imaginary toward explaining human development locates the imaginary in a dyadic space of the mother and child, which is then extended through language into the ontology of other and self. As I argued chapters 2 and 3, the neoliberal social rationality does not turn on this kind of dyadic epistemic space and, accordingly, ideological interpellation does not capture neoliberal processes of subject formation, racialization, or racism. In aiming to render the market the site of veridiction across all aspects of social life, the neoliberal social rationality intensifies and multiplies differences far beyond the dyadic relation of self and other that structures liberalism's histories of xenophobia. The neoliberal social fabric becomes a fractured conglomeration of diffuse, fungible differences. The more intensified those differences become, the more superficial they are. The less historical or psychological depth is attached to them, the better they float across context and meanings—and the cooler and cooler one is!

REREADING SOCIAL DIFFERENCE

It is unsurprising then that we are so deeply confused about social difference in neoliberal cultures. The ongoing, constantly repeated mantras of celebrating diversity leave us not merely perplexed, but profoundly confused. What could it possibly mean, in a culture so deeply structured by its cathexis to xenophobia, to act as if racial differences or nonnormative sexualities are suddenly something to embrace and even celebrate? As our students sometimes tell us, often without intending to do so, the categories of social difference that have been so critical to the work of feminist and leftist social theorists have lost a good deal of their meaning.

Rather than read this simply as the failure of feminism or our students, I want to follow out the possibility that the confusion itself is caused by a transformation in the categories in neoliberal cultures. If we take seriously the argument about neoliberalism no longer functioning through ideological interpellation, then these categories of social difference and our modes of cathexis to them must also be thoroughly reconsidered. One of our most pressing tasks as critical, feminist theorists is thus to elaborate these transformations of concepts and cathexes in the specific categories through which contemporary neoliberal cultures specify and regulate social difference.

The effort to do so, however, has mired much of our feminist critique in ideological trappings. Still living out the fears and realities of the heated debates about the competition of victimization, we continue to be haunted by the politics of *ressentiment* in our attempts to articulate the differing vectors of social difference.[6] In broad strokes, two recent scholarly developments offer a snapshot of the contemporary formulations of this persistent problematic: the ongoing, heated debates about intersectionality and its meaning, relevance, constraints, and codes; and the emergence of language such as precarity and abandonment.

The ongoing debates about intersectionality often seem to spring from a failure to recognize the substantially different disciplinary epistemologies through which intersectionality is formulated.[7] Consequently, the participants in these debates often seem to speak across one another, understanding Kimberlé Crenshaw's coining of intersectionality in critical legal studies to refer to remarkably different objects, problems, and dynamics. I thus agree with Roderick Ferguson's recent assessment that many of the debates are structured by a fundamental confusion and disagreement about the ontological status of linguistic referents and the will to truth that animates them.[8] For example, particular analyses alter immensely according to whether one takes intersectionality to refer to a classically liberal project of amelioration through inclusion, a description of the multiply embodied character of a historically produced identity category, an attempt to analyze the complex process of naming particular and mutually constituting historical vectors, or a synecdoche for "race."

Emergent roughly alongside these debates, the broader turns to concepts and figurations such as precarity and abandonment initiate a way to sidestep the vagaries of identity categories and analyze broader historical, political, and economic vectors of disenfranchisement. While I am concerned, as I noted in the introduction, with the singular cathexis to pain (and subsequently the dead-end dyad of victim and guilt) that the language of precarity, abandonment, and bare life so often implies and initiates, I agree with the turn to a broader rubric of analysis that can speak effectively to the variegated material instantiations of social difference without canceling the crucial differences among and between them. Moreover, given my long-standing approach to social difference as a historicized dynamic (especially the racializing of sexuality and the sexualizing of race), I continue to conceptualize social difference as an active vector of material, social life, rather than as a static category of identity.

As I turn to the reconfiguring of social difference in the neoliberal episteme, therefore, I aim to articulate the problematic in a language that still finds some traction in neoliberal social rationalities. This means we must be able to speak both in and beyond the traditional categories of social difference (gender, class, race, sexuality, and the infamous etc.). That is, given the sociohistorical fugue in which I place my analysis of our shared historical present, we must become nimble enough to articulate the material instantiations of social difference that jam the neoliberal machine of fungibility, while still calling out the exact contours of that resistance when and where and how it appears, despite the appearance of being "old fashioned" and woefully uncool.

With grave doubts about whether I have become that nimble, I offer the language of "somatic xenophobia" to articulate this persistent resistance to neoliberal fungibility across the precise instantiations of that resistance in the variegated social field. No book or theory or singular perspective can or should pretend to address all forms of oppression. Accordingly, I understand my sustained focus on the persistence of racialized difference and racism in the US neoliberal social fabric as one of those multiple iterations. Wanting to sidestep the problems of victim-competition and its accusations of omission, I hope the language of somatic xenophobia will amplify the amazing work of so many activists and scholars in various sites of simultaneous precarity and resistance, especially that of disability and trans* cultural politics.[9]

In the rest of this chapter and chapter 5, I analyze this transformation in categories of social difference directly and explicitly. To do so, I focus on the four traditional categories through which cultures of liberalism articulate, in differentiating and mutually constituting manners, social difference and that continue to structure, albeit in shifting and often obfuscating ways, neoliberal social fields: gender, class, race, and sexuality. I argue that the differentiated historical ontologies of each of these categories render them differently transformed in neoliberal cultures. Through the Lacanian registers of the imaginary and the real, I argue that, despite the transformation of gender and class into cool neoliberal accessories, somatic xenophobia persists in the neoliberal episteme in the singular form of race that is always already sexualized.

Accordingly, in this chapter, I turn to gender and the transformation of class into consumerism. To do so, I focus on two contemporaneous examples, one from popular culture and one from academic culture: metrosexuality and the theory of gender performativity. Through these, I argue that gender in the mainstream culture of the United States has become a kind of playground for the neoliberal social rationality, offering up superficial spaces that are easily evacuated of any historical meanings and that are thus served up for endless self-enhancement and manipulation.[10]

Intensified through a transformation of class into consumerism, gender has become a perfectly fungible kind of social difference, floating freely across more intractable manifestations of race and sexuality. Metrosexuality cuts gender loose from sexual difference and thereby, at least allegedly, from homophobia. Gender becomes a playful accessory to the subject of interests' endless drive for cooler and cooler images—especially of itself. As a consumerist practice, gender-as-consumerism-run-amok enacts the neoliberal circuit of the drive, obfuscating yet further the role of class in neoliberal social ontologies and becoming a vehicle for the process of rendering social differences fungible. In the following chapter, I turn to race as a sexualized vector of social difference that presents more obstinate instantiations of long-standing, somatic xenophobia to the celebratory evacuations of the neoliberal machine.

GENDER: THE NEOLIBERAL PLAYGROUND

Milton Friedman, the recipient of the Nobel Memorial Prize in Economic Sciences in 1976 and University of Chicago economist, is widely hailed as "the grandfather of neoliberalism." Along with colleagues such as Gary Becker and T. W. Schultz, Friedman developed and disseminated the core economic principles of the Chicago School brand of neoliberalism, which was exported across the world.[11] For example, in his *Capitalism and Freedom*, published in 1962, Friedman extols the merits of the free market as the social guarantor of individual freedom—the heart and soul of any liberal democracy. In this classic text of neoliberal theory, he lays out the essential problem of the twentieth century as a veering from nineteenth-century "true" liberalism, thus positioning neoliberalism as a return to those nineteenth-century values. The primary corrective, as Friedman sees it, is a return to "freedom" as the fundamental value of liberalism to supplant and thus repair the damages wrought by those early-twentieth-century bastardizations of liberalism, namely, "welfare and equality."[12] For Friedman, of course, the meaning of this "freedom" boils down to a matter of "individual choice." The individual is transformed from citizen to consumer: the individual's ability to choose becomes the fundamental concern of society and the open, free market ensures and protects this much better than the laws of government.

Arguing against welfare and equality and for the free market, Friedman locks onto a central value that drives this system, a value that neoliberal cultures and some of their most allegedly avant garde movements (including various forms of leftist social theory, most especially queer theory) have also embraced: nonconformity. The fundamental fear of neoliberalism is not equality, as it is for the twentieth-century liberals, but conformity. Writing most directly against state socialism and stoking the Cold War fears of the time, Friedman extols the values of nonconformity over and over again. He argues that the capitalist free market can and does fund dissent from governmental policies, but that socialist economies cannot. While agreeing with the anticommunism of McCarthyism, therefore, he disagrees with its process: the private market protects against injustice (CF, 20–21). And it does so much more smoothly than any governmental policies (or witch hunts) because the market always ensures individual choice—and thus nonconformity. As he tells us through an exemplary metaphor:

> The characteristic feature of action through political channels is that it tends to require or enforce substantial conformity. The great advantage of the market, on the other hand, is that it permits wide diversity. It is, in political terms, a system of proportional representation. Each man can vote, as it were, for the color of tie he wants and get it: he does not have to see what color the majority wants and then, if he is in the minority, submit. (CF, 15)[13]

Here, we have the full transition from citizen to consumer that exemplifies the transition from liberalism to neoliberalism: to vote is to purchase. And because a man (clearly a gendered subject here) can "vote" however he wishes, in Friedman's mind, the market frees us from the onerous problem of conformity.

Nonconformity both ensures individual choice—the gold standard of social progress for neoliberals—and, of course, keeps the market churning along: the free market demands innovation, endlessly. Friedman's argument is quite straightforward: only the free market can ensure individual freedom of choice; to fuel the free market, we must have endless innovation and diversity; to ensure innovation and diversity, we must stimulate competition; therefore, to ensure individual freedom of choice, diverse innovation, and competition, we must cultivate and encourage nonconformity as the grandest value of free market democracies. This is the heart of Tom Frank's analyses of the co-optation of cultures of cool in marketing strategies in the 1960s and 1970s. But rather than read that as a kind of ideological manipulation (or, worse, a conspiracy theory), I offer Friedman's text here as an example of the kind of social rationality increasingly driving all modes of living in neoliberal cultures. More specifically, I offer it as exemplary of the fundamental transformation in social values of neoliberal cultures that is slowly rendering us way too cool. This excessively cool detachment has been enabled primarily through the social difference we call "gender" and the unhinging of consumerism from class.

It has now been twenty-five years since Judith Butler developed her Althusserian reading of gender, extending the insights about the role of "the family ISA" in assigning gender subject positions. Taking up Althusser's own examples about the intensity of ideological interpellation at the site of birth,[14] Butler showed how such intensity was fraught with anxiety, especially the particular anxiety about homosexuality. I won't rehearse the arguments: they are so well known and have gathered such authority that they seem to interpellate us, leaving us unable to think without or beyond the (unseen) framework of gender as performative interpellation. The impact on queer theory, where *Gender Trouble* is still regularly positioned as a founding text, was particularly intense, as Butler helped to frame sexuality as a distinct socio-psycho-political dynamic requiring specific tools and modes of analysis.

Butler's arguments had such a tremendous impact, in part, because they capture so much of the constructed yet simultaneously binding character of this strange phenomenon, gender. Moreover, in her insistence on the performative character of interpellating practices, Butler provided some opening through which to conceive political resistance against the heterosexist, patriarchal norms of gender, namely, through the "cracks" of always imperfect gender performances. There is no perfect repetition, especially for the unnatural phenomena of gender. For feminists and queers, this came as a considerable relief. For neoliberals, it played into the kinds of marketing tools already well afoot by 1989, as Tom Frank's work aptly shows. And now, in the mid-2010s, for critical social theorists, it should prod us to theorize beyond interpellation and identification as the exhaustive horizons of subject formation and to historicize the cultural ascendancy of gender as a kind of playground for the endless stimulation that neoliberal subjects of interests crave.

Although Butler later regretted and sometimes tried to move beyond drag as the exemplar of her theories of gender performativity, the ways that her work was taken up through this singular example are instructive for us now. Fusing Jodi Dean's argument that neoliberalism functions through imaginary, rather than symbolic, identities with Tim Dean's provocative critique of Butler as developing gender exclusively as an imaginary phenomenon, I argue that Butler's early theories of gender performativity and their remarkable impact—both inside and outside the academy—surprisingly capture the fundamental transformations underway in neoliberal social rationalities.

Recall that, for Jodi Dean, the dynamic of social formation in the neoliberal episteme is not the fulfilling of a prescripted, socially anchored identity, but rather the endless pursuit of cool, ever new, interesting, and stimulating poses: we become purely what Foucault calls "subjects of interests" when we are most superficially oriented and stimulated. Especially when set loose in the circuit of the drive, unhinged from any teleology of desire, we loop endlessly through the superficial stream of images that we increasingly call "happiness." As imaginary identities, we seek and respond to intensifying practices that are thoroughly aestheticized and, even more particularly, visually cathected: we are pursuing cool, ever new, interesting, and stimulating *looks*, images-as-identities. In the social rationalities and practices of the neoliberal episteme, cognitive registers shift from the symbolic to the imaginary: image is everything, as Nike and every other marketer know all too well. And gender, with the constructed, liberatingly superficial spin that the fetish of drag gives it, is the perfect vehicle for such endeavors. Gender is the neoliberal playground.[15]

In this context, when Tim Dean critiques Butler's concept of performative gender as constricting gender to the aesthetic problematic of *mimesis*, he may actually help to articulate how gender is beginning to function in neoliberal social rationalities and practices. Tim Dean's project is to locate the precise ontological error in Butler's reading of gender as performative. Rightfully extending her concept of drag beyond the realm of gender, Dean demonstrates this category error through the infamous reading of *Paris is Burning*. As Dean puts it, "According to Butler, almost every conceivable kind of identity can be a form of drag insofar as, being imitable, identity is revealed to be itself imitative."[16] This restricts our analyses of subject formation to "the level of imaginary representations" and, in turn, "restricts vital political questions to the arena of ego identifications" (BS, 71). (This echoes Viego's concerns about dominant readings of racialization and racism that I sketched at the end of chapter 2.)

Pursuing his project of offering a more robust, Lacanian understanding of transgender and transsexual identifications (a problematic pairing), Dean corrects Butler's ontological error "by factoring the Lacanian real" (BS, 71) back into the questions of gender and sexuality, a project with which, as will become clear in the following chapter, I am entirely sympathetic. But Tim Dean's work also allows us to see, however inadvertently, how Butler's theorizing of gender captures, also inadvertently, a fundamental transformation underway in the neoliberal episteme: we are purely and only how we appear and the more interesting we can appear, the more successful and cooler we are! And gender, especially understood as the endless donning of cool new fashion accessories, is the most fabulous way to intensify our ever so cool appearances.[17]

WELCOME, METROSEXUALITY

The cultural emergence of metrosexuality in the United States and United Kingdom in the early 2000s offers a particularly apt example for analyzing these transformations. Proclaimed the coolest, latest thing on the cover of the *New York Times Magazine* in 2003, metrosexuality came on the scene as the coolest, latest thing the neoliberal market had cooked up. Of course, the fashion industry had known this for some time: any good neoliberal knows that a style has already lost its edge by the time it reaches the cover of the *New York Times Magazine*. Still, the play of androgyny and, particularly, the making cool of effeminate masculinity in metrosexuality became confusing cultural phenomena for feminist and queer theorists, for a short while. (Metrosexuality was officially proclaimed dead in 2012, since it is passé to note that which is fully mainstream; and, as the cartoon in the *New Yorker* in 2013 shows, it is clearly mainstream.)[18]

On the one hand, following Butler's lead, gender-bending had been hailed (pun intended) by feminists as one of the ultimate barometers of social change, a sure sign that the patriarchy was crumbling. But as metrosexuality has become cool and hip, nothing seems to be changing: economic indicators such as the gender gap in employment, wages, and salaries have not substantially changed; the wedding industry is flourishing and about to be boosted in unforeseen ways as same-sex marriage is gradually legalized; and the assault on women's reproductive rights and justice is intensifying across the United States. So, what is going on? How is it that gender-bending has been co-opted as the latest, coolest thing by the neoliberal market? And what does this tell us about the transformation in categories of social difference as well as processes of subject formation in neoliberalism?

To analyze this, I first return to Judith Butler's *Gender Trouble*, which became remarkably popular roughly a decade before the cultural emergence of metrosexuality. Arguably the most culturally challenging aspect of Butler's work in *Gender Trouble* was her link of gender binaries and normativity to a heterosexist concept of sexuality. This was, of course, not news to feminists, who had been analyzing and articulating the endemic connections of sexism and heterosexism, sometimes alongside white supremacy, for some time by 1989. The 1970s were overflowing with feminists, across a range of ideological and political affinities, calling out the constrictive roles that patriarchal sexism forced upon women, including quite directly the constitutive roles of heterosexism and white supremacy. The names doing such work from a wide variety of (often conflicting) cultural standpoints far exceed any single, exhaustive list: Shulamith Firestone, Kate Millett, Robin Morgan, Susan Brownmiller, Gloria Steinem, Cheryl Clarke, June Jordan, Audre Lorde, Angela Davis, bell hooks, the Combahee River Collective, Catherine MacKinnon, Andrea Dworkin, *etc.* (A very different kind of twist on the now infamously Butlerian "etc.") I particularly emphasize Hortense Spillers's remarkable essay "Mama's Baby, Papa's Maybe: An American Grammar Book," published in 1987, which thoroughly racializes gender as a critical tool of chattel slavery and colonialism (an argument María Lugones continues to develop). In this historical light, it is quite puzzling why and how Butler's arguments became so popular, especially given the esoteric and rather torturous prose of *Gender Trouble*.

I do not claim to solve this puzzle, nor do I want to invoke the ridiculous kind of reductions that would be required by such a claim to do so. Rather, I offer a couple of speculations about linguistic, philosophical, and cultural transformations to offer a context in which to read the remarkable popularity of a thoroughly academic book such as *Gender Trouble*. As with any kind of historical reconstruction, the speculations I offer are partial; one can always find counterarguments and paths less taken for any genealogical analysis. My effort is not to offer the "true" reading of *Gender Trouble* and its widespread reception. I am not interested in arguing further about whether the theories of gender performativity Butler develops are "correct" or "true," as I hope is already clear in my discussion of Butler in chapter 2. Rather, I am interested in why and how they became so fascinating and provocative to so many of us, in and beyond the academy.

Therefore, I want to historicize (very briefly) the text of *Gender Trouble* and its most salient theory, gender performativity, as an exemplar of many of the critical transformations involved in the broader cultural unleashing of gender as the neoliberal playground. Not claiming any kind of cultural causality, I read *Gender Trouble* as exemplifying several conceptual and categorical transformations that are underway in neoliberal social rationalities and practices, especially as we find them enacted in the United States and United Kingdom in the late 1990s and early 2000s. That is, I argue that *Gender Trouble* may be a quintessentially neoliberal text.

On the one hand, the abstraction of Butler's argument offered a clear schematic of the hegemonic chain of signifiers that transcended some of the cultural, historical, and even personal contexts that enabled easier dismissals of some of the previous feminist analyses. The canonization of *Gender Trouble* as one of the founding texts of queer theory, however, impels us to see how Butler's arguments enabled the disarticulation of gender from both sexism and sexuality, and most certainly from such old-fashioned, decidedly uncool concepts as patriarchy and white supremacy. These shifts in language from the unabashed use of "patriarchy," "white supremacy," "heterosexism," and "homophobia" in the 1970s and early 1980s to the more domesticated "heteronormativity," "gender performativity," and, eventually, "homonormativity" and "queer" in the 1990s and 2000s indicate more than merely stylistic predilections. They indicate a substantive shift in the register of analyses from deep historical structures of domination toward more abstracted and ahistorically rendered cultural iterations of normativity.

While we feminists may still be highly habituated to reading gender through heterosexual interpellation and its endemic sexism, the emphatic embrace of denaturalizing gender as a culturally mediated and repetitive performance seems to make gender more pliable for the workings of neoliberalism. As neoliberal social rationalities render the role of history less and less culturally valued or even legible, this notion of "culturally mediated and repetitive" becomes quite thin. Consequently, the connection of gender to long-standing structures of sexism, heterosexism, and even white supremacy is simply lost. Liberated from the heavy baggage of interiority and symbolically scripted roles, with their fixed sexual expressions, gender can float freely as the most playful of signifiers. Once we understand that gender is performative, it seems we can just begin performing it to our endless entertainment and expansion of wardrobes (despite Judith Butler's screams of protest).

We can now see how Butler's *Gender Trouble*, while not framed as an analysis of gender in the neoliberal episteme, maps out many of the philosophical moves involved in this kind of unmooring of gender from deep political and historical structures. Grounded in Nietzschean critiques of causality and subjectivity, the text easily reads as a quintessentially postmodern liberation of gender from all forms of constriction and domination. *Gender Trouble* can be read as a playbook of neoliberal celebrations of and incitements toward nonconformity, a playbook read most assiduously by many of us (myself included) taking on the next historical mantle of coolness, queer theory. The feminist insistence on an endemic connection of gender back to sexism and heterosexism thereby increasingly falls on deaf ears. We sound like historical throwbacks, caught in those dark days when oppression reigned over (presumably dowdy, certainly prude) feminists who lacked any sense of humor—or of style. So uncool. We are cast into that "Siberia of feminism," as Angela McRobbie so aptly analyzes the kind of analysis eschewed wholly from the grand celebrations of gender in the postfeminism era of the neoliberal episteme.[19] And, in the terms of my broader efforts here, the category of gender begins to exemplify the cultural embrace of social difference as fungible, as evacuated of any political heft or historical weight—as o so cool.

Bringing this to bear on the cultural ascent of metrosexuality, we see how the social barometers regulating gender-bending practices in the early twenty-first century are fraught with ambivalence and anxieties about this tension between normative sexuality and normative gender (with any connection to sexism and racism utterly erased). From its inception, the phonic echo of heterosexuality in metrosexuality ensures the ongoing heterosexuality of the metrosexual man.

Mark Simpson's official coining of the term in his essay "Meet the Metrosexual," on *Salon.com* in July 2002, followed by a self-interview in 2004, is laced with homophobic insistences that he—and the metrosexual man he is "outing"—is not homophobic. The subtitle to the essay reads: "He's well dressed, narcissistic and obsessed with butts. But don't call him gay." Simpson then proceeds to parody coming out—"Ladies and gents, the captain of the England football squad is actually a screaming, shrieking, flaming, freaking metrosexual. (He'll thank me for doing this one day, if only because he didn't have to tell his mother himself.)"—as well as AIDS, claiming he was "contact traced" by the *New York Times* to be "Patient MetroZero."

These capture the general flavor of the two posts, which are filled with historical references (Oscar Wilde, Norman Mailer, The Village People) to show how gay culture cornered the market on narcissism long before metrosexuality. While these references overtly support the claim that the metrosexual is post-homophobia, the caricatures of gay culture are all too well worn as homophobic tropes. By the time Simpson provocatively suggests that the metrosexual, following on the middle-class slaying of the nineteenth-century dandy, is actually killing sexuality itself, only one message is legible: the metrosexual ambivalence about sexuality altogether. Very cool.

I do not belabor Mark Simpson's clearly playful, ironic, and very cool posts on *Salon.com* in order to call him out as a homophobe. (That would, obviously, be so uncool.) Rather, I read these posts and the broader cultural phenomena they are describing as examples of the kind of political confusion that so often attaches to gender-bending practices in these neoliberal times. With names such as David Beckham and Brad Pitt and films such as *Fight Club*, *American Psycho*, and *Spiderman* attached to the term, "the metrosexual" clearly refers to straight (mostly white) men who are indulging gay aesthetics.

Setting political questions aside, the metrosexual is explicitly defined by two intertwining characteristics: an unabashed narcissism and the drive to spend and consume as recklessly as necessary to feed the image. As Simpson describes this "new" cultural phenomenon, the metrosexual "might be officially gay, straight or bisexual, but this is utterly immaterial because he has clearly taken himself as his own love object and pleasure as his sexual preference."[20] In this emphasis on unbounded narcissism, the metrosexual becomes the quintessentially imaginary identity, obsessed with cultivating the endless adoration of others. Allegedly freed entirely from homophobia and any other boorish concern with politics (or history), the metrosexual is the ideal subject of interests.

Still, insofar as metrosexuality emerges as a kind of transitional phenomenon in neoliberal transformations of gender and thus in neoliberal transformations of social difference into apolitical, fungible coolness, the ambivalence about sexual normativity and gender normativity persists across its various cultural iterations. For example, the regulative role of heteronormativity is more pronounced, if still fraught with ambivalence, in the contemporaneous, extremely popular television show *Queer Eye for the Straight Guy*, which aired under that precise title and theme from 2003 to 2005 in both US and UK versions.

The premise of the reality show was basic: it showed how good heterosexual men can be coached into becoming more sensitive—and more aesthetically savvy and appealing—heterosexuals precisely through the aesthetic sensibilities of homosexual men. The role of heteronormative sexuality in these gender-bending practices thereby becomes clearer: (1) so long as heterosexuality is not under any serious threat, there are presumably no limits to the play of gender as a fabulous fashion accessory that can be intensified and consumed ad infinitum; (2) the reworking of masculinity into ever more appealing and interesting aesthetic modes is welcome as an enhancement of heterosexual desire and pleasure; (3) if the homosexual can deliver this reworking of straight masculinity, then homosexuality can become more and more enmeshed in the perpetuation of more interesting, savvy heterosexuality that will, in turn, be all the more culturally powerful.

Without the distracting protestations against homophobia of Simpson's posts, *Queer Eye for the Straight Guy* shows more clearly how the crucial stake in metrosexuality is the transformation of masculine heterosexuality into a more aesthetically interesting and varied phenomenon; it is not any challenge to normative heterosexuality itself. The exciting aspect of the show, which captured the attention, imaginations, and perhaps even fantasies of a widespread (if largely straight, female, white, middle-class) audience, was the amplification of masculinity as a fresh site for the inventiveness of gender—of neoliberal gender unleashed from any concerns about sexism or heterosexism, but still quite happily playing into heteronormativity. Good ole fashioned heteronormativity could begin to flourish through gender variance, bolstered by the apolitical stance that adheres to all cultural positions of normativity.

Of course, the emergence of this fresh gender playground primarily in the professional classes to which metrosexuality is marketed confirms the kinds of class stratifications we have come to expect of the neoliberal iteration of the modern episteme. But as Simpson emphasizes, metrosexuality turns primarily on a man's spending priorities and habits, not on his class position.[21] The metrosexual becomes an exemplary neoliberal subject of interests not only because he embraces gender for endless experimentation and enjoyment, but also because he does so through unabashed and ever joyful consumerism. He confirms the fantasy of instant wealth directly by enacting it: one's spending habits need not correlate to one's class position, as the ongoing fetishizing and purchasing of remarkably expensive tennis shoes by lower-class, working-poor communities show.[22] The role of class, which has never been a recognized or comfortable category for liberalism and its adamant myth of meritocracy, intensifies in neoliberalism into the role of spending and consumerism.

UNCOOL DIFFERENCES

This slide from class to consumerism in metrosexuality does not mean, however, that class no longer matters. Class structures continue to modulate the neoliberal social field, shaping and limiting the transformation from class to consumerism, from sexuality to consumerism, and from race to consumerism. Some differences remain intractable.

Not all differences are cool. Not all differences can be aestheticized, scrubbed clean of historical residues, evacuated into glorious superficiality, and transformed into an oh so cool accessory. The historical ontologies of bodies are not so easily erased. The *soma* resists, demarcating our various social differences according to scales of malleability. Some differences, written into bodies and psyches by long patterns of sustained, systemic xenophobia, remain intractable to the allure of superficiality and fungibility enacted in neoliberal social rationalities. These more obstinate differences, these recurrent instances of somatic xenophobia, carry a historical ontology that cannot be so easily expunged.

Attention to the different historical ontologies attached to various categories and instantiations of social difference thereby offers a crucial way to parse contemporary politics around various issues, such as reproductive rights, same-sex marriage, disability rights, transgender rights, prisoners' rights, and immigration. In the line of thinking I am advancing, these issues are mediated by the kinds of histories that shape and inform the different bodies involved. While that in and of itself is far from a new argument, the neoliberal intensification of liberal categories of social difference substantially confuses our abilities to read those histories. Unmoored by the cool motor of fungibility from historical cathexes to xenophobia, the variations among particular iterations of social difference are flattened.

Put differently, the neoliberal command to "celebrate diversity" aims to decathect the histories of explicit, if still disavowed, xenophobia that stratified the social fabric of liberalism. These ugly histories are just bad historical hangovers—totally uncool. But this does not mean that they do not continue to shape and inform arguments over various forms of social difference and their attendant political rights, as we see in the ongoing assault on women's reproductive rights, the proliferation of anti-immigrant sentiments and politics, the persistence of only redemptive representations of disability, and the inability to cognize the complexity of trans* lives beyond anything more than a fretful aberration. If we are to intercede in this confused social landscape in the name of justice and ethics, we must develop analytic skills to decipher this interplay between historical xenophobia and its aestheticized erasure.

We must begin, with Hortense Spillers, to think through the terrifying histories of our American grammar.

FIGURE 4a.1 Miles Davis. Copyright © Hulton-Deutsch Collection/Corbis.

INTERLUDE 4

The Birth of Cool

Writing about Miles Davis as a mere Interlude of Cool is just plain wrong. Acclaimed as birthing "cool" itself, he with his legendary status is rightfully the topic of innumerable studies—biographical, musicological, historical, and political. Brilliant, immensely talented, and deeply passionate, Miles Davis altered the course of contemporary American music, several times. He was uncompromising in all matters, aesthetic and political, living at that rare high heat that only the most intense aesthetic expressions afford. He was and always will be the icon of old-style cool.

While early critics may have debated his virtuosity as a trumpet player and later critics accused him of selling out, one clear attribute sets Miles Davis apart from his peers: change. As Ian Carr quotes him: "I have to change. It's like a curse."[1] From his birthing of "cool jazz," in contrast to the "hot jazz" of bebop, in the late 1940s to his introduction of fusion at the Newport Jazz Festival in 1955 and on *Kind of Blue* in 1959 to his fusing of jazz, rock, and funk on *Bitches Brew* in 1969 and his full embrace of all-things-electric in the 1980s, Miles Davis changed music—"at least fiver or six times," by his own count.[2]

But he never did so through romanticized notions of pure creativity or the sheer force of "genius." Miles Davis understood himself as immersed in the wide histories of music. In an early interview with *Down Beat* in 1950, he explains the necessity of knowing musical history: "You've got to start way back there before you can play bop. You've got to have a foundation."[3] This unquenchable thirst for *all* kinds of music defined Miles's life. Although disgusted with the "prejudice and shit" of Juilliard,[4] he recognized the value of the technical knowledge he gained there. From those early days in New York City, when he would "go to the library and borrow scores by all those great composers, like Stravinsky, Alban Berg, Prokofiev" (M, 61), to much later days of being enthralled with the theoretical innovations of Karlheinz Stockhausen and Paul Buckmaster, Davis engaged music in all its layers, angles, and forms.

Early on in the late 1940s, he is shocked that "a lot of black musicians didn't know anything about music theory" (M, 60) and, later, that Jimi Hendrix couldn't read music. But he never shames them for it.[5] He simply recognizes the different approaches, bridges the gaps, and makes way for the one thing that matters most to him: creativity.[6] It is little wonder that a man with such a voracious appetite for all music works with legendary figures from the 1940s, 1950s, 1960s, 1970s, and 1980s. Miles constantly pushed forward, constantly changed.

One further aspect of Miles Davis's life makes him the exemplary figure of old-style cool for me and this project: his unflinching commitment to call out race and racism. His autobiography, *Miles*, is filled with stories of racism: early childhood memories of being called "Nigger! Nigger!" on the street; stories of East St. Louis race riots in 1917; the constant and often violent police harassment as an adult; the refusal to appear on late night television talk shows because the white hosts and producers do not recognize their own racism; humorously told stories of ignorant white bigots at the Reagan White House's dinner for Ray Charles; and so on and so on and so on. While he describes his father as "a Marcus Garvey man" (M, 22), Miles claims he did not come to a political consciousness of race and racism until he returned from Paris in 1949. Despite his descent into a hellish four years of heroin addiction, Miles emerged in 1955 at the Newport Jazz Festival to become not only the defining figure of jazz, but also the defining figure of black resistance. As Amiri Baraka explains: "In a sense Miles embodied a black attitude that had grown steadily more ubiquitous in the fifties—defiance, a redefined, contemporary function of the cultural traditional *resistance* of blacks to slavery and then national oppression. . . . Miles was not only the cool hipster of our bebop youth, but now (late 50s) we felt he embodied the social fire of the time."[7] Miles never looked back.

His interviews across the 1960s and 1970s are filled with scathing critiques of racism and racist institutions, ranging from police practices to music producers and promoters to media representations and deeply held social narratives. The infamous interview with *Playboy* in 1962 reads as a primer in race consciousness. Calling out bigoted whites for their ignorance and always, always refusing to play the Uncle Tom, Miles Davis never ignored, erased, or kept silent about the deep racial stratification of US culture.[8]

Still, my celebration of Miles Davis as the icon of old-style cool is not without hesitation or complexity. As with so many icons of this ever so masculinist aesthetic, cool, his life and autobiography are filled with a hedonism and sexism that are often difficult to stomach. Always a fashion maven and a boxer, Miles developed a love for fast, expensive cars, drugs of various sorts, and beautiful, sexy women.[9] While these all fall, perhaps too easily, into a pattern of lives that are set free from social controls by fame and wealth, the stories about sex and women, including his violent outbursts, become increasingly intense in his autobiography. We must heed Pearl Cleage's anger and not sidestep the sexism and violence that also filled this too cool man's life.[10]

On the one hand, the stories of his wild orgies during his retirement from the music business from 1975 to 1981 are perfectly in step with the kind of excessive pleasures that filled this life: Miles Davis was a man who sought the limits of all experiences, repeatedly. He could not turn away from the allure of intense pleasures, even in their self-destructive extremes. But the sexism of these stories as an endless stream of nameless female bodies colludes with the monolithic concepts of "women" that pepper the entire autobiography, especially the closing pages on various racial "kinds" of women. The role of women in Miles's life vacillates between the two classic positions of all sexist men: the pedestal and the bed. The classic contradiction, then, is the way this stereotyping of "women" clashes with his vehement anger about precisely this kind of racist generalizing about "blacks" as a monolithic phenomenon. His politics were, so to speak, lacking in self-critique.

To call Miles Davis the icon of old-style cool is thus not to celebrate him uncritically. It is not to position him as The Magical Negro who saves us from the neoliberal bastardization of cool. There is no way back to Miles. But the ways that race and sex came together in his life speak to the kinds of deep social conflict that must animate any historical sense of cool. Nothing superficial, and rooted deeply in the histories of music and politics, Miles Davis was not merely a rebellious young hipster. He was after change—deep, abiding, persistent, ongoing, and always intense change. And the register in which he exerted his power to make such change was singular: creative, ingenious, often mind-blowing music.

I'll give him the last word, speaking in about 1955, just as he is birthing cool:

> Wherever we played the clubs were packed, overflowing back into the streets, with long lines of people standing out in the rain and snow and cold and heat. It was something else, man. And a whole lot of famous people were coming every night to hear us play. People like Frank Sinatra, Dorothy Kilgallen, Tony Bennett (who got up on the stage and sang with my band one night), Ava Gardner, Dorothy Dandridge, Lena Home, Elizabeth Taylor, Marion Brando, James Dean, Richard Burton, Sugar Ray Robinson, just to mention a few.
>
> When this group was getting all this critical acclaim, it seemed that there was a new mood coming into the country; a new feeling was growing among people, black and white. Martin Luther King was leading that bus boycott down in Montgomery, Alabama, and all the black people were supporting him. Marian Anderson became the first black person to sing at the Metropolitan Opera. Arthur Mitchell became the first black to dance with a major white dance company, the New York City Ballet. Marlon Brando and James Dean were the new movie stars and they had this rebellious young image of the "angry young man" going for them. *Rebel Without a Cause* was a big movie then. Black and white people were starting to get together and in the music world Uncle Tom images were on their way out. All of a sudden, everybody seemed to want anger, coolness, hipness, and real clean, mean sophistication. Now the "rebel" was in and with me being one at that time, I guess that helped make me a media star. Not to mention that I was young and good looking and dressed well, too. Being rebellious and black, a nonconformist, being cool and hip and angry and sophisticated and ultra clean, whatever else you

want to call it—I was all those things and more. But I was playing the fuck out of my horn and had a great group, so I didn't get recognition based only on a rebel image. I was playing my horn and leading the baddest band in the business, a band that was creative, imaginative, supremely tight, and artistic. And that, to me, was why we got the recognition. (M, 197–98)

CHAPTER FIVE

Reading Race as the Real

THE SECURITIES AND PUNISHMENTS OF NEOLIBERAL COOL

RACIALIZING THE (SEXUALIZED) DRIVE

"What is foreclosed in the symbolic will return in the real." As Tim Dean warns and reminds us, Lacan repeats this mantra over and over in his 1955–56 seminar, *The Psychoses*.[1] For Dean, this leads to an extended inquiry into sexuality as it grounds and cathects us to the real. Laying out the conceptual and textual arguments in *Beyond Sexuality* and the cultural enactments in *Unlimited Intimacy*, Dean thoroughly demonstrates how the Freudian and Lacanian readings of sexuality are irreducible to the (repetitive) cultural reductions of sexuality to genitality, identity, or representation. Located in the Lacanian register of the real (or what we might call the drive in the Freudian schema), sexuality is fundamentally chaotic, turbulent, disordered, and disordering. It resists signification, registering in consciousness only through the trace that it leaves as the limit of the symbolic order. The cultural interpellation of the symbolic order thereby occurs through the constitutive disavowal of the real. This leads us very easily to conceptualize sexuality as regulated by sexual difference and sexual object-choice, resulting in the registers of identity politics that saturate US mainstream discourse. But these formulations fundamentally transform sexuality with their claims of intelligibility. As an asignifying field, sexuality as it "resides" in the unconscious and cathects the real knows none of these formulations.

For Dean's purposes, this radically decenters heterosexism as the natural or normal course of sexual development. As he writes, "If there is no signifier for sexual difference in the unconscious, then as far as the unconscious is concerned heterosexuality does not exist."[2] It turns out we can add a fourth characteristic to Freud's list of concepts that the unconscious does not know—the unconscious knows no negation, no contradiction, nothing of time, *and nothing of heterosexuality*! Heteronormativity, read through Dean, emerges only at the level of symbolic interpellation—the site of subjectification that renders all humans fundamentally self-alienated. Pushed into identity categories that are critical to the functioning of the symbolic order, all humans are, therefore, fundamentally alienated from this unconscious desire that exceeds signification and cultural representation. Heteronormativity thereby becomes part of the violence of the symbolic order against all subjects, not "merely" those engaged in nonheteronormative sexual activities. Consequently, we get an entirely different sense of the anxiety caused by Freud's persistent claim that all humans are fundamentally bisexual: sexuality—sexuality per se—is fundamentally, as an unconscious drive, without form, order, or intelligible aim.

Sympathetic and indebted to Dean's work, I want to amplify it, especially through a different orientation to race.[3] I remain convinced that sexuality is never embodied in the kind of singular and often abstracted manner that haunts so much of queer theorists' compelling analyses of and speculations about it, especially those deriving from psychoanalytic frameworks. I do not mean that we must limit ourselves to a muted form of positivism that demands empirical indices to account for the infinite permutations of particular embodiments and enactments: I am committed to and epistemically framed by abstract and speculative modes of thinking. My alteration and expansion of Dean's account emerge, rather, from my long-standing feminist conviction that, in the long sociohistorical ontology that continues to frame the United States, sexuality is always already racialized and race is always already sexualized.

In this relentless insistence, I take my point of departure from black feminists of the 1970s and 1980s. As Angela Davis, Hortense Spillers, and bell hooks, among many others, argue, the psychosexual history of chattel slavery continues to animate the complex sociopsychic dynamics of both race and sexuality in the United States.[4] For each of these thinkers and numerous others, the historical weight of the systemic raping of black slaves (both female and male) by white slave owners locks the psyche of United States's culture in the vicious, persistent dynamics of racialization and racism that are always also sexualized.

Spillers's articulation of this is particularly instructive for the profound impact this psychosexual-racial history has on the entire modern episteme in the United States. As she articulates it in her classic essay "Mama's Baby, Papa's Maybe: An American Grammar Book," "The sociopolitical order of the New World, . . . with its human sequence written in blood, *represents* for its African and indigenous peoples a scene of *actual* mutilation, dismemberment, and exile . . . a *theft* of the *body*."[5] The scene of this theft is profoundly sexualized and eerily epistemological. With a focus on the "ungendering" of the African female (and, by implication, male) flesh, Spillers extends the impact of this "primal scene" of rape (enacted in many ways) to the impossibility of representing the unthinkable violence of the entire episteme of chattel slavery (categories, taxonomies, economics, and practices) that "altered human tissue" (MBPM, 207). As she puts it, "Even though the captive flesh/body has been 'liberated,' . . . dominant symbolic activity, the ruling episteme that releases the dynamics of naming and valuation, remains grounded in the originating metaphors of captivity and mutilation" (MBPM, 208). Thinking through this distinctly "American grammar," I insist that the exquisite twisting of bodies and undergoing of *jouissance* that we might name "sexuality," when thinking it in the register of the real, are always already a profoundly racialized act in the psychosocial episteme of the United States.

This directly impacts the meaning of the drive as the circuit in which neoliberal subjects of interests endlessly (and quite happily) loop. It now assumes not only the sexualized meanings of its Freudian legacies, but also these deeply racialized contours of the legacies of chattel slavery. Again, the early work of queer theory is both crucially instructive and disturbingly limited for thinking through what it means to read the drive as both sexualized and racialized.

As sexualized, the drive becomes a primary heuristic for Leo Bersani's classic "Is the Rectum a Grave?," published in 1987. Working amid the onslaught of AIDS and drawing from the rich archive of Bataille, Freud, Foucault, and Gayle Rubin, Bersani argues for what became known as the antisocial thesis, namely, that we who are labeled as perverts in this bourgeois episteme must embrace the "anticommunal, antiegalitarian, antinurturing, antiloving" aspect of sex in all its self-destructive, self-shattering *jouissance* "as a mode of ascesis."[6] While written in Freudian language, the text emphasizes the explicit and graphic location of sexuality's unmooring and resistance to socially scripted identity categories in the body, namely, the anus.

This somatic indexicality is central to the Lacanian development of this Freudian concept. When Lacan specifies the kinds of partial drives (anal, oral, scopic, invocatory), he does so through erotogenic, somatic registers: the anus, the mouth, the eye, the ear. He explicitly accentuates the physical kind of stimulation located only in the circuitous character of the orifice as our embodied instantiation of these drives.[7] The drive is structurally ateleological precisely because its circuitous form enlivens repetition, rather than arrival, as the site of pleasure. The somatic indexicality is thereby crucial: it is the circular structure of the mouth, the ear, and the anus that renders them physical sites of intensified stimulation and thereby exemplars of the circuit of the drive.[8]

Tim Dean then develops this fundamentally somatic characteristic to show how sexual experiences are not able to be folded neatly into any of the structures of the whole with which so many cultures freight them. As a closed circuit, the drive can never be synthesized into any greater whole; as a sexualized experience, the circuit of the drive renders sexuality as partial, never harmonized into any whole—whether of identity, self, relationship, cultural or religious ideal, nationalist mandate, and so on. Sexual experiences are disaggregating experiences, radically so, which is how Dean reads them through the Lacanian real.[9]

Given the early date of work such as Bersani's, I find the ongoing occlusion by the Slovenian school of Lacanian social theory (especially Slavoj Žižek and Jodi Dean in this project) of this emphatic instantiation of the drive in somatic, and especially sexual, orifices quite troubling.[10] This fundamental abstraction from the *soma* skews the analysis of social difference per se into the register of the imaginary, where both queer and Slovenian schools of Lacanian social theorists agree that the binary logic of inclusive and exclusive representation traps the persistent struggle of identity politics in an impossible site of meaningful change. At the same time, however, we can also see a striking formal parallel between these two modes of Lacanian analysis, namely, the reduction of all social differences other than the particular designated psychosocial formation of the respective analysis (for example, proletarianization for Jodi Dean and sexuality for Tim Dean) to the register of the imaginary and, subsequently, the discounting of identity politics.[11] Rather unnervingly, all of these accounts fail to give any sustained attention to the powerful force of racialization, which, I argue, must be endemic to any consideration and use of the Lacanian drive, especially in the American grammar.[12]

I thereby share my point of departure with that scholarship labeled "queer of color critique," which argues that this mutually constitutive relation between sexuality and race must be the self-evident point of departure for analyses of historical, aesthetic, and sociological formations. These analyses are developing into a thorough and persuasive argument for the persistence of race and sexuality as mutually constituting, historical vectors of social formation and its persistent, often structural inequities.[13] This is a crucial intervention. Focused primarily on marshaling the historical evidence, however, these analyses often fail to offer accounts of the onto-psychological dynamics involved in these social formations. They fail to address the deep patterns of social cathexes animating these historically racialized and sexualized formations.

By bringing this argument about the mutually constituting relation of race and sexuality into the psychoanalytic registers of the real and the drive, I hope to develop a lexicon that can account for the deep patterns of social cathexes to sexualized racism that continue to animate US culture, if in increasingly convoluted manners. Cast far beyond subjectivity as reduced to identity markers, the real and its vocabulary allow us to think both sexuality and race as powerful forces that ontologically refuse the reduction to historical categories of identity—or remedies cast purely in their terms. They allow us to heed the lessons about the somatic indexicality of the drive from queer theory and, moving beyond queer theory, to conceive race as the complex embodiment of what Stuart Hall calls a long, historical "common disaster."[14]

Finally, neoliberalism, of course, twists all of this. Alongside the intensifying of values, concepts, and categories of liberalism that I have been tracking, the neoliberal social rationalities and practices also transform these historical ontologies of sexuality and race. I have already argued that the neoliberal episteme, functioning primarily through the imaginary, intensifies gender into an oh so cool accessory. Animated particularly through the neoliberal intensification of class into consumerism, gender subsequently helps to domesticate cultural representations of nonnormative sexuality, especially those that go under the now fully legible categories of gay and lesbian. In this chapter, I extend these arguments to focus on the persistence of racism in the contemporary United States.

First, I examine how the neoliberal intensification of class into consumerism is a thoroughly racialized phenomenon; through analyses of "the ghetto tax" and the accelerating racial wealth gap, I show how fundamental class stratifications have been exacerbated through neoliberal economic and political reforms. This indicates that there are racialized limits to the neoliberal transformation of class into consumerism. I then turn to the neoliberal transformations of nonnormative sexuality and racial difference through an analysis of the contemporaneous emergence of the same-sex marriage movement alongside the carceral state; I speculate that this contemporaneous expansion of rights to a particular kind of same-sex relationship and contraction of rights from a clearly racialized portion of the population capture the kinds of transformations underway in gender, sexuality, class, and race in these dizzying neoliberal times. Finally, I conclude by elaborating my fundamental conviction and provocation that, amid these confusing and kinetic neoliberal times, a singular vector of social difference in the United States remains, obstinately, at the level of the real: race.

RACIALIZED CLASS INEQUITY: A LIMIT OF NEOLIBERAL CONSUMERISM

Long-standing, arguably endemic patterns of class inequity are materially built into categories of race and the social stratifications they have historically subtended in the United States. The neoliberal intensification of class into consumerism is subsequently enacted very differently across racialized groups. For example, the kinds of obfuscation of class position in spending practices and priorities such as those I located in metrosexuality do not occur symmetrically across racial groups.

First of all, the divisions between "luxury" and "necessary" purchases have long been differentiated along race and class lines in the United States, correlating to the differentiating concepts of both "security" and "welfare." The racialized stereotypes of the Welfare Queen, with Cadillacs in the yard and food stamps in the grocery store, proliferated during the Reagan 1980s—two decades prior to the celebration of metrosexuality and white straight men spending beyond their means. But rather than reclaiming the Welfare Queen as the proto-neoliberal, the racialized condemnation of "welfare" (which has now been extended to anti-immigrant diatribes) consistently excludes corporate welfare. Indeed, the gap between those who receive state welfare via wages (including housing and food aid) and those who receive state welfare via tax breaks continues to be intensely racialized.[15] On the other side of the schematic of welfare and security, the proliferation of gated communities, both physical and cyber, has served up an endless array of markets for the selling of "security," especially as exacerbated by jingoist nationalism in the post-9/11 years. The more one has to lose, it seems, the more one is obsessed to secure it—and the more one will participate in racist stereotypes, assumptions, and schematics of security.[16] The #BlackLivesMatter movement (and especially the @KilledByCops Twitter account) is finally exposing this epidemic of grossly underreported racialized violence occurring in these various guises of "security" across the United States.[17]

As my quip about the Welfare Queen as the proto-neoliberal suggests, spending and consumer practices are increasingly dislodged from material class positions: we are all encouraged to spend beyond our paychecks in these neoliberal times. True to the Foucaultian analysis of neoliberal rationalities as intensifying practices, values, and categories of liberalism, this obfuscates the persistent role of class stratification in ensuring the historical racial schemas of the United States. For example, the repeated celebration of the emergence of the black middle class encourages us to embrace the neoliberal mantras of (privatized) individual fiscal responsibility as the singular explanation for any income disparities. But this creates considerable cognitive dissonance when confronted with the increasingly widespread information on a systemic, accelerating wealth gap. Given voice in 2011 by the Occupy Movement's "99%" slogan, the suspicion that the wealthy are getting wealthier each and every year is surely growing in the United States.[18] But it seems to be more difficult to realize that this accelerating wealth gap carries forward the racist social stratification of the nineteenth century. Indeed, the categorical obfuscation of this racialized and racist phenomenon (for example, through allegedly "color-blind," facially neutral practices such as those I analyze below) seems to aid and abet the material intensification of this long-standing racist social stratification.

Thankfully, scholars from various disciplines are collecting and analyzing the intensified racial patterns of this accelerating wealth gap. Before turning to this research, I first recall my discussion of statistics at the close of chapter 3, wherein I extended Mary Beth Mader's analysis of the numerical standardization of objects as fundamental to the social rationality of neoliberalism. Abstracted from referentiality altogether, the numerical epistemology of the statistic enables the formalization of social objects, including especially social difference, into fungible units appropriate to the metric of ratio-calculative normativity. As I turn to the research on the accelerating racial wealth gap, I want to keep this account of statistics and its historical emergence as well as epistemological formalization front and center. It is unsurprising, of course, that research on wealth distributions and factors should articulate its findings through the neoliberal lexicon of statistics. Moreover, the malleability of statistics for a variety of ideological spins is not news. In my overarching effort to think about the aporia of ethics, however, I emphasize the limits of numerical formalization endemic to the epistemology of statistics itself. While such an epistemology is a powerful heuristic and can clarify various kinds of social phenomena, it is never sufficient to the analyses or full psychosocial digestion of those phenomena. If we are to think ethically in these neoliberal times, we have to sort through what it means to reach beyond these limits and encounter complex sociopsychic histories that are decidedly not fungible.

In 2013, the Pew Research Center published a jarring report, "King's Dream Remains an Elusive Goal," that shows accelerated gaps between whites and both African Americans and Hispanics (to use the language of the US Census Bureau on which the Pew Center depends) in both income and wealth:

INCOME GAPS	1970		2011
Whites-African-Americans	$19,000		$27,000
Whites-Hispanics	$15,000		$27,000
WEALTH GAPS	**1984**	**2011**	**2009**
African American wealth as percentage of white wealth	9%	7%	5%
Hispanic wealth as percentage of white wealth	13%	9%	6%[19]

In 2012 dollars, this means that "in 2011, the typical white household had a net worth of $91,405, compared with $6,446 for black households [and] $7,843 for Hispanic households."[20]

Similarly, using a different set of data, a recent study at Brandeis University found, from 1984 to 2009, "the total wealth gap between white and African-American families nearly triple[d], increasing from $85,070 in 1984 to $236,500 in 2009."[21] The graph from those findings offers a very similar trend of proportional changes found in the Pew Report, if with different numbers attached (see figure 5.1).

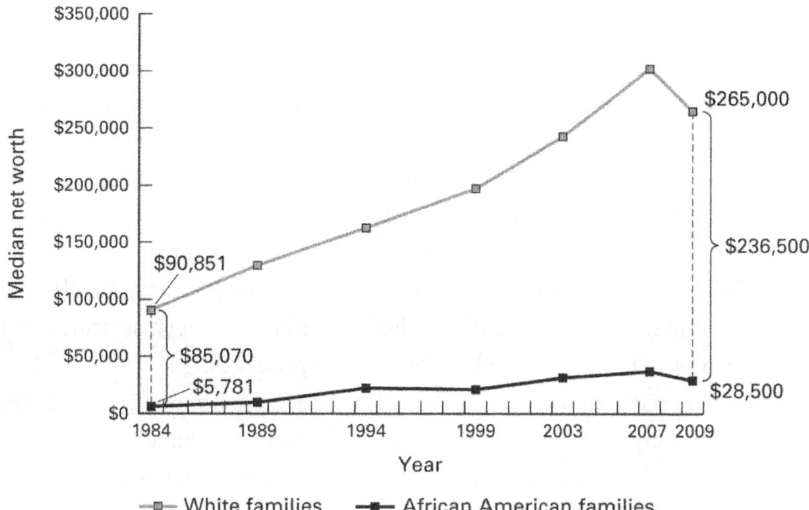

FIGURE 5.1 The growing racial wealth gap.
Source: Shapiro, Meschede, and Osoro, "The Roots of the Widening Racial Wealth Gap."

The emphasis in these studies is on the net worth and wealth (two interchangeable terms), not just income. As the Brandeis researchers explain, "Wealth—what we own minus what we owe—allows families to move forward by moving to better and safer neighborhoods, investing in businesses, saving for retirement, and supporting their children's college aspirations. Having a financial cushion also provides a measure of security when a job loss or other crisis strikes."[22] While there is most certainly still an astonishing racialized income gap, the focus on wealth allows scholars to ascertain a wide variety of financial vectors that constitute the overall racialized gap in material, economic security.[23] Moreover, as the work of Devin Fergus illustrates, the focus on wealth enables an analysis of neoliberal transformations in systems of racist inequalities that the exclusive focus on exclusionary practices of employment obfuscates. In the Lacanian lexicon, the focus on wealth enables an analysis of the shift from the liberal practice of exclusion that is explicit in the symbolic order—often written literally in the legal code—to the neoliberal eclipse of the symbolic through facially neutral categories, setting us free to pursue the cool in the imaginary unleashed. In effect, the focus on wealth allows an analysis of neoliberal racism.

Fergus focuses on four central factors contributing to the racial wealth gap: housing, transportation, education, and employment. This choice, of course, is intentional: these have historically been the primary arenas in which racist discrimination in the United States has been both enacted and contested. The progress narrative of liberalism proclaims that each of these areas has been corrected, erasing legal exclusion on the basis of race through a variety of post–Civil Rights Acts. Particularly through a focus on practices of consumption (housing and transportation), however, Fergus demonstrates how a "ghetto tax" has been systematically levied since the mid-1960s to enforce the long-standing racist stratification of the United States through facially neutral practices.

Focusing particularly on the industries of auto insurance and housing mortgages, Fergus exposes "the network of informal shadowy subsidies . . . that central-city residents pay for goods and services, which are often used to offset the costs of wealthier and less deserving residents outside the inner city."[24] The auto insurance industry, for example, began screening applications through zip codes, rather than explicit categories of race, in the 1970s and has wound up charging black drivers from 37.5 percent to 83.5 percent more than non-Latino white drivers, despite the record of the driver.[25] Despite public campaigns against such practices, the use of zip codes to determine rates of fees and interest has actually become more widespread across a variety of credit markets, leading scholars to investigate the increasing role of financial services and fees—from car loans to mortgages to credit card debt—in the accelerating racial wealth gap.

The housing crisis of 2008, which precipitated the Great Recession of 2009–11, demonstrates this most powerfully. Despite the federal laws that were passed in the late 1960s and 1970s to eliminate practices of redlining in the mortgage industry,[26] "researchers have documented the emergence of a 'dual mortgage market,' in which communities of color are more likely to be served by subprime lenders, even as overt discrimination in mortgage lending has decreased," as Carolina Reid explains.[27] This means that communities of color systematically pay more for their mortgages and encounter a range of hidden fees, obstreperous application processes, and risky subventions.

While this already indicates a racialized disparity written systematically into the financial industry's practices, Devin Fergus traces how, despite the post–Civil Rights explicit illegality of explicitly racist practices, the gradual deregulation of the mortgage and banking industries enabled this acceleration of the racial wealth gap.[28] This broad deregulation illustrates how the neoliberal social rationality uses facially neutral categories, codes, and practices that nonetheless produce racially differentiated effects. The Tax Reform Act of 1986, for example, eliminated most nonmortgage-related deductions from the tax code, thereby pushing citizens of the United States to purchase homes; twenty years later, blacks and Latinos are issued subprime mortgages at outrageous credit rates that result in the historically unforeseen racial wealth gap in the United States in 2011.[29]

These examples, alongside an endless stream of such phenomena across all kinds of industries and markets (credit cards, student loans, payday loans, home insurance, mortgage insurance, and so on), show how the "color-blind" rhetoric of neoliberal diversity merely obfuscates the persistent racial stratification in economic practices in the United States.

Despite the post–Civil Rights progress narrative of liberalism that legal exclusion to major institutions (education, housing, transportation, and employment) has been corrected, these analyses expose the costs of racial inclusion. Caught up in the neoliberal incitement to spend beyond one's paycheck, we neoliberal subjects of interests cannot discern class position from consuming practices: the more we spend, the cooler we are. Race no longer matters. But when it comes time to pay those bills or to play the shell-game of rotating credit, one's zip code suddenly matters. Functioning through facially neutral categories and practices, the financial sector of the United States enacts neoliberal racism doubly: it obfuscates the persistence of race as a primary vector through which US society is financially stratified and segregated, while simultaneously—and precisely through the tools of denial that enable that obfuscation—accelerating the racial wealth gap and deepening the systemic obstacles of poverty in black and Latino communities.

Following my insistence that neoliberal social rationalities are not fully captured by ideological critiques, I insist here that this is not merely a kind of duping of black and Latino communities by a white wealthy minority in power. While such an analysis explains some of the dynamics, especially as the top 1 percent of the wealthiest continue to increase their wealth,[30] it does not address the internalizing of neoliberal vocabularies, practices, and arguably values by *all* racial communities in the United States. As Fergus speculates, the resounding call to responsibility in black communities across the United States often comes in the call for "financial literacy," grossly contorting the historical fight for freedom as the fight for better, more prudent fiscal practices.[31] Even antiracist politics, including those emerging from communities of color, sometimes speak the language of neoliberalism.

Tellingly, we hear exactly this kind of call for fiscal responsibility and the belief in economic opportunity as the solution for all social ills in then Senator Obama's famous speech on race in March 2008. Framed by its rhetorical genre of a presidential campaign's attempt to control the damage of a media blitz, the speech explicitly condemns and disavows Reverend Jeremiah Wright's "profoundly distorted view of this country—a view that sees white racism as endemic."[32] In disavowing that view, Obama articulates the very slides from liberalism into neoliberalism that I have tracked across this book: he begins with the liberal promise of the US Constitution to perfect itself by healing the errors of slavery and slowly moves toward two primary explanations for the ongoing anger, violence, and poverty of black communities, namely, legalized discrimination (especially regarding employment) and the lack of economic opportunity. He then amplifies the ways that economic disenfranchisement creates anger and resentment on all sides of racial divides, thereby pointing to middle- and lower-class whites as most often the ones articulating racist views. The problem, then, is not race: it is economic opportunity. And the answer, in a rhetorically bizarre conclusion, is privatized, individualized sentimentality: Obama concludes with the story of a young white woman (whose name we learn is Ashley) who, by refusing to play the racist card as a child, focused on economic disparities and, subsequently, convinced an elderly black man (nameless) to join Obama's campaign.

In one of the most celebrated public speeches on race and racism in the twenty-first century, Obama articulates the neoliberal view of race and racism, replete with its ambivalence and confusion. Without a single mention of police violence against people of color, he frames racism primarily as a kind of anger and resentment fueled by a lack of economic opportunity. Therefore, the solution to lingering racism is upward mobility, which will transform the anger and resentment, through personal, private, and sentimental exchange, into peace and tranquility: if we can all just make enough money, we will happily join hands and sing Kumbaya together.

But this is clearly not the entire story of race and racism in the early twenty-first century in the United States, and Obama's other speech about race (prior to the protests against the killing of Michael Brown in Ferguson, Missouri, in August 2014 and the full-blown emergence of the #BlackLivesMatter movement in the fall of 2014) belies this: in July 2013, upon the acquittal of George Zimmerman for the murder of Trayvon Martin, Obama stepped forward to *identify* with Trayvon Martin. In so doing, Obama talks poignantly about the long history of violence and racial profiling against black men, especially young black men, that persists in the United States.[33] This identification with young black men then becomes the kernel of his response to the protests of the #BlackLivesMatter movement as it unfolds across the fall of 2014. While the speech about Trayvon Martin also concludes on the notes of hope and progress, the ongoing and widespread violence against black communities is shoring up a very different kind of narrative—one that is still developing as I conclude this book.

What is foreclosed in the symbolic returns in the real.

REAL RACE: THE LIMITS OF NEOLIBERALISM

Racial difference, cathected with the long violent history that I am calling the real, jams the neoliberal machine. Carrying the deep historical violence of settler colonialism, the transatlantic slave trade, the violent practices of chattel slavery, and the range of racist immigration codes and practices that have marked US history since its inception, racial difference continues to function as the ongoing repository for xenophobic violence and our cultural cathexis (however disavowed) to it. As so many texts from the twentieth century teach us, we would be incoherent without race. It structures who we are.

In liberalism, this can be formulated as the impossibility of privatizing race. In contrast to homosexuality, race bears its marks biologically. That "hair, skin and bone" that W. E. B. Du Bois called out so long ago render the historical violence that attaches to these biological differences impossible to privatize. While homosexuality can thus become normalized through the privatizing schemas of citizenship, as Roderick Ferguson argues, race is endemically marked in the body.[34] Unlike religion, class, gender, and sexuality, we cannot climb out of our bodies: we cannot privatize race. We cannot erase it in the name of inclusion and progress. We remain deeply cathected to it, admittedly or not. It grounds and structures, in Lacanian language, the core fantasies of liberalism: tolerance and neutrality.

In neoliberalism, however, the challenge of social differences is not privatization and the erasure from the public sphere in the name of Sameness. The challenge is to make social differences cool. The erasures and evacuations thus occur in different registers. Articulated in a somatic obstinacy, the fundamental problem of race in the neoliberal episteme is its stubborn, persistent reminder of an unspeakably violent history. Impermeable to the neoliberal seduction of cool superficiality, the historical stain of systemic violence by one group of people against another group of people cannot be formalized. As the biological marker of this historical violence, race is not and can never become fungible. It persistently brings the long and current history of somatic xenophobia along with it. Race jams the neoliberal machine.

The remarkable emergence of the #BlackLivesMatter movement in the fall of 2014 intensifies and expands consciousness of this systemic racist violence in manners unprecedented since the ascendancy of neoliberal social rationalities across the 1980s. While there are many aspects of this movement that may develop into critical new interventions, the exposure of the systematic character of extrajudicial killings of black people in the United States is one of its most important aspects thus far (as of December 2014). The scores and scores of names of those killed by cops (whether employed by the state or private security firms) that are now circulating globally with constant repetition undercut one of neoliberalism's most important forms of racism, namely, the rendering of racist violence as aberrant and singular.

Prior to the fall of 2014, US popular mainstream culture was being punctuated regularly by the spectacle of overt violent racism, such as the tragedy of the killing of Trayvon Martin in the spring of 2012 and its ensuing trial-as-media-event of summer of 2013. As allegedly singular events, these acts of racist violence were positioned as aberrations that, as singular exceptions, simultaneously cathected crucial registers of both liberalism and neoliberalism. As singular, a racist act of violence reinvigorates both the liberal fantasies of superiority and the neoliberal celebrations of coolness: it recathects the *objet a* of xenophobia that supports liberalism's core fantasies, but it also produces a space in which the circuit of neoliberalism can claim itself as the site of true progress. Given the neoliberal erosion of the symbolic function, this fleeting recathexis with overt xenophobia no longer functions exclusively as the "dirty little secret of enjoyment" that energizes and enables the grander narrative of denial known as tolerance.[35] In the neoliberal overlaying of liberalism, this fleeting recathexis also functions as a kind of embarrassment, a bad historical hangover of bygone times, the bigotry of eras long past.[36]

Because it is situated as a singular act of racist violence, the neoliberal subject of interests can cast it as historically archaic, a throwback to the unfortunate times of overt racism. Progress thereby speaks not in the syntax of tolerance and inclusion, but in the active proclamation of cool detachment. It is through this kind of cool detachment that the neoliberal mantra "celebrate diversity" circulates. The mantra functions as an anxious proclamation: "we are cool." But it also functions always as a command: "be cool." Chill out. Relax. The singularity of this repeated racist violence assures us—albeit over and over and over—that we need not *do* anything, politically or ethically. It's all cool.

It is particularly unnerving, in this vein, that Trayvon Martin's death produced a new fashion icon: the hoodie. While the production of this dress code was part of savvy political maneuvering to expose the absurdity of racial profiling, it also aestheticized politics in ways that neoliberalism facilitates so smoothly.[37] The effect of the hoodie—of a readily accessible fashion accessory—as a political tool is, in keeping with the emptied content of neoliberal cool, ambivalent. On the one hand, it rather brilliantly exposes the generic and irrational character of racist readings of the social landscape, wherein a singular kind of clothing signifies a racialized threat that must be confined. But it also dangerously aestheticizes the protest against this kind of racist profiling, granting easy access to the affect of political protest by simply donning a hoodie. I hope that the hoodie was just the beginning of a widespread social movement that will continue to expand and intervene in the limited neoliberal lexicon for race and racism. But the problematics I have outlined are cautionary notes for living amid this fugue of liberalism, with its deep reservoir of all too real xenophobia, and neoliberalism, with its adamant proclamation of diversity and seductive invitation to coolness.[38]

It is not surprising that the neoliberal social rationality offers no lexicon for encounters across racial difference, especially encounters that stir this historical violence, whether directly or obliquely. Bigots are disavowed, cast as ignorant, uneducated, locked in a time long past, totally uncool, despite the dirty truth they speak (that recathects the xenophobia of liberalism and its fantasy of tolerance). Cool neoliberals are way past bigotry. Speaking the language of diversity, multiculturalism, and colorblindness, neoliberal social rationalities erase any vocabulary of social difference that speaks its historical roots in violence. This means that neoliberal social rationalities have no language for race as a persistent, somatic marker of historical violence and xenophobia. In the United States, this is all too painfully clear: people of all races (especially, perhaps, but not exclusively white people) do not know how—and do not want—to talk about race. It's all long past, it's over, and it has nothing to do with the coolness of now. Emptied of the historical register that cathects us to it, race is also emptied of all signifiers: it's a blank space. And yet a blank space that somehow, unnervingly, haunts us. And scares us.

This loss of language aligns with the reading of neoliberalism as functioning in the Lacanian register of the drive. In the Lacanian schema, desire is structured by the power of signification and, in these terms of negotiating social difference, the faith in the ability to root out xenophobia at the level of the symbolic (for example, through legal codes), thereby recathecting the fantasy of tolerance. But Lacan develops the concept of the drive precisely to articulate, in necessarily convoluted manners, that which resists all signification. By reading neoliberalism in the register of the drive, we find ways to read the neoliberal episteme for its silences, its aporia.

As I turn to my final set of cultural examples, I focus on two of these aporia that, I argue, are deeply intertwined: the loss of language for racial difference as cathected to historical racism and the loss of language for ethics. Through an analysis of the simultaneous historical emergence of the racist carceral state and the political movement to legalize same-sex marriage, I argue that the politics of consumerism easily wins in the neoliberal episteme, while an ethics of race fails to find any social traction at all. Consequently, I locate the doubled, mutually constituting aporia of racism and ethics that becomes my final meditation of this book. Immune to symbolic investiture, race in the neoliberal episteme is the real. It may then be only an ethics of the real that can grab a hold of us now.

Without giving up the long-standing historical evidence that race is always sexualized and sexuality is always racialized in the United States, I argue that these two vectors of social difference are transforming differently in this neoliberal social field, as it overlays, intensifies, and transforms the various practices, concepts, and categories of classical liberalism. To show this, I return to my analysis of the racist carceral state that I began in chapter 2 and place it alongside another major cultural development of the same period, namely, the political movement to legalize same-sex marriage. These two social and political phenomena emerge out of the same historical period, from the 1980s to the 2000s, during which neoliberal social rationalities became more and more deeply rooted in US culture. By placing them alongside each other in this shared historical period, I show how the various ways that sexuality and race have been positioned and constituted in relation to class and gender affect their differentiated transformations in the neoliberal episteme. I argue that the simultaneous historical emergence of the racist carceral state and the political movement to legalize same-sex marriage exemplifies a biopolitics of cool, whereby the malleability to become the neoliberal cool allows the expansion of social life and incitement to make one set of people live (in very particular ways), while the failure to become the neoliberal cool, despite having birthed cool itself, becomes a mode of social abandonment that lets another set of people die.

Accordingly, the representations and economics that have enabled the imminent political victory of legalizing same-sex marriage exemplify the transformations of social difference underway in neoliberal social rationalities and practices, while the social ignorance of the burgeoning carceral state exemplifies the aporetic status of race in that same neoliberal social field. Without ascribing a causal argument (that would somehow place blame on the political movement to legalize same-sex marriage for the social erasure of the burgeoning and racist carceral state), I aim to locate the kinds of sociopsychic transformations that are occurring in our dominant concepts of sexuality that enable the acquisition of rights, while communities of color are being systematically—and silently—stripped of them. By bringing these two historical emergences together, I hope to force the ethical question of this social silence about the racist carceral state and the more general aporia of race, a question I am calling an ethics of the real.

FROM METROSEXUALITY TO SAME-SEX MARRIAGE: IMAGINE THAT!

I begin with the political movement to legalize same-sex marriage. In contrast to the more recent trend of scholarship on the politics and economics of the carceral state, queer critiques of the homonormativity and homonationalism endemic to the movement to legalize same-sex marriage are well circulated.[39] To implicate myself here, as I wrote in the epilogue to *Queering Freedom*, the institution of marriage is "too white, too reliant on sexual identity, and too immersed in the class structure for us to look upon the extension of its domains as an unqualified success."[40] The queer outrage against the political and economic capital expended in this movement to legalize same-sex marriage turns on the myriad kinds of pressing social problems that it does not address and will not improve: widespread lack of health care; violence against immigrants; transphobia; incarceration rates; racism; and so on. I cannot explore each of these critiques here and cannot reduce their complexity to one simple analytic schema. At a general level, however, these critiques (including my own) turn on a latently ideological critique aimed at a partial but dominant set of the minoritarian population ("white, affluent gays and lesbians") that is wrongfully pursuing economic and political aims that render other parts of the community ("queers," a racialized, classed, and sexualized label) either untouched or, much worse, further disenfranchised and alienated.

In 2014, with the imminent victory of this movement on the horizon, these structurally ideological, neo-Marxist critiques form part of a classic, if poignant, political story that once again affirms the eventual benevolence of classical liberalism and its protection of the common good. The story goes like this: hailed as a civil rights victory, the legalization of same-sex marriage plugs directly into the language of classic liberalism, while its vocal opponents plug directly into the well-trod leftist language of ideological critique. That is, the legalization of same-sex marriage folds neatly into the progress narrative and identity politics of perfecting the union by extending rights to a wrongly excluded minority, leaving its neo-Marxist critics still screaming on the sidelines—or in the dustbin's ashes, as it were.

My efforts here are not to debunk the credence of these long-standing queer, neo-Marxist critiques, but to expand our reading of the movement and its imminent victory beyond these frameworks of liberalism and implicitly Marxist ideological critique—once more, in an effort to find a language that holds some social cathexis in neoliberal semiotics, rationalities, and practices. As with all political movements that turn on changes in the legal code, the framework of liberalism is certainly alive and well in this movement and will very likely carry the day in a longer historical framework: thirty or forty years from now, the legalization of same-sex marriage will likely be told as part of the onward march of civil rights and the queer critiques of it, if told at all, will simply seem quaint. As I have argued throughout this book, however, while these discourses of classical liberalism and Marxist ideological critique are still animating our episteme, they are not the dominant vocabulary of the neoliberal social rationality. (They are but two voices in this fugue.) To understand the political movement to legalize same-sex marriage and its imminent victory as a neoliberal phenomenon, I reorient our analyses to the socio-psychic modes of affect and cathexes regarding sexuality.

To understand the differentiated transformations that are underway in our social concepts of sexuality, I offer an account that comes out of that neoliberal social rationality and its various vocabularies of cool. From that perspective, the question seems to be less about whether we should allow same-sex couples to marry and more about how they look, how they spend, how interesting they are. The question within the neoliberal social rationality is: How have queers—to use a word that has been evacuated of all social critique of sexual identity and now refers to any kind of nonstraight sexuality, including but not exclusive to gay and lesbian—become so alluring? How have queers become so cool?[41]

My effort, therefore, is to speak in a language of neoliberalism. And so I return to my analysis of metrosexuality to argue that the issue of same-sex marriage has cathected the neoliberal imaginary along the same lines as that of metrosexuality, namely, the expansion of gender norms to embrace a wider, often more emphatically celebratory class of consumers. The only difference is that the operative barometer in same-sex marriage is homonormativity, rather than the heteronormativity structuring metrosexuality. As the work of Lisa Duggan, Michael Warner, and many others amply shows, homonormativity is but a mere extension of heteronormativity in neoliberalism: with the legalization of same-sex marriage, all gays and lesbians can quickly become homo-neoliberals.

The homonormativity at work in movements to legalize and normalize same-sex marriage answers perfectly the fundamental demands of neoliberalism, namely, privatized responsibility and intensified entrepreneurialism. Consequently, the images of monogamous, longtime, committed gay and lesbian couples getting married that are splayed across television screens and newspapers from time to time, as the ping-pong game of legalization bounces across states, provide precisely the right mix of "responsible," committed couples who are, well, pretty interesting to *watch*. The gender variation satiates the enterprising urge to intensify gender aesthetics and expressions: Does the couple both have on wedding gowns? Is one in a suit and another in a dress? Are they both sporting beards? Meanwhile, the tying of the knot leaves the most fundamental anxiety about security nicely reaffirmed. As many have quipped, whence the need to protect marriage through "Defense of Marriage Acts" when the desire to get married by same-sex couples so clearly reaffirms the social power of marriage? As gay and lesbian parenting also continues to increase in visibility and acceptance, we must begin to realize that neoliberalism is far from threatened by homonormativity. To the contrary, gay and lesbian married parents seem to be its latest and best ally.

The social registers of metrosexuality and same-sex marriage are thus intimately intertwined and tell us a great deal about the elasticity of gender as it is modulated by consumerist class politics in neoliberal social fields. Same-sex marriage is not, in this light, fundamentally about sexuality. While it may appear to step beyond the norm of heterosexuality, strict heteronormativity is no longer the fundamental social value at stake in neoliberalism. To flourish as a powerful social rationality, neoliberalism must ensure that two values are internalized in the formation of subjects: an unwavering commitment to economic productivity, writ across all registers of life as we increasingly judge our lives through financial barometers and metaphors; and an undying desire to make and remake one's self as an alluring image that intensifies and entices further image-creativity, preferably through a market of some sort.

Put in a Lacanian lexicon, neoliberal social rationalities and practices flourish where the register of the imaginary and its boundless play of comparative, calculating image-intensification eclipses the regulations of the symbolic and its bifurcating, normalizing law. In this regard, the (symbolic) legalization of same-sex marriage is merely an effect of (imaginary) transformations in gender and consumerism that I tracked through metrosexuality. Read through this reorientation of the social field away from the power of the symbolic toward the free-floating play of the imaginary, same-sex marriage is being legalized in these neoliberal times because consumerism has unhinged gender from antiquated concerns about heteronormative sexuality.

Same-sex marriage is, thereby, a distinctly *neo*liberal phenomenon. On the one hand, it extends the reach of the classic, liberal marriage contract, privatizing yet more nonremunerated labor and continuing the social organization most apt for capitalism. Given the long-standing position granted homosexuality as a wildly nonproductive threat to Western culture's most treasured value of utility, this is a remarkable feat of domestication. It is crucial, therefore, to see how it manages this feat of "normalizing" homosexuality, a task that is categorically unthinkable in classical liberalism (and consequently, once more, the bigots and homophobes are cast as cultural artifacts of a bygone era). As a neoliberal phenomenon, same-sex marriage becomes not merely normal, but exciting and alluring: the domestication of gays and lesbians not only inscribes the value of economic productivity at the very heart of this obstreperous mode of living, but it does so by turning it into an exciting, creative, and intense market. The historical coincidence with metrosexuality thereby becomes critical to the success of the political movement to legalize same-sex marriage.

Marriage can be quite boring, as any honest person in a long-term monogamous relationship can easily attest. It would thus appear that the neoliberal embrace of endless self-fashioning loses one of its best outlets with this broad incursion of monogamy and domesticity into gay communities and aesthetics. The historically simultaneous emergence of metrosexuality alongside the normalizing of same-sex marriage frames this problem differently. Precisely when gays (and lesbians, perhaps, but we all know who really tends the gates of fashion) become more boring, metrosexuals emerge on the scene to heighten and intensify gender creativity: whew, we can still *look good*! (And maximize the reach of both the beauty and the wedding industries' markets.)

As I argued in chapter 4, the cultural emergence of metrosexuality indicates the ascendancy of class-as-consumerism in the social register of gender. It unleashes gender as a fantastically superficial playing field of images and neoliberal subjects of interests, unhinged from any archaic (liberal) connections to heteronormativity or sexism. By linking the movement to legalize same-sex marriage to the cultural embrace of metrosexuality, I am arguing that the normalization of same-sex marriage tells us more about the unleashing of gender, especially when modulated by class-as-consumerism, than it does about sexuality in the neoliberal episteme.

As the mainstreaming of metrosexuality and the normalization of same-sex marriage show, gender is not a register of contemporary living in which we find a substantive expression of difference. Rendered a fungible difference that can intensify one's image and interests, gender has arguably become the exemplary vehicle for the transformation of social difference in neoliberal social fields.[42] And same-sex marriage is one of its best vehicles. While the legalization of same-sex marriage brings substantial material change to many lives of gays and lesbians, the huge political movement that has altered popular opinion on this issue depends on the broader cultural embrace of gender as a playful accessory in order to normalize homosexuality. The insistent focus on *images* of normal gays and lesbians—most often white, always in couples, sometimes with a dog—becomes legible through the expansion of gender, such as we find in the mainstreaming of metrosexuality. It is because gender is the neoliberal playground that same-sex marriage can be hailed (yes, hailed) as the great civil rights victory of these neoliberal times.

FROM THE IMAGINARY TO THE REAL: THE RACIST CARCERAL STATE

The simultaneous emergence of metrosexuality and the same-sex marriage movement serves as an exemplar of the neoliberal embrace of the imaginary. It instructs us on the consumerist freeing of gender from old concerns about sexuality, liberating both markets and excited, interest-maximizing subjects to participate in them. But, read negatively, it can also tell us something about what it never addresses, about its silences, about its constitutive aporia. In distracting us with the proliferation of "Equal Signs" and such, what has the same-sex marriage movement kept us from apprehending, much less addressing? If we read it through its omissions, this widespread cultural embrace of the imaginary can also tell us something about the overwhelming, widespread cultural silence about a historically simultaneous institutional emergence: the carceral state.

At least partially emergent in and through that silence, the prison industry has boomed by remaining off the radar of that which the neoliberal social field celebrates, intensifies, and encourages. Therefore, I argue that the historical simultaneity of the political movement to legalize same-sex marriage and the carceral state is not mere coincidence. To the contrary, it exposes both the transformation of class into consumerism and the harsh limits of that transformation precisely where the research on the accelerating wealth gap locates it, namely, race. We must, therefore, wrangle with the historical fact that, in the same period in which the same-sex marriage movement focused intense cultural, psychological, political, and economic energy on the extension of civil rights to gays and lesbians, the prison system systematically exploded into a machine that strips civil rights from citizens at an alarming and still increasing rate. This, too, I argue is a distinctly *neo*liberal phenomenon.

In an effort to speak in a neoliberal lexicon, I offer a *statistical image* of this historical coincidence (see figure 5.2). My concern is with the image and the response it might stir, not with any claim to exactitude in the facts it represents. Whether parsed in rates of incarceration or raw number of people incarcerated, the explosion of the US carceral state since the mid-1980s is undeniable. I chose the raw numbers of people incarcerated in order to correlate with the numbers of those possibly affected by each state's legalization of same-sex marriage. In order to quantify that possibility, I used the long-standing rule-of-thumb estimate that one in ten (10 percent) of a population is gay or lesbian. I then charted 10 percent of each state's population at the time of legalization. That this number, ten, resonates with the Talented Tenth extolled by early-twentieth-century African American communities unnervingly points to the dynamics that no graph can pretend to capture: does the legalization of same-sex marriage somehow replenish the *tenth* of the forces of social production and reproduction that the carceral state kills?[43]

Scholars have already established conceptual and historical connections between neoliberal economic policies as well as practices and the emergence of the carceral state. As Bernard Harcourt demonstrates, amplifying Foucault's arguments from *The Birth of Biopolitics* through a long historical framework that goes back to eighteenth-century French practices of regulation and penality, neoliberal concepts and practices intensify a classically liberal configuration of state, market, and penality. In short, liberalism witnesses the naturalization of the economic order, carried in the nominal concept of the "free market," which then demarcates and facilitates the expansion of the penal sphere as the proper realm for state regulation. Neoliberal concepts and practices intensify this, developing into "the logic of neoliberal penality [that] has facilitated our punishment practices by weakening any resistance to governmental initiatives in the penal domain because that is where the state may legitimately, competently, and effectively govern."[44] Extending Harcourt's argument, we can see how the United States holds the highest rates of incarceration and raw number of incarcerated in the entire world

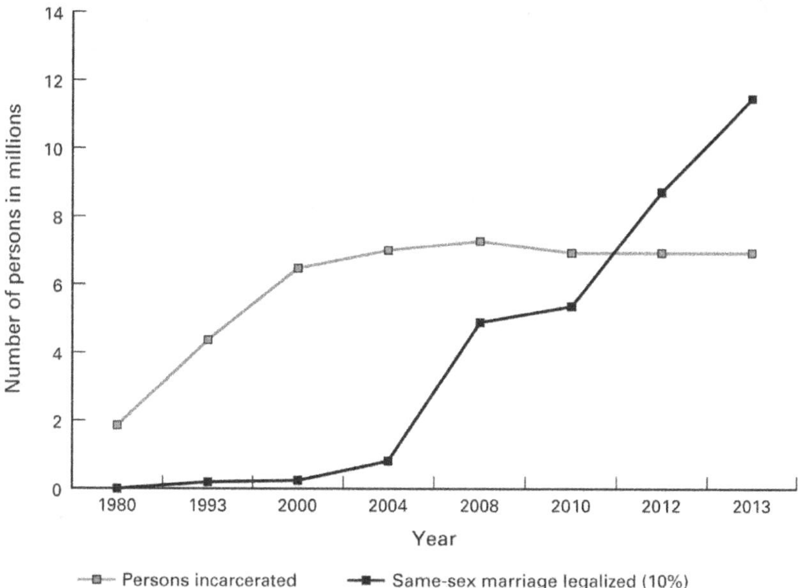

FIGURE 5.2 The historical simultaneity of the political movement to legalize same-sex marriage and the carceral state.

through this remarkable fiction that the market is "naturally" and properly free from the law. The deregulation of the financial sector has aided, abetted, and enabled the still increasing expansion of the penal sphere, not through any strict or direct causality, but through sharing this same neoliberal episteme.

Harcourt thereby provides the historical framework in which to understand the emergence of the carceral state as, in precisely the Foucaultian terms of intensifying liberal concepts and practices that I have employed throughout this book, a distinctly neoliberal phenomenon. Despite discussions of the incoherence of criminalizing tax fraud differently from welfare fraud (IM, 206) and the acknowledgment of Milton Friedman's opposition to the War on Drugs (IM, 231–33), however, Harcourt never turns to any robust analysis of race, which I am arguing is the driving force of the carceral state—or, more exactly, the racist carceral state. As Loic Wacquant, Dorothy Roberts, Angela Davis, and Michelle Alexander have been arguing for some time, we must face the enduring fact that the carceral state is fundamentally and endemically a racist and racialized institution. Structurally connected to the long, enduring history of chattel slavery and its unspeakable violence, the carceral state is fundamentally constructed to continue and expand the warehousing of people of color, especially black male bodies, in the United States.

Both Loic Wacquant and Michelle Alexander offer precisely this kind of structural argument. As Wacquant argues in a variety of essays and books, we must understand the carceral state as economically, politically, and sociologically growing out of the practices of slavery in the seventeenth through nineteenth centuries, the practices and laws of Jim Crow in the nineteenth and twentieth centuries, and the urban emergence of the ghetto in the twentieth century. As he puts it, for example, in "From Slavery to Mass Incarceration," published in 2002:

> Not crime, but the need to shore up an eroding caste cleavage, along with buttressing the emergent regime of desocialized wage labour to which most blacks are fated by virtue of their lack of marketable cultural capital, and which the most deprived among them resist by escaping into the illegal street economy, is the main impetus behind the stupendous expansion of America's penal state in the post-Keynesian age and its de facto policy of "carceral affirmative action" towards African-Americans.

Wacquant analyzes these phenomena primarily through a Weberian lens, emphasizing how these four "peculiar institutions" have constructed the meaning of race in the United States, particularly through systemic labor extraction, caste division, and social death. As Angela Davis and Dorothy Roberts have argued for some time and as Michelle Alexander has more recently accentuated, the contemporary prison enacts and enforces this social death through denying prisoners cultural capital, social redistribution, and political participation. And, as all of these scholars emphasize, the primary demarcating characteristic of these rates of incarceration is race. We cannot confront the carceral state if we do not confront it as a racialized and racist institution.

The thread I want to bring forward into these analyses of the racial carceral state is the obstinacy that race presents to neoliberal social rationalities and practices. On the one hand, neo-Marxist analyses, especially as incisively articulated by Angela Davis, still hold great traction. The prison industrial complex, as she names it, is clearly an ongoing form of class warfare. Moreover, as I indicated in chapter 2, in light of my arguments against interpellation as capturing the modes of social cathexes in the neoliberal episteme, the penal criminalization of the black body appears to be the last full stand of interpellation, notably a punitive and legal form, in these neoliberal times. Given these social and economic formations, the appeals to abolition in the name of a more ideologically pure form of democracy are a crucial political response to this abhorrent institution and its many tentacles. But it is not the only possible response. Nor is it a response that finds much traction or social cathexis with neoliberal subjects of interests. In an effort to expand and amplify our outrage, I aim to call out the racist carceral state as a distinctly neoliberal phenomenon that enacts distinctly neoliberal forms of racism.

In calling it out, I do not pretend to understand or master or fully analyze this unethical phenomenon. Rather, using the sharp contrast with the sheer verbosity (symbolically and literally) of the political movement to legalize same-sex marriage as a point of departure, I close with a meditation on the overwhelming silence about the racial carceral state. Even in light of recent growing interest in the issue (if we take the long run of *The New Jim Crow* on the *New York Times* Bestseller List as an indication), the United States has not paid any sustained attention to the burgeoning prison industry or its structurally racialized operations. As Alexander herself argues, "Despite unprecedented levels of incarceration in the African American community, the civil rights community is oddly quiet."[45] In a culture now fully immersed in the constant communication of social media in its remarkable variety, this kind of silence speaks volumes.

To return once more to a Lacanian lexicon, I read this silence as the failure to signify, the failure to enter into codes of signification that render phenomena legible to individuals and societies. For liberalism, the long historical violence that constitutes race as a salient category of social difference was spoken, if only to be disavowed, through the twinned fantasies of tolerance and neutrality. As I showed in chapter 3, these fantasies are unraveling in the neoliberal episteme: utility no longer serves as a dominant social metric, and xenophobia is summarily dismissed by the intense celebration of diversity. In this adamant practice of color-blindness, the carceral state cannot possibly surface as an explicitly racialized and racist institution. At the same time, in the neoliberal lexicon, there is no language for the kind of systemic, violent xenophobia that undergirds such a phenomenon. And so it goes unspoken, unnoted. It forms a fundamental, even constitutive aporia across which the neoliberal episteme, with all its frivolous fungibility and diversity, splays on and on in o so cool manners.

I have argued in this chapter that, in the United States, the long, violent, and persistent history of chattel slavery and its sexualized antiblack racism makes racial difference ontologically intractable to the fungible machine of neoliberalism. Totally uncool to recognize, racial difference can force encounters with social difference that are not celebratory, not easily co-opted by any market, and not rendered fungible. Racial difference is, thereby, the site where neoliberal social rationality grinds to a sudden halt, where its incitements toward frenetic stimulation and enterprising novelty fall short and a psychic gap opens up in the social fabric. Contrasting sharply with the neoliberal iterations of race as "diversity" and racism as "aberration," the kind of racism we find in the tragedies emanating out of the destruction of Hurricane Katrina, for example, exposes a qualitatively different kind of historico-social ontology. A kind of intractable, decidedly nonfungible difference, it tears open the gorgeously superficial social fabric of the neoliberal episteme, splitting it open into gaping holes that jam the machine of fungibility and the market's promised ease and comfort. It is here that we see the punitive force of interpellation reenter the neoliberal social scene, enforcing prescriptive limits to the alleged neoliberal celebration of diversity and constructing the tragically booming racist carceral state. Exposing all the diversity talk as only so much hollow banter, these gaping psychic holes open onto another source of sociopsychic energy. Like Schelling's *katabole*, they recathect the deep, unconscious xenophobia that we have allegedly left so far behind.[46] But we have no language for it.

Despite this aporetic state, the lasting material and sociopsychological harm executed in and through the racist carceral state does not somehow go away. It persists. Race and racism persist. And in the Lacanian language of the real, they fester and grow more virulent. If we are to find some way to respond, we must find our way out of the language of politics, with all its ideological entrapments and the constraint of power as a singular rubric. We must find a way to speak this unspeakable in a manner that moves us, personally and socially. We must confront the twinned aporia of neoliberalism: race and ethics.

FIGURE 5a.1 Kehinde Wiley, *Portrait of Andries Stilte II* (2006). Oil and enamel on canvas. 96 x 72 inches. Copyright © Kehinde Wiley. Used by permission.

INTERLUDE 5

Real Cool, Now

Kehinde Wiley's portraits of alpha-male black and brown bodies in Rococo settings mess with history and race and cathexis in all the ways I am imagining the Real Cool now, in these dizzying neoliberal times. Huge, oversized canvases filled with intricate, colorful designs that spill over into ornate, gilded frames form the perfect landscape to make the black body regal, at last: he waltzes forward with unnerving calm and panache. He is sooo cool.

The lore around Wiley's paintings bespeaks the kind of turning upon the real of history that I speculate is a site of ethics: Wiley's repeated origin story of the idea for the portraits in a found FBI wanted bill on the streets of Harlem points to the histories of enslavement, incarceration, and disenfranchisement that linger and stain the black body; the street-casting of anonymous black and brown men both enacts a vexed attempt to render erased lives glorious and fuels the neoliberal fantasy of instant wealth and fame; the transnational move to the streets of Africa, from Nigeria to Senegal, to Rio and São Paulo, to Afghanistan and Israel globalizes the subject matter, if sometimes doing so precisely through marketing techniques.[1] There is so much to explore here.

But for this brief and concluding interlude, I just want to look at the paintings. They are so jarring. To come upon one in a museum—especially a museum of lower profile (and thus expectation) in a mid-size city, such as Austin, Texas, or Columbus, Ohio—is to have one's entire

FIGURE 5a.2 Kehinde Wiley, *Antoine, "The Grand Batard de Bourgogne"* (2011). Oil on linen. 78.3 x 60.6 inches. Copyright © Kehinde Wiley. Used by permission.

experience reset, reconfigured, recentered around a vertiginous engagement with the history that art and museums carry forward, if obliquely and critically. There is simply something so *wrong* about the canvases: the obvious and candid and bold rescripting of the European aristocratic practices of portraiture. We should be able to write it off as yet another conceptual artist gone a bit too far down the road of political correctness or multicultural representations. But it is so much more than that: the paintings are gorgeous, filled with stunning painterly detail, rich historical vocabularies, and a contemporary punch in the gut.

Since at least the late 1980s, theorists, artists, and curators have positioned the black body as the real—that kernel of desire and experience which drives systems of signification by refusing to signify at all.[2] In stark contrast to the intense confrontation with the sexualized racist violence of chattel slavery that we find in Kara Walker's contemporary work, Kehinde Wiley surprises, jars, and then makes us laugh. Framed in these absurdly large, gold scaffoldings, the floral backgrounds are reassuring with their quaint, innocent reminiscence of antique wallpaper. This should be hanging in our grandmother's or great-grandmother's living room. But that echo of calm interiority is far from contained:

FIGURE 5a.3 Kehinde Wiley, *Morpheus* (2008). Oil on canvas. 108 x 180 inches. Copyright © Kehinde Wiley. Used by permission.

the leaves or flowers or birds sprout out over the body being portrayed, demanding more attention! More attention! He is *inside* our grandmother's living room: he is *inside* us.

And that's all good, because he is so fabulous, so regal, so badass, so, so cool.

FIGURE 5a.4 Kehinde Wiley, *Mark Shavers* (2010). Oil on canvas. 48 x 36 inches. Copyright © Kehinde Wiley. Used by permission.

In interviews, Kehinde Wiley often describes part of his work as taking a classic poststructuralist turn, namely, the turn to examine the frame of representation itself.[3] A twenty-first-century artist, he's taking that turn several degrees further and demanding that we, the neoliberal purveyors of art and theory and books in the affluent parts of this world, turn to look at ourselves—our deepest historical selves in all our repressed and suppressed mess and nastiness. And, without overstepping the violence and pain that are there, to be surprised and, perhaps, even laugh. (Or at least chuckle.)

CHAPTER SIX

Stop Making Sense

THE APORIA OF RACE AND ETHICS

Queer theory seduced me with one clear argument: the incisive, multifaceted dismantling of identity. While mostly taken up as a sustained critique of identity politics, early queer theorists unraveled sexuality across multiple registers to expose its ontological inability to sustain the construction of a coherent identity—qua identity. Most incisively, those emerging out of psychoanalysis, such as Leo Bersani, extended the fundamentally inchoate character of sexuality to entail the impossibility of a cohesive, singular "sexual identity." This was, after all, how queer theory broke from gay and lesbian studies in the academy.

For much of that early work, as I have showed in my analysis of the popularity of *Gender Trouble*, this dismantling of sexuality was articulated primarily along the axis of gender, which was reconceptualized as an effect of sexual norms. Despite the insistence on the racialized limits of this gender-sexuality critique by theorists such as Cathy Cohen and José Muñoz, however, the radical rethinking of identity has not been taken up along the axis of race. While we have much excellent work on the sociological and historical twining of sexuality and race, we have yet to reconsider race as a concept in its endemic relation to the destabilizing, inchoate dynamics of sexuality. We have yet, that is, to reconceptualize race away from, if not without, identity categories and all their political, historical, and sociopsychic baggage. In this final chapter, I attempt to offer a way to do this. By extending my thinking on the limits of ideology, interpellation, and the register of the imaginary for our concepts of race, I argue explicitly how we must move beyond these identity categories if we are to engage an ethically meaningful lexicon in this neoliberal episteme.

To move beyond identity categories in these times of persistent racism is dangerous, to say the least. We in the contemporary United States are deeply, deeply confused, if not verging on a kind of madness, when it comes to matters of race. Whether uttered in mono- or multiracial settings, speech about race and racism sets off all kinds of psychosomatic, historically material, and deeply suppressed dynamics that will spin most conversations into a twisted, carnivalesque funhouse. Despite the pure excess of material evidence that we are living in an extraordinarily racist and violent culture, we seem to have no language for it. And this makes us remarkably anxious.

I have mapped this sputtering as the faltering of classical liberalism's symbolic and its core fantasies of tolerance and neutrality. Central to that sputtering is the linguistic transition from discourses of antiracism and identity categories (such as "white," "black," "Native American," "Latino," and so on) to those of color-blindness and diversity. While advocates of the latter two, color-blindness and diversity, may locate themselves on opposite ends of the political spectrum, the move to postracial signifiers sutures them to two sides of the same coin. This move from explicitly calling out racism to the erasure of race from our social vocabularies exemplifies the slide toward fungibility that enables the neoliberal aestheticizing of social difference. While the impulse to insist on a return to the older, identity-based language of "white supremacy" and "antiblack racism" is understandably alluring, it no longer holds the social traction or meaning required to intercede in the sly forms of contemporary racism: it may be necessary, but it is insufficient.[1] By putting pressure on this linguistic transition as a substantial, historically new transformation in our modes of signifying race, I offer some insight into why we—all of us, despite racial identification—are so anxious about race in this contemporary US neoliberal episteme. Moreover, I offer some speculation on what this anxiety might tell us, especially if we read it with Lacan as a signal of the real.

THE SOCIAL ANXIETY ABOUT RACE

The US mainstream culture of the early twenty-first century is riddled with stories of its past that it would simply prefer not to hear. This is, of course, not unusual: a driving force of cohesion in arguably all cultures is the embrace of a positive image and historical narratives to support it. Amid the social landscape of neoliberalism and its cultural moniker of diversity, however, the suppression of systemic histories of violence in the United States is no longer intentional or conscious: the suppression itself is erased. Increasingly naturalized, the cultural amnesia is becoming so deep that we seem more and more unable to remember, unable to reconstitute what Foucault called "counter-memories," unable to recollect lost and forgotten information and then to rekindle painful, unwanted memories. (If the #BlackLivesMatter movement is to intervene and develop a critically new antiracist lexicon, it must move beyond the localization of police brutality, avoid the temporality of crisis, and recathect these deep, long histories of systemic racist violence that the neoliberal episteme renders so uncool.) As Glenn Ligon puts it, regarding responses to his artwork (specifically a show in Memphis about civil rights in 2008): "I know this focus on the past is all 'old school'; that we are in a post-civil rights era and, as one art student said to me at the opening, 'Who wants to think about all of that stuff?' I suspect he meant to say, "Who wants to think about all of that stuff *again*?'"[2] The answer is clear: no one.

And so we walk around in states of latent anxiety, avoiding any kind of social contact that might provoke these suppressed histories of violence and systemic disenfranchisement to surface. To be called racist in the contemporary mainstream United States is arguably one of the most shameful of social possibilities. Unlike with the fear of outright guilt for being caught as a racist that might describe "old-style" racism, we now seem just to fear the shame of such a public accusation.[3] With the symbolic order sputtering, actual instances of racism fade into ideological debate: the act or thought itself recedes into the hall of mirrors, and the reflection of the mirrors is all that matters.[4] This is, of course, unnerving. Given the long histories of racism alive and well in a wide variety of institutional apparati and the social habits they instill and reenforce, we all inhabit a deeply racist culture. But we are gripped with fear about being caught in the act, an act that we no longer recognize. Without any language to address the fear, a pervasive anxiety has taken hold.

For the Lacanian analyses I am advancing here, this is unsurprising. In his 1962–63 seminar, *Anxiety*, Lacan situates anxiety as signaling the real. Describing it as the moment when "the subject is seized, concerned and implicated in his inmost depths,"[5] Lacan reads anxiety as a signal of the real erupting into a subject's signifying universe. Having described it as spurred by experiences in which "all words cease and all categories fail" in his 1954–55 seminar, Lacan pursues the intricacies of this "signaling of the real" in exquisite detail in the 1962–63 seminar.[6] He thereby locates several features of anxiety that shed considerable light on the contemporary US neoliberal inability to speak a meaningful language of race and racism.

First of all, Lacan follows Freud's linking of anxiety to the uncanny to insist that experiences of anxiety do not pass through signification: we cannot speak them; they do not emerge from a distinct *objet a* that causes our desire; they do not distinguish us as particular identities. Not signified, however, anxiety is nonetheless framed, and this problematic initiates Lacan's formal analysis of it. To elaborate the effect of this framing, Lacan uses the same metaphor he had previously used to examine the structure of fantasy, namely, the reorientation that occurs if we place a painting in a window. As Lacan elaborates his use of this metaphor, he emphasizes the formal analysis it affords: "No doubt an absurd technique were it a matter of better seeing what's in the painting, but that's not what it's about. Regardless of the charm of what's painted on the canvas, it's about not seeing what stands to be beheld outside the window" (A, 73). The technique retrains the focus of our sight from the content of the painting to the significance of the background—or framing—of where and when we behold the painting. Moreover, it forces one's "vision" away from the content and toward the formal framing of vision itself, with a particular emphasis on how the frame obscures and reorients the interplay of background and foreground.

Taking this as a heuristic for reading the linguistic transition from explicit antiracist identity categories to the neoliberal postracial language of diversity and color-blindness, I am interested in the transition itself in language about race, not in what is lost or gained in one specific set of signifiers vis-à-vis the other. It is the shift in the frame itself that is stirring anxiety. More specifically, following Lacan's emphasis on the obscuring effect of this reframing, I argue that it is the blockages that occur in this shift in the frame that are stirring anxiety, namely, the blockage of the long, violent history of racism that generated (and continues to generate, if in a twisted manner) the concept of race. We are, as an entire culture in this neoliberal episteme, losing our old language for and social cathexis to these histories.[7] For Lacan, this attention to the framing of anxiety affords a formal account of the structure of anxiety, rather than an account driven by the specific contents of the experience. A fundamental requirement for any account involving the real, this formal account of anxiety may also spur important ways to reconceptualize race, which is stirring our anxiety so intensely.

Anxiety, as anyone who experiences it regularly will attest, is perhaps most unnerving because it lacks any distinct object. One cannot diagnose the cause and address it directly: anxiety comes upon us obliquely and is only appeased in the same stealth manner. It thwarts intentionality, unnerving us further. Following Freud with his usual exquisitely concise formulations, Lacan distinguishes anxiety from fear precisely because it lacks any proper *objet a*. Lacking any proper object such as those that cause one's desire, however, anxiety "*is not without an object*" (A, 89). Rather, it lacks the lack that renders desire a subjectifying and individualizing phenomenon. This is partially what renders anxiety an affect that can describe a cultural disposition, rather than a singular emotion experienced individually, such as fear.[8]

This careful formulation that anxiety "is not without an object," which Lacan literally writes on the blackboard in the seminar, forces us to reconceptualize the kind of object that stirs anxiety. As Dylan Evans puts it, anxiety "involves a different kind of object, an object which cannot be symbolized in the same way as all other objects."[9] Because anxiety resists symbolic interpellation, whatever brings anxiety into circulation does not function in the same manner as that which causes desire. Since there is no exact cause of anxiety, the kinds of phenomena that can trigger it are endless: objects, events, memories, unusual odors, particular genres of music, sartorial preferences, strange and amorphous feelings in the gut. Literally anything can stir unconscious associations that then animate latent anxiety. Impossible to map with traditional schemas of causality, the so-called objects or causes of anxiety are always only partial insofar as the claim to locate an object or cause is itself an act of substituting and forcing signification onto that which fundamentally resists it.[10] In the neoliberal social landscape of race and racism, this means that the latent anxiety about racism can be triggered by an endless and amorphous set of possible phenomena that, in turn, cannot be demarcated as the distinct cause of our anxiety. No wonder we are simultaneously so confused and angry about charges of racism. Our language constantly fails to address the anxiety, and so it persists and festers.

Put slightly differently, this also means that the experience of anxiety is depersonalizing. Again reading Freud, Lacan writes: "Anxiety is a rim phenomenon, a signal that is produced at the ego's limit when it is threatened by something that must not appear" (A, 119). Connecting this in a variety of ways to the real as that which does not lack the lack that marks signification, Lacan specifies this as phenomena that are "unsuitable for egoization" (A, 120). Not passing through the chains of signifiers through which we become subjects, the formal objects that stir anxiety are "designated as phenomena of depersonalization" (A, 119). Related to the uncanny in both Freud's and Lacan's texts, anxiety is a deeply unnerving affect because, among other characteristics, it does not fall into the habitual tracks of the ego and its mode of subject formation as an identity.

This offers a profound caution against falling back into identity categories to conceptualize and talk about race. It is not only that the language of identity categories is a throwback to a mode of speech with fading social traction and altered meaning, but also that it repersonalizes that which is not personal. When I argue that race functions as the real in the contemporary US iteration of the neoliberal episteme, I mean that race makes all of us, despite our racialized identities, anxious. Unhinged from its location as the *objet a* of classical liberalism's core fantasies of neutrality and tolerance, the long violent history of xenophobia that animates the concept of race is now precisely that which cannot enter signification in the neoliberal episteme. We cannot speak it. We increasingly cannot even recognize it or its absence. It is, to gloss Lacan's reading of the unconscious alongside Hortense Spillers, the censored chapter of our American grammar.[11]

ETHICS WITHOUT DIFFERENCE

To turn toward this deep cultural anxiety about race is thereby to turn to the real, where I complete the Lacanian analysis of the fugue of liberalism and neoliberalism that I have been developing across this book. To bring forward the full force of this turn, let me back up and recollect the argument thus far, with apologies for the repetitions.

In chapter 3, I argued that the neoliberal episteme initiates a shift in social authority and subjectivity such that we can very helpfully understand the neoliberal subject of interests as functioning in the drive, where the symbolic function (as well as interpellation) is eclipsed. I then proceeded to argue that the twinned core fantasies of liberalism, tolerance and neutrality, are sputtering. Their respective *objet a*, utility and xenophobia, are losing traction, respectively, through the neoliberal socioeconomic command to proliferate and maximize interests and the neoliberal cultural mantra of diversity. As social difference, particularly, transforms from a marker of historical xenophobia (however disavowed in the name of neutrality) to the formal metric of fungibility, we are encouraged to cathect with any and all forms of social difference with remarkable coolness. We are, that is, encouraged in this neoliberal episteme to rewire some of our most fundamental modes of social cathexes from xenophobia to coolness. While it appears, as I argued in chapters 4 and 5, that we may be able to do so around particular forms of social difference (gender, sexuality-as-mediated-by-gender, class-as-consumerism), other forms (race and class) remain intransigent. Putting this in the Lacanian heuristic of the symbolic, imaginary, and real, I argued that we can locate those forms which bend to this transformation in social cathexis in the imaginary, while locating those obstinate forms in the real.

When Lacan positions anxiety as an affect that signals the real, it should be of little surprise that neoliberal subjects of interests experience profound anxiety around race. Inculcated with the neoliberal celebration of diversity, we are encouraged, begged, and commanded to approach any and all forms of social difference as aesthetic, fungible units of cool. But the anxiety gives us away. The anxiety around even talking about race—much less encountering differently racialized cultural formations or personal experiences that bring the long, intense, historical force of racism to the surface—belies our cool. With the core fantasies of tolerance and neutrality faltering, we do not know how to respond when confronted with this persistent xenophobia. As Lacan puts it, "The real supports the phantasy, the phantasy protects the real."[12] In the wake of these fantasies' faltering, we have no script for racial encounters and are left with nothing but a stammer. When we are confronted with the real, our anxiety blows our cool. But the lack of an object explicitly animating anxiety also opens onto different ways of conceiving these problematics, particularly in a register of ethics.

If race functions as the real, an ethics of the real may still grab a hold of us. Driven by the problem of social cathexes, I want to speculate about a language of ethics that might still find some traction with neoliberal subjects of interests. My aim in this turn to ethics is not, however, recuperative: by no means do I suggest that we ought to reanimate systems of alleged universality, whether religious or secular, that have been central to the nightmare of liberalism's imperialism and domination under the cloak of idealism. Rather, my turn to the register of ethics is part of an effort to ask how and why the very cathexes of social problems once deemed "ethical" have been domesticated, defanged, and decathected into problems of politics, and even more fundamentally, into problems of economics.

As I put it in "The Queer Thing About Neoliberal Pleasure," how is it that prolonged ethical dilemmas of our neoliberal times—namely, the structured production of gendered and racialized poverty, complete with horrific human rights violations and environmental destruction—have been retooled into problems of ideologically driven politics and competing versions of sound economic policies? How and when and where did ethics get supplanted by politico-economic rationalities? How and when and where did the very question of values, especially those that might govern our relationships to ourselves and to others, collapse into the neoliberal barometer of success? And, if this is a viable diagnosis of the contemporary moment in the overdeveloped populations of the world, how can we recathect languages of values as a way to a different kind of ethics? As a way to respond to this structural violence that involves us, willingly or consciously or not?

This is not merely a disciplinary turn, although my training in philosophy orients me, generally and loosely, in the direction of ethics. To the contrary, I would argue that the proliferation of ethics centers through the discipline of philosophy has, largely, bastardized the kind of ethics I am trying to speak here into another form of rational calculation and problem solving that is palatable to the neoliberal US academy. By focusing on the transformations in subjective formation underway in neoliberal social rationalities and practices, I have argued at length that ideological critiques of neoliberalism fail to engage the depth and breadth of these sociopsychological transformations. Consequently, we must find our ways out of the language of politics, if we are to interrupt the multiple forms of violence carried out through the smooth, cool neoliberal surface that now passes for subjectivity.

Moreover, the widespread cynicism in the United States about electoral politics indicates the deeply ideological (and subsequently bifurcated) character that politics has assumed in mainstream US culture. For cool neoliberal subjects of interests, the language of politics holds no traction. With the language of morality captive to that ideological political field, we seem to be increasingly left with no meaningful language in which to speak, discuss, critique, or cultivate social evaluations beyond the metric of the market. Ethics is an aporia, formally positioned in the same manner as race and racism are in this neoliberal episteme.

So, what has traction? How to avoid recourse to old-fashioned liberalism or ineffective Marxism and speak in a vocabulary of social evaluation that still connects with and moves the cool neoliberal subject?

As I hope is clear by now, the neoliberal episteme aims to erase social difference. But it does so in the name of coolness, not of sameness. For social theorists drawing upon European intellectual traditions of various stripes, this ushers in an entirely different kind of epistemological, ontological, and sociopsychological set of dynamics, questions, and difficulties. Particularly for what I specify as the post-Hegelian lineage of ethics, the cornerstone of subject formation has been rooted in the encounter with an Other: the fear of an explicit object defines the xenophobia that animates liberalism's avowal of tolerance and neutrality. Consequently, the struggle with the Other or the problem of difference has absorbed much of twentieth-century social theory. Given the ongoing and flourishing scholarship in feminist, postcolonial, race, and queer theory as well as the burgeoning scholarship in contemporary European philosophy on thematics such as Deleuzian multiplicity, Levinasian alterity, and even the Lacanian real, it appears that the twenty-first century is largely heightening if also complicating this obsession.

But such language and alleged problems of difference and otherness no longer hold the same kind of singular traction with neoliberal subjects of interests. To stay with Hegelian parlance for a moment, in the spirit of the infamous Master/Slave dialectic, we neoliberals are all masters now, unconsciously trained to encounter difference only insofar as we can own it as another cool accoutrement. In the aesthetic language of cool fungibility, difference no longer presents the kind of contrapuntal force that symbolically interpellated subjectivity relies upon for greater and greater self-consciousness and self-actualization. Difference no longer tracks along the logic of noncontradiction that renders it a formative moment of negation in the interpellative account of identity formation. The neoliberal aestheticizing of difference into fungibility retools our conceptions of social difference such that difference no longer arrives with the kind of political force that feminists, antiracists, and anticolonialist theorists have trained us to ferret out. Cannibalized before arrival, difference no longer poses the kind of negativity required by post-Hegelian systems of ethics: it no longer functions, for example, as the inversion of our ego ideals, à la Fanonian or Irigarayan analyses. Rather, evacuated of any historical cathexis, we consume difference as rapidly and repetitively as possible: the more superficial it is, the better and faster we can stuff our mouths! For post-Hegelian traditions of ethics, the neoliberal aestheticizing of difference precludes the emergence of ethics insofar as it precludes the dialectical encounter of negativity. From this angle, neoliberalism appears every bit as nihilist as early critics of postmodernism warned.

By speculating about an ethics of the real as a possible ethics of racial justice in the United States, I attempt to intervene in this presumed nihilism. An ethics of the real offers an epistemology, syntax, and cathexis that do not turn on the central role of authority in traditional ethics.[13] Given the erosion of authority—or, in Lacanian parlance, the eclipse of the symbolic function—in the neoliberal episteme, forms of traditional ethics that rely on an authority to enforce a law or set of laws find no traction in the neoliberal subject of interests. Whether religiously or secularly articulated and whether externally or internally derived, no ethics of judgment holds cathexis in neoliberal social rationalities and practices: the neoliberal subject of interests will not be found guilty. The neoliberal subject is, however, as I have suggested, still prone to shame and filled with anxiety—affects that have no proper object, no Other. And affects that psychoanalytic social theorists associate with the real.

KANTIAN ETHICS REVISITED

As Alenka Zupančič describes it, Lacan admired Kant because he so poignantly and forcefully captured the impossibility of ethics. Positioning ethics as distinct from morality precisely through disallowing any role for motivation, Kant elegantly articulates the pure form of duty. While critics (to this day, including disgruntled undergraduate students) insist that Kant thereby renders ethics "too ideal" and impossible, Lacan admires him for the discovery of "the essential dimension of ethics,"[14] namely, the existential and epistemic impossibility of the ethical act.

Existentially, given the normative anthropology of Kant's system, subjects filled with pathos cannot become ethical without giving up their very subjectivity. That is, insofar as a modern, western anthropology with deep roots in Christianity frames Kant's thinking about ethics, he understands the human condition as animated by desire, which is then cathected by the dance of interdiction and transgression. For this kind of subjectivity, which also constitutes the subjectivity of liberalism, the categorical imperative demands the impossible, namely, the sacrifice of one's very self as subject. Defined by our desires, feelings, motivations, and cathexes, we modern liberal subjects hear the purely formal character of the ethical act as a sacrifice of our very subjectivity: if we can only act ethically by giving up all recourse to motivation, cathexis, and pathos, then we seem not to be able to act ethically at all without giving up our very subjectivity—or, even more extremely, our very humanity. The purely ethical act is possible only for nonhumans—whether gods, angels, or robots. Kant courageously spells out the impossibility of ethics for humans, that is, for humans understood as animated by desire (and its articulation in the eighteenth and nineteenth centuries, the will and intentionality).

Railing against this, liberal modern subjects may take some solace in the twin of this existential impossibility, namely, the impossibility of knowing the true ethical act. Kant articulates this as the fundamentally noumenal character of the true ethical act, which he parses more specifically through the concepts of the pure will and freedom. Existentially impossible, these concepts are also, Kant argues, fundamentally unknowable. Moreover, the unknowable characteristic of one's motivations to act ethically is precisely what protects the ethical from reduction to mere duty: the ethical act will always align with duty and, thus, our originary motivation to act ethically will forever be obscured by the possibility that it is merely this insufficient motivation of fulfilling one's duty. The ethical motivation qua ethical can never be distinguished at the level of the act itself, since all ethical acts should also conform perfectly with duty (assuming the cultural law of the duty is itself ethical). This epistemically aporetic character leads most readers of Kant to posit a kind of asymptotic, regulative idealism, whereby the purity of the ethical act and the freedom that attends it become ameliorating ideals. That is, by striving for them, we structure our lives and ways of living in the best manner possible. Rather than emphasizing the endemic failure to attain the ideals, Kant argues that the impossibility of knowing or acting in a purely ethical manner *ought* to serve as an internal structure for constantly striving to make ourselves better. It is, as I said, a quintessentially modern and liberal system.

But a Lacanian reading of these existential and epistemic impossibilities does not soften the blow quite so readily. Rather than domesticating these aporias into regulative ideals, Alenka Zupančič reads them as articulating a Lacanian ethics of the real. As she elaborates, Kantian ethics is not simply an ethics of asceticism and sacrifice. It involves, rather, a fundamental transformation in the anthropology that undergirds such concerns. As Zupančič elaborates, the paradox of Kantian ethics "is not that pleasure is forbidden to the ethical subject but, rather, that it loses its attractive power for such a subject" (ER, 8). The Kantian ethical subject undergoes an ontological transformation such that the question of pleasure—of motivation, cathexis, and pathos—no longer holds any affective or epistemological force. Again, as Zupančič puts it, "We need have no fear that entry into the realm of the ethical will require us to sacrifice all the pleasures we hold so dear, since this will not even be experienced as a loss or sacrifice—'we' will not be the same person as before" (ER, 8). No longer the subject animated by desire and its vortex of ego-centrism, the Kantian ethical subject is no longer attached to her pathos and thus does not fear losing it. The Kantian system of ethics turns on this ontological change in subjectivity.

Strongly echoing the depersonalization Lacan locates in anxiety, this ontological change in subjectivity makes this Lacanian reading of Kantian ethics particularly rich for the neoliberal episteme, as I have developed it. By following out various implications of reading neoliberal subjectivity as circulating in the Lacanian drive, I have articulated the neoliberal subject of interests as a subjectivity no longer animated fully or singularly by desire. On the one hand, this means that the neoliberal subject is not the subject Kant is addressing or the subject hailed by Kantian ethics; paradoxically, on the other hand, this also means that the neoliberal subject may be more obliquely prone to the kind of ethics-without-pathos that Kant articulates. In other words, I want to speculate on the possibility that a Lacanian reading of Kantian ethics—or what I call, following Zupančič, an ethics of the real—may provoke a way back into a language of ethics for neoliberal subjects precisely, albeit ironically, because it shuns motivation and all its personalizing effects. Immune to the dynamics of authoritarian interpellation (whether rationally, internally generated ideals of altruism or religiously, externally enforced mechanisms of guilt), cool, neoliberal subjects are detached and decathected. Without pathos, they already inhabit the scene of the drive, where an ethics of the real erupts.

AN ETHICS OF THE REAL AS AN ETHICS OF RACE

Without desire, without cathexis, without difference, without pathos, cool neoliberal subjects cruise the circuit of the drive, endlessly if uninterrupted. When I speculate that this renders us more prone to an ethics of the real, I do not mean that we can willfully bring such an ethics into being. The real is defined as precisely that which resists all signification: we certainly cannot intentionally bring the real before us. Again, as Zupančič puts it, "The paradox of the real or the event lies in the fact that as soon as we turn it into the direct goal of our action, we lose it" (ER, 237).[15] Undoing the active and passive logic of willful subjects of desire, the real is not subject to causality. Ironically, however, such concerns about bringing the real intentionally into our direct experience belong to the liberal, modern, willful subject—not the cool, detached neoliberal subject of endless interests. Cruising the circuit of the drive, the cool, detached neoliberal subject is prone to an ethics of the real.

While this detachment can make us more susceptible to encounters with the real, the tendency to turn them into spectacle seems to have become the dominant neoliberal response. As Žižek shows in his analysis of 9/11 in *Welcome to the Desert of the Real,* while we could respond to the planes crashing into the Twin Towers as an eruption of the real, the endless repetition of the image for days and even weeks across media screens defanged it into a spectacle—indeed, an icon—ready for consumption. (By making it a spectacle, it also entered that quintessentially neoliberal temporality of crisis.) The undoing of the active and passive logic of causality does not, therefore, mean we can simply be passive about encountering the real. While we cannot bring it willfully before us, we can attune ourselves to its constant and persistent, if latent, force.[16] Our relation to the real may be oblique, but it is a relation nonetheless. We can remind ourselves vigilantly that the real persists, thereby altering the moments of its eruption from "shock and awe" or speechless surprise into a language of ethics.

Encounters with the real and, consequently, any ethics of the real thereby produce the epistemic conundrum of articulating a noncausal relation. As Zupančič formulates it, the Real is "essentially a by-product of the action (or inaction) of the subject—something the latter produces, but not as 'hers,' [not] as a thing in which she would be able to 'recognize' herself" (ER, 238). By reading an ethics of the real in the contemporary United States as an ethics of (endemically sexualized) race, I understand this noncausal encounter with the real as articulating the kind of nonagential response to the long, intense history of sexualized racism that makes us vigilant about this violence without ascribing intentionality or the morality of accountability. We were not alive in the seventeenth, eighteenth, or nineteenth centuries, and we do not understand ourselves as racists; but this does not mean that we cannot consciously call attention to the harsh realities of these violent histories and their ongoing, persistent repercussions and reinventions. An ethics of the real is not the aim of our actions, but it can still be understood as the effect of our actions. We can attune ourselves to these effects: we can, that is, consciously attend to and reconfigure the long unconscious habits of suppressing these intense histories of somatic xenophobia.

This involves a kind of vigilant reminding that is more visceral than intellectual. We must never forget that the real does not signify; even more so, it resists and even undercuts signification, especially those signifying practices that promise wholeness, fullness, a return to Paradise Lost. As Amy Hollywood articulates in her provocative readings of the Lacanian real alongside Bataille, the real locates a turn to ethics for Lacan precisely as a rejection of the fantasies of wholeness as we find them in historical narratives of progress and salvation. She thereby associates the real "with that in history that is unassimilable to its meaning-giving and salvific narratives."[17] This recuperative tendency in historical narratives, structured by epistemologies and politics of recognition, becomes a primary obstacle to encountering the ethical, that is, to encountering the sprawling and shattering mess of violence, suffering, anguish, horror, and also joy that Lacan calls *jouissance.*

Jouissance is that exquisite description Lacan gives of pain so intense that it becomes pleasurable and pleasure so intense that it becomes painful. It marks encounters with the real as they unnerve and decenter us. These encounters are simultaneously alluring and repellant, generative and destructive. We cannot consciously control or want them, lest they become a sadomasochistic power trip bent on suicide. We can, however, talk *about* these kinds of encounters that litter our racialized and sexualized pasts and presents. And in so doing, we can open ourselves to the ethical transformation that their eruptions bring.

Given the resistance to signification that defines the real, attempts to concretize encounters as moments of possible ethical transformation are tricky, to say the least. I persist, nonetheless, in my speculation that an ethics of the real offers a way—albeit a complex and difficult one—to generate a meaningful language of ethics in the contemporary US neoliberal iteration of the modern episteme. As a visceral attunement to the *jouissance* of history, I insist that this must be articulated in the United States as an ethics of endemically sexualized race. This means, in short, a sustained and intensified attention—in whatever form or media—to the vast histories of sexualized racism that litter our cultural psyche. This kind of sustained effort both exposes the fantasies of classical liberalism and, perhaps more urgently, interrupts the neoliberal aestheticizing reduction of subjectivity to the drive, even if violently. This kind of raw, unmediated encounter with the real, where the real is the racialized history of liberalism's relation to difference as a historically violent and threatening phenomenon, may harbor sufficient force to rip through the aestheticizing social dynamics of neoliberal cultures.

As forms of *jouissance*, these are mostly scenes of violence, but not entirely. The encounters that also stir intensive pleasures are perhaps even more important than those that stir intensive pain. First of all, to limit ourselves to understanding these scenes of racialized *jouissance* of history as only violent may entrap us in the deep habits of blame and (ultimately narcissistic) guilt and their vapid cycle of apology. Second, the characterization of *jouissance* as a pleasure so intense that it becomes indistinguishable from pain constitutes a substantially different experience that resists the flattened-out, hyperstimulated, endlessly streaming acts of consumption that neoliberalism sells (quite successfully!) as "pleasure."

Jouissance cannot be maximized or intensified, tweaked or manipulated: it is not an object of willful choice. As Tim Dean puts it, *jouissance* indicates that rare experience of pleasure that radically disarms the self, not the identity-confirming, self-enhancing domesticated pleasure that saturates neoliberal cultures.[18] This disarming of the self takes me back, once more, to Lacan's seminar on anxiety, where he discusses the impossibility of willfully ordering *jouissance* as an origin of anxiety. Going back to "the God of the Jews" and the text of the Bible, he muses: "*God asks me to jouir, to enjoy*. . . . [But] to *jouir* on order is all the same something about which each of us can sense that, if there's a wellspring, an origin, of anxiety, then it must be found somewhere there. To the imperative *Jouis*, I can only reply one thing, and that is *J'ouïs, I hear*, but naturally I don't *jouir* so easily for all that" (A, 80). We cannot will *jouissance* and yet we are ordered to do so; consequently, we become anxious.

This lacing of anxiety with this impossibility to will *jouissance* becomes all the more provocative for my reading of race and racism when paired with the habitual ascription of *jouissance* to the Other.[19] A regular theme in Lacan's seminars, he again refers to it in the seminar *Anxiety* in the context of explaining the structure of a nightmare. Lacan explains: "The nightmare's anxiety is felt, properly speaking, as that of the Other's *jouissance* . . . the creature that bears down on your chest with all its opaque weight of foreign *jouissance*, which crushes you beneath its *jouissance*" (A, 61). Continuing my line of thinking that the long, violent, sexualized history of racism is the nightmare of the United States,[20] what kind of twisted relation to this *jouissance* of the Other do we now inhabit in this neoliberal episteme?

Given the neoliberal torsion of race and ethics into concepts wrung dry of their lifeblood, what happens when we speak from the racialized *jouissance* of history? What happens when we speak from the space of intensified pleasure and pain that no longer has a cultural register? While realizing the thorny problem of articulating that which resists signification, I conclude with an example of the kind of phenomena that stir this deep racialized *jouissance* of history, namely, a meditation on New Orleans and the remarkable nonevent of the early twenty-first century in the United States: Hurricane Katrina.

NEW ORLEANS: REAL COOL, REAL, NEOLIBERAL COOL

It was the city of sin: "N'Awlins," as anyone who has ever been there should pronounce it. The place where people went to lose themselves, to unwind a bit, perhaps even unhinge a bit. To take a walk on the wild side—let loose and indulge, or more likely overindulge, in some of those deliciously forbidden pleasures. Full of funk, it was a city that defied the most treasured boundaries of the larger US culture: sexualities ran amok, crossing all racial and gender lines; liquor flowed freely in the streets; exotic and enticing odors spilled out of Creole kitchens; and music of soulful jazz and blues was simply everywhere. Even funerals became street celebrations: the ongoing practice of jazz funerals remains one of the most iconic images of New Orleans. Thoroughly racialized as a black and Creole city, New Orleans functioned as a site of promised *jouissance* for the country. It was our unconscious. It was real cool. It was the Big Easy.

But, finally, the ease it held out to this nation of good, upstanding citizens with proper jobs and the patriotism to protect them was too much. The ease with which it offered its unbridled pleasures was more than the nation could handle. Unlike in Vegas, where people work their tails off to run fancy hotels, put on extravagant shows, and keep lucrative casinos moving, the denizens of the Big Easy never really worked at all—they just did what they liked to do and made enough to get by.[21] The ease of their lives was itself too easy, too slack, too indulgent, no proper signs of guilt or even shame. The only viable sign of productivity, the capital generated by this economy of sin, was embezzled by the legendary corruption of the place.

And so when the big storm came, it was something of a psychic discharge for the nation. When that overwhelming mass of turbulent wind and water, engorged by the unusually warm surface water temperatures of the Gulf of Mexico, destroyed this singular site of thoroughly racialized and sexualized *jouissance*, it was something of a relief. In the days of televisual obsession following August 29, 2005, we were engulfed by images of the storm, the refugees, the looters, the horrors (fantasized and real) unfolding in and around the overwhelmed Super Dome, and the unbelievable, unforeseen, gross inefficiency of national and local relief efforts. Amid all that, a very quiet, muffled, slightly ashamed sigh of relief was audible. It was gone: the true City of Sin—the city of utter indulgence and zero productivity—was gone. When the right-wing nuts proclaimed it "God's wrath against this City of Sin," they spoke a kernel of truth that, precisely through disavowing it, provided some catharsis for the upright citizens of the United States. Dismissed as crazy, overzealous talk, it still provided a verbal affirmation that this place of excessive and shameless indulgence was gone: the bigots, once more, spoke the true xenophobia of our long history that the neoliberal language of diversity has stripped from us.

This is hardly the story of Katrina that has been told. The preferred narrative is that of a natural disaster that has been healed by renewed commerce, an exemplary neoliberal twist on the liberal narrative of white benevolence and redemption. Professional organizations of all stripes, including the coolest academic ones, pride themselves on holding conferences in post-Katrina New Orleans, salving their moral conscience by spending dollars. This has become the quintessential neoliberal articulation of the classically liberal theme of helping the downtrodden: we now prefer and are encouraged at every turn to "do good" through clever practices of consumption. Choose the shade-grown coffee at Starbucks, to gloss one of Žižek's favorite examples, to add a little zip of altruism or generosity or even "ethical activity" to the regular morning java jolt.[22]

In the case of Katrina, the benevolent, white, middle-and-upward class need only schedule conferences and small vacations in the cleaned-up French Quarter to glide into town, yet again, in the usual shining armor to rescue and redeem the poor black underclass who got wiped out by nature (somehow, again). Or, in an even more enticing and alluring neoliberal twist, the hipsters need only colonize various parts of the city, materially and in media, to enshrine New Orleans as one of the edgiest cities of cool.

The gaping holes of racism in this nice neoliberal fable, however, are glaring: it exemplifies neoliberal racism. Far from ameliorated or erased, structural racism in this region has intensified, sometimes exponentially, as the racist effects of the poststorm economic infrastructure around education, housing, and employment demonstrate. As Vincanne Adams catalogues and argues in painful detail, Katrina became the perfect neoliberal storm, privatizing charity in an abhorrent twist that allows crony capitalism to make profit on the manipulation of the needy into ever needier states. Functioning as a kind of negative to the bright luminosity of the nation-changing, world-changing event of 9/11, however, those few horrific days of August 2005 and the tragedies that continue to ripple out from them are largely forgotten in the United States.

Indeed, the dark illegibility of the lives lost in Katrina to both death and transiency seems only to sharpen the exquisite, ongoing charting of those lives directly affected by 9/11. Unlike the meticulous obituaries in the *New York Times* of those killed in the Twin Towers, there has never been any meticulous public archiving of the approximately eighteen hundred killed by Katrina. Many dead were likely never logged in any legal record at all. Decayed or waterlogged beyond recognition, many were likely disposed of without any attempt to decipher identity, much less contact any kin. The last eighty-five of such unclaimed bodies were finally entombed by a group of private funeral home owners, taking on responsibilities shirked by the state, in August 2008—three years after the storm.[23]

In similar fashion, the diaspora caused by the tragic storm has also fallen off the national radar. Scattered to every corner of the United States and beyond, the former denizens of New Orleans are now largely believed to have resettled into either new locations or a kind of ongoing transiency. It is estimated that Katrina displaced one million people who were resettled into fifty-five hundred cities across the United States. For the African American population, settled in the most far-flung locations, ranging from Las Vegas, San Francisco, and Seattle to Chicago and Boston,[24] the return to New Orleans lags considerably behind the general population. Statistics, such as they are, show that New Orleans has returned to 78 percent of its pre-Katrina population, including newcomers to the city. However, it is estimated (and this estimation is much fuzzier) that 32 percent of the African American population has yet to return.[25] From the Middle Passage to the Great Migration of the early and mid-twentieth century to Katrina, African Americans continue to live a diasporic existence. But none of this is charted or tracked any longer: it is naturalized into a mere shift, if somewhat unusual, in demographics and populations.

Here is the story I am interested in telling: the transformation of New Orleans from a city of real cool through an overwhelming encounter of the real to a site of neoliberal cool, filled with ever-so-hip, fungible difference that is more ready than ever for the market. That is, I conclude this book with what Foucault might call a countermemory of New Orleans and Hurricane Katrina that reads them as exemplifying the kinds of transformations underway, in all kinds of gradations and differentiated articulations, through the neoliberal intensification and transformation of liberalism across the United States. This exemplary status is bestowed not only by the horrible tragedy of the hurricane, which I position as an encounter of the real, but by the location of that human-enabled storm in a site of unmatched racialized *jouissance.*

Hurricane Katrina was, in so many ways, the Perfect Storm. It was human-enabled in at least two ways: as an effect of carbon-induced climate change produced (at least partially) by the neoliberal intensification of consumerism, the storm landed in a region where the levees were—and remain—grossly neglected.[26] But as the site of real cool, the Big Easy was a city where such negligence and its racialized connotations were always already naturalized. The denizens of this site of unmatched racialized *jouissance* were fully and wholly *of the place* and thus unable to protect themselves against the ravages of nature. The widely circulated images of post-Katrina black bodies stranded in floodwaters thereby easily fed into the long-standing racist trope of the black body trapped in nature, especially in water. As Kara Walker's exhibit *After the Deluge* from 2006 illustrates so clearly, the powerful black body has a long history of being positioned metonymically with the fearsome power of the ocean.[27] Consequently, the horror of a massive hurricane wiping out a black population finds easy purchase in this long-standing metonymy.

The idiom of nature thereby readily emerges to carry forward the racist representations and responses to the tragedy, while absolving any upright citizen from any responsibility. Fully "naturalized" both as a freakish storm and as a racialized and thus infantilized city, the tragedy of Hurricane Katrina striking New Orleans aligned remarkable ingredients to become an overwhelming, forceful encounter of the real. But rather than being stripped of language, rather than falling silent in an admission that the real is happening, the machines of racism immediately locked into gear. From the apocryphal but self-fulfilling stories of raping and pillaging at the Superdome to the iconic, blackface images of Aunt Jemima and the Coon, the long-standing reservoir of racism gave us the language we needed to explain and absolve: "savages live in nature and so die of nature."[28]

To live out an ethics of the real may require one of the very most difficult things for cultures of classical liberalism and neoliberalism: to fall silent, as an act of ethics. More specifically, it is to fall silent when encountering the suppressed history of racialized *jouissance* that is the real in these neoliberal times. In the instance of Katrina, this would surely mean to resist all the racist images, tropes, and representations of black savagery and white benevolence. It would mean to resist all these attempts to signify—to make sense of—that which ontologically strips us of language. It would mean to heed one command: stop making sense. These racist tropes function as fetishes, enlivening the memory trace of a vanquished (alleged) threat and thus promising to return us to wholeness.[29] But like Paradise Lost, there is no wholeness to which to return: the United States is structured by racism. It tells us all who and where and how and why we are. It is our symbolic, even if sputtering and twisting into much more convoluted concepts and explanations.

In these heady neoliberal times of erasing history and shunning authority, we are incited to fly without that symbolic. And so we might try to make Katrina cool. Or make our embrace of New Orleans hip. But that's just a mean trick: How could we be hip so quickly in a place that has undergone such profound pain and loss? And how could we be hip so quickly in a place that still reverberates with remarkable, deeply rooted *jouissance* of creativity and funk? The heightened, intensified superficiality of such a claim to cool in the face of such deep memories and scars makes my head spin. If we are to come to any ethics of justice that can move beyond the ideological hall of mirrors, we must find our ways back through the debris of history—still, again.

An ethics of the real knows this. Honoring it, without making sense of it, an ethics of the real tends to the open wound that is the ongoing, persistent racism in this country. In the example of Hurricane Katrina, it tends to the intensive losses of homes, livelihoods, communities, and meaningful lives that continue to occur in its wake *and* to the unspoken, even unnoticed erasure of these losses. But not in the name of redemption, salvation, or recuperation to wholeness. Moreover, this is only an example, and an ethics of the real is animated by the vigilance of its repetition. If I and all the social theorists that I have drawn upon capture even part of what is happening in this neoliberal episteme, we are living in times when we will encounter the real with greater and greater repetition. To remain vigilant about this so as to remain attuned to all that might reverberate out of it is to live an ethics of the real.

NOTES

INTRODUCTION: A VERY UNCOOL BOOK

1. hooks, *We Real Cool*, 147.
2. See ibid., on the masculinity of black cool, and Walker, *Black Cool*, especially essays by Olopade, Harper, Davis, Thomas, Ryder, Lewis, and Amah on these long historical roots of coolness in black strength and resistance.
3. Of course, Marxists (especially Marcuse) have argued for some time that this kind of commodification is inherent in capitalism. Rooting myself in Foucault's analyses of neoliberalism, I argue we must develop non-Marxist readings of these various transformations.
4. See hooks, *We Real Cool*, and Fraiman, *Cool Men and the Second Sex*.
5. Prime examples of the advocacy work include Fukuyama, *The End of History and the Last Man*; and Sachs, *The End of Poverty*. Prime examples of the critical work include Brown, "Neoliberalism and the End of Liberal Democracy," in *Edgework*; Dean, *Democracy and Other Neoliberal Fantasies*; Dean, "Drive as the Structure of Biopolitics"; Habermas, "Toward a Cosmopolitan Europe"; Harvey, *A Brief History of Neoliberalism*; and Stiglitz, *Globalization and Its Discontents*. For an excellent recent overview of various "forms" of neoliberalism, see Wacquant, "Three Steps." See also Mirowski and Plehwe, *The Road from Mont Pelerin*, for a thorough account of the widespread impact of the Mont Pelerin Society on academic disciplines.
6. It is little wonder, then, that the very issue of naming "neoliberalism" has rightfully become a subject of some debate. Heeding the arguments of both Elizabeth Povinelli and Lauren Berlant that we gain much from calling this contemporary period "late liberalism," so as to capture the kinds of sociopolitical

transformations such as multiculturalism and cultural recognition, I nonetheless persist in calling this social rationality under investigation "neoliberalism." This by no means distances it from liberalism; to the contrary, my analysis is grounded in Foucault's argument in the 1979 lectures that the "new" aspects of neoliberalism derive from an intensification of categories and practices of liberalism, not any kind of clear break from it.

7. Locating this problem, Bernard Harcourt argues in *The Illusion of Free Markets* that a nominalist approach offers an effective method to intervene in this politico-semiotic problematic. For Harcourt, the dominant categories of analyses of neoliberalism—namely, "free market" and "regulated" alongside "natural order" and "discipline"—have come to stand in for the practices they are allegedly describing. Through a brilliant comparison of late-eighteenth-century French regulations of the bread market with late-twentieth-century regulations of the wheat market at the Chicago Board of Trade, Harcourt exposes how these categories have become freighted with ideological proclivities, consequently skewing our view of what is happening (in the past and present) in the wide array of activities shaped by market rationalities.

8. I refer to Althusser's foundational essay, "Ideology and Ideological State Apparatus," in *Lenin and Philosophy*. Of course, Althusser argued this is always the case, demonstrating how there is no outside to ideology. I return to these arguments in great detail in chapter 2.

9. I offer only a brief sampling of this vast scholarship, from older classics to more recent work: Alexander and Mohanty, *Feminist Genealogies, Colonial Legacies, Democratic Futures*; Mies, *Patriarchy and Accumulation on a World Scale*; Parrenas, *Servants of Globalization*; Ehrenreich and Hochschild, *Global Woman*; Peterson, *A Critical Rewriting of Global Political Economy*; Hawkesworth, *Globalization and Feminist Activism*; Cabezas, Reese, and Waller, *The Wages of Empire*.

10. See, for example, his classic *Capitalism and Freedom*.

11. For prime examples of this Marxist critique of neoliberalism, see Harvey, *A Brief History of Neoliberalism*; Duggan, *The Twilight of Equality*; Giroux, *Against the Terror of Neoliberalism*; and Goldberg, *The Threat of Race*. The work of Chandan Reddy, especially his *Freedom with Violence*, and Jodi Melamed, especially her *Represent and Destroy*, both draws implicitly on Marxist analyses, especially the workings of ideology and interpellation. Finally, the explicitly non-Marxist analysis that I am deriving from Foucault here also addresses current trends in queer theory that analyze neoliberalism through Marxist lenses, including turns to the utopic as a queer temporal horizon. See especially Rosenberg and Villarejo's special issue of *glq*, "Queer Studies and the Crisis of Capitalism," as well as Hennessey, *Profit and Pleasure*, and Floyd, *The Reification of Desire*.

12. In the 1982 preface to *Capitalism and Freedom*, Friedman writes: "Only a crisis—actual or perceived—produces real change. When that crisis occurs, the

actions that are taken depend on the ideas that are lying around. That, I believe, is our basic function: to develop alternatives to existing policies, to keep them alive and available until the politically impossible becomes politically inevitable" (xiv). The economic and demographic transformation of New Orleans after the crisis of Hurricane Katrina demonstrates this kind of neoliberal strategy perfectly; I conclude the book with a discussion of these phenomena.

13. Most scholarship, such as that of Harvey, Giroux, Stiglitz, and Duggan, locates the emergence of neoliberalism primarily in the Chicago School of the 1960s. See Ong, *Neoliberalism as Exception*, esp. 10–12, and Dean, "Enjoying Neoliberalism," esp. 48–50, for excellent overviews of these genealogies of neoliberalism.
14. I have in mind the broad sweep of scholarship inspired by Giorgio Agamben's concept of bare life (in *Homo Sacer*) and Judith Butler's concept of precarity (in *Precarious Lives*), including the work of Berlant, Esposito, Negri, Povinelli, and Virno. I am implicitly returning to a concept of biopolitics derived more directly from Foucault's work and its emphasis on various modes of normalizing populations; my analysis of the transformation in the social aesthetics of cool in mainstream US culture is one of these modes through which particular kinds of living are "made to live" in particular ways and other kinds of living are "left to die."
15. Dean, "The Biopolitics of Pleasure," 477. As he elaborates, Dean wonders how and why "the question of pleasure, so central to Michel Foucault's work on power relations, has been skirted by those who have developed his inchoate remarks on biopower for an understanding of our contemporary political situation" (477). While Dean focuses on Italian scholars such as Agamben, Esposito, Negri, and Virno, I argue that the same occlusion informs scholars in the United States such as Povinelli, Butler, and Berlant, as well as work out of queer theory and critical ethnic studies that focuses primarily on violence, such as that of Jodi Melamed and Chandan Reddy. See also my essay from 2012, "The Queer Thing About Neoliberal Pleasure," for musings on the thematic of pleasure through exploring why Foucault locates both sexuality and neoliberalism at "the heart of biopolitics."
16. The use of Foucault in the very act of occluding pleasure is particularly surprising in Povinelli's turn to *The Use of Pleasure* in *Economies of Abandonment* precisely to develop the bifurcation "between those who reflect on and evaluate ethical substance and those who are this ethical substance" (11). While this works for her own project, it is far from the primary focus of Foucault's volume, namely, the problematic of practicing pleasure. Her reading of Ursula Le Guin's "The Ones Who Walk Away from Omelas" performs a similarly gross occlusion of the major theme, namely, the unmitigated joy and happiness of the Omelas. As I hope is already clear, I find Povinelli's work compelling and provocative, but regarding this specific occlusion of pleasure it is so via negation.
17. See Winnubst, "The Queer Thing About Neoliberal Pleasure," for my argument that queer theory's allegiance to antinormativity may render it one of neoliberalism's best songs. See also Wiegman and Wilson, "Queer Theory Without

Antinormativity," for broader considerations of how queer theory might move away from and without this long-standing commitment.

18. Since the #BlackLivesMatter movement has emerged in the fall of 2014, Obama has given several more statements and interviews regarding the protests against the failure to indict the police officers who killed Michael Brown, John Crawford, and Eric Garner. While I have inserted some analysis of the #BlackLivesMatter movement (as of December 2014) across the book, I do not track Obama's responses.

1. EXCAVATING CATEGORIES: FOUCAULT'S *BIRTH OF BIOPOLITICS*

1. Foucault, *The Birth of Biopolitics*, 271. Hereafter cited parenthetically in the text as BB.
2. Thomas Lemke's early reading of these lectures in 2001—seven years before they were translated into English—laid the groundwork for Wendy Brown's reading of them, both of which functioned as authoritative summaries of the lectures for some time; see Lemke, "The Birth of Bio-Politics"; and Brown, "Neoliberalism and the End of Liberal Democracy," in *Edgework*. Scholarship has continued to proliferate since the translation of the lectures into English in 2007. See especially Dilts, "'From Entrepreneur of the Self' to 'Care of the Self,'" on the role of these lectures in the transition to the later volumes of *History of Sexuality*. See Nealon, *Foucault Beyond Foucault*, for the argument that Foucault's work ought not be divided into periods and themes.
3. Han, *Foucault's Critical Project*, 114.
4. See Foucault, "Truth and Power."
5. See Nealon, *Foucault Beyond Foucault*, 19, for a helpful delineation of Foucault's primary problems with ideology as a conceptual framework for critique. See also Han, *Foucault's Critical Project*.
6. For an excellent example of this kind of analysis, see Delaney, *Times Square Red: Times Square Blue*, which is also marked by a distinct tone of nostalgia that often accompanies Marxian critiques.
7. Foucault calls the German form "ordoliberals" because the primary theorists published in the journal *Ordo*. It also helps to distinguish them from the neoliberals in the United States. See also Brown, "Neoliberalism and the End of Liberal Democracy," for a discussion of this language.
8. I have developed some of the implications of this narrowed conceptualization of Protestantism through the work of Georges Bataille, who argues (following Max Weber and R. H. Tawney) in *The Accursed Share*, volume 1, that it is Calvinist theology, not Lutheran, that introduces commerce into the heart of Protestantism and its infamous work ethic. For a reading of this in relation to Foucault's lectures on neoliberalism, see Winnubst, "Sacrifice as Ethics."

9. For a sustained examination of this point, see Sheth, *Toward a Political Philosophy of Race.*
10. Foucault discusses the transformation as occurring both in practices, such as shifts in agriculture and so on (BB, 33), and in "the heads of the economists" (BB, 30), including Adam Smith explicitly later in the lectures.
11. In one of his earliest discussions of "truth" as a matter of discursive practices, rather than correspondence, Foucault argues that Mendel's insights about genetics had to begin to shape contemporary discourses before they could be fully "true"; see Foucault, "Discourse on Language."
12. Labor is, of course, also fundamental to John Locke's account of classical liberalism and social contract theory; see Winnubst, *Queering Freedom*, chap. 1, for an analysis of this. Suffice it here to say that the liberal strains in Marxist analyses are worth reconsidering in light of Foucault's lectures.
13. Granted, Milton Friedman does analyze structures of distribution, but only to discount the need to do so, in *Capitalism and Freedom.*
14. Foucault draws extensively on Chicago School theorists for these developments, especially Gary Becker and T. W. Schultz.
15. It is worth noting that Foucault links the transformation—namely, "a policy of growth focused precisely on . . . the form of investment in human capital" (BB, 232)—directly to the considerable economic growth of Western and Japanese societies since 1930 (BB, 232).
16. See Huffer, *Mad for Foucault*, 67–74, for an incisive argument that this dominant reading turns on both a problematic translation of Foucault's French into English and a distinctively Anglo-American concept of identity.
17. See especially Zupančič, *An Ethics of the Real*, for a provocative explication of this Kantian dilemma as the ethical dimension of the Lacanian Real. I return to this at length in the final chapter.
18. Foucault cites the physiocrats of France, the English economists, and even theorists like Mandeville; see BB, 275.
19. For compelling work on Foucault's analysis of race and racism and extensions of it into Foucaultian analyses of race and racism, see McWhorter, *Racism and Sexism in Anglo-America* and "Foucault and Race;" and Sheth, *Toward a Political Philosophy of Race.*
20. I have in mind particularly the work of Giroux, Goldberg, Duggan, Delaney, and Melamed.

INTERLUDE 1: OLD SCHOOL COOL

1. Goyette, "Joe Cool," 1971.
2. Ibid.
3. As Rheta Grimsley Johnson writes: "Schulz describes himself as 'a secular humanist' from late 1980s onward, despite being reared in the Lutheran faith

and being active in the United Methodist Church in early adulthood." Grimsley, *Good Grief*, 137.

4. Mendelson and Melendez, *There's No Time for Love, Charlie Brown*.
5. Ibid.

2. RETHINKING DIFFERENCE: THE LIMITS OF INTERPELLATION

1. A slogan used by Margaret Thatcher in the 1980s, "TINA" has become a standard shorthand way of dismissing any attempt to think beyond capitalism. Of course, there have been and still are plenty of backlashes against this view by scholars and activists; I am only characterizing the view of mainstream US culture.
2. Hall's insights in this essay are remarkable, particularly concerning the fraught theoretical times of the 1980s, when poststructuralism emerged right alongside Thatcherism in the United Kingdom and the Reagan Right in the United States. His overview of Marxist theory in the twentieth century locates precisely when and where Marxist critique has altered in an effort to remain relevant to the rapidly transforming circuits of capital. I must note that his analysis of how Marxist critique will always revert to the primacy of production over the market gives me pause about its tracking of the neoliberal transformations Foucault charts in the 1979 lectures. See Hall, "The Problem of Ideology," 38.
3. Ibid., 27, 26.
4. Ibid., 27.
5. Ibid., 30.
6. Ibid.
7. Given the argument that I will elaborate that Althusserian interpellation fails to capture the shifting modes of social authority and subject formation underway in neoliberal social rationalities, these conceptual roots of queer theory may render many of its analyses insufficient or even irrelevant to neoliberal social rationalities. Indeed, queer theory's fetishizing of nonnormative genders and sexualities as sites of resistance may, given the protracted arguments about subject formation and social difference underway across this book, become one of neoliberalism's best songs. For a very condensed version of this argument, see Winnubst, "The Queer Thing About Neoliberal Pleasure." For a recent turn to this question of moving beyond antinormativity for the field of queer theory, see Wiegman and Wilson, "Queer Theory Without Antinormativity."
8. Given his tragic early death, the metaphor of canonization is particularly poignant for Muñoz.
9. Butler, *Gender Trouble*, 33.
10. Althusser, *Lenin and Philosophy*, 119, my emphasis. Hereafter cited parenthetically in the text as LP.
11. Muñoz, *Disidentifications*, 3.
12. Ibid., 11.

13. The essay was originally published in Calderon and Salvidar, *Criticism in the Borderlands*.
14. Alarcón, "The Theoretical Subject(s)," 289.
15. Ibid.
16. Muñoz, *Disidentifications*, 7.
17. Ibid., 11–12.
18. As he tells us in the opening sentence of the essay, he agreed to write this essay because of the criticisms "for discussing Lacan in three lines" (LP, 133) in a previous essay from 1963. In a letter to a translator in 1969, we hear more of this fraught historical context within the French Communist Party: "There is a danger that this text will be misunderstood, unless it is taken for what it then objectively was: a philosophical intervention urging members of the PCF to recognize the *scientificity* of psycho-analysis, of Freud's work, and the importance of Lacan's interpretation of it" (LP, 129). I note these historical conflicts because the allergy, if not hostility, to Lacanian analyses persists in so many of the intellectual and political worlds in which I travel.
19. See Butler, *Gender Trouble*, 42–46.
20. For an account of this in Althusser's thinking, see Montag, *Althusser and His Contemporaries*, esp. chaps. 7 and 8. Montag does not argue against this concept of social authority and thereby, albeit inadvertently, gives the kind of Althusserian reading of Foucault that I suggest Judith Butler's early work helped to instigate.
21. Dean, *Democracy and Other Neoliberal Fantasies*, 61. Hereafter cited parenthetically in the text as DNF.
22. See Nealon, *Foucault Beyond Foucault*, 10–13, for a discussion of this confused reading of Foucault, particularly in the specific self-fashioning aesthetics of contemporary neoliberalism.
23. Althusser's list of these ISAs is instructive: "the religious (the system of different churches), the educational (the system of the different public and private 'schools'), the family, the legal, the political (the political system, including the different parties), the trade-union, the communications (press, radio and television, etc.), the cultural (literature, the arts, sports, etc.)." LP, 143.
24. See Žižek, *First as Tragedy, Then as Farce*, 53–54.
25. In addition to Butler and Muñoz, these kinds of cultural repetitions also structure the early work in queer theory of Eve Kosovsky Sedgwick. For a clear example, see her classic list of "family activities" in "Queer and Now," in *Tendencies*.
26. See Passavant, "The Strong Neo-Liberal State," for an excellent overview of the scholarship in political theory, especially Foucaultian accounts, of whether the neoliberal state is "big," "small," "weak," or "strong." In a manner that seems sympathetic if not symbiotic with my account of the carceral state as a racializing mechanism, Passavant argues that the neoliberal state has not declined in force, but has transformed in the ways that it governs. Arguing that the figure of the criminal is twinned with the figure of the consumer in neoliberal

governance, Passavant shows how a logic of risk and security has come to structure the prison: "While the prison during the Fordist era was justified on grounds of correctionalism, today, incarceration is justified based on the incapacitation of those whose presence in society is seen simply as too risky" (15). I thank an anonymous reviewer of the press for bringing Passavant's scholarship to my attention.

27. Put more pedagogically, while Charles Mills's remarkable work in *The Racial Contract* remains required and crucial reading, it is insufficient to conceptualizing neoliberal processes of racialization and racism.
28. In *The Illusion of Free Markets*, Bernard Harcourt shows how one of the opaque twists in neoliberal logic is the demarcation of the penal system as the space where state law reigns boundlessly, having been removed from the space of the market.
29. This continues to structure the debates about same-sex marriage, whereby liberal advocates argue that it is gays and lesbians' "turn" to receive rights, having waited "behind" African Americans and decidedly "ahead of" immigrants. For an excellent analysis of this problematic logic, see Reddy, "Time for Rights?"
30. I return to Alexander's work, as well as that of Loic Wacqant and Angela Davis in chapter 5.
31. See Jodi Melamed's much acclaimed essay "The Spirit of Neoliberalism: From Racial Liberalism to Neoliberal Multiculturalism," for an example of this kind of fundamentally ideological reading of neoliberalism that, first, serializes the historical development from liberalism to the Civil Rights Movement to neoliberalism and, secondly, argues that the carceral state is part of an ideological bifurcation of the population into neoliberals and prisoners. While this is an excellent and insightful analysis, the reliance on ideology and interpellation constrains the understanding of neoliberal racialization and, consequently, also the possibilities of interrogating and resisting it.
32. Cacho, *Social Death*, 8. Cacho develops a compelling analysis of how the categories of "social death" constrain our most well-intentioned attempts to contest them.
33. See Zack, "The American Sexualization of Race." This also introduces heterosexuality as the mode of monetizing race.
34. Clearly, nonwhite bodies have nonetheless become excellent entrepreneurs in various kinds of markets in this neoliberal episteme, enacting the kind of confusion around race that animates my inquiries across this book. For a clear example, see Freeman, "The 'Reputation' of Neoliberalism." Thanks to an anonymous reviewer of the press for bringing Freeman's work to my attention.
35. For my own account of whiteness precisely through these texts, see chapter 2 of *Queering Freedom*. The analyses of that book are framed by the classically liberal episteme and also constrained to the symbolic and imaginary functions. Some of them, therefore, remain relevant to the neoliberal iteration of the modern

episteme under analysis here. I track the most important connections in chapter 3, where I analyze the core, constitutive fantasies of classical liberalism.

36. Viego, *Dead Subjects*, 3. I am greatly indebted to and inspired by Viego's work in *Dead Subjects* in thinking through what it means to conceive of race exclusively at the level of the Imaginary. I recommend his remarkable book for a much more sustained meditation on this, especially as it has been encouraged and incited by the dominant school of ego psychology in therapeutic practices in the United States. I note, particularly, his cautionary tales for academic theories, which run rampant these days, that explicitly and implicitly rely on this kind of conceptual framework, especially in the tendency to psychologize the racialized subject.
37. Ibid., 16.
38. Ibid.
39. Moraga and Anzaldúa, *This Bridge Called My Back*, 261.
40. See Hall, *Race*.

INTERLUDE 2: INSTANT COOL!

1. John Lennon wrote and recorded "Instant Karma! (We All Shine On)" on January 27, 1970. The song was released to the public ten days later. It is one of the fastest released songs in music history. The song has been covered many times, most notably by U2 on the album *Instant Karma: The Amnesty International Campaign to Save Darfur* in 2007. The song also inspired the title of a novel that became a movie and a television miniseries: *This Date in History: Instant Karma*. See http://929dave.radio.com/2012/01/27/this-date-in-history-instant-karma/#ixzz1toFylFyI.
2. That it was and continues to be encapsulated by Lennon's relationship with Yoko Ono furthers my query in chapters 4 and 5: how have our categories of gender, sexuality, and race transformed in and through this neoliberal social rationality?

3. FROM INSTANT KARMA TO INSTANT WEALTH: THE FANTASIES AND CATHEXES OF THESE NEOLIBERAL TIMES

1. See Dean, "Drive as the Structure of Biopolitics," for the provocation to read Foucault's subjects of interests as inhabiting the Lacanian drive. While this framing of neoliberal subjects as existing in the circuit of the drive does not clash with her earlier argument that neoliberal subjects are controlled through the imaginary, rather than the symbolic, I find the opening ushered by the notion of the drive far more provocative for this project and the direct concern with ethics. To root all subjectivity in the imaginary effectively renders all modes of evaluation political, but the drive also initiates the real, which is a register of ethics.

2. By developing a Lacanian analysis of these dynamics, I aim to excavate some of the affective dynamics that may be animating the interrelations between these various categories that are, in turn, evacuating our concepts of social difference and obfuscating the erasure of ethics that is occurring in the practices, values, and categories of neoliberalism. I thus want to avoid two possible diversions: (1) the tedious debates around the viability of using Lacanian concepts as tools of social analysis; (2) the need to engage all of Lacan's dizzying corpus before using any of it for social analysis. Taking my cues from the work of Tim Dean, Alenka Zupančič, Jodi Dean, and Slavoj Žižek, I approach Lacan in the same manner that I approach all theorists, namely, as helpful interlocutors who offer fresh analytic and speculative lenses for various problematics.
3. See Lacan, *Four Fundamental Concepts*, where he distinguishes the circuit of the drive from the linearity of desire as a fundamental indifference to the object. He writes: "Even when you stuff the mouth—the mouth that opens in the register of the drive—it is not the food that satisfies it, it is, as one says, the pleasure of the mouth" (167). The drive thus functions quite differently from desire, which Lacan diagnoses as the structural lack that relentlessly pursues the impossibility of wholeness that the phallic symbolic appears to promise. See especially "The Mirror Stage," "The Signification of the Phallus," and "The Subversion of the Subject and Dialectic of Desire in the Freudian Unconscious," all in *Écrits*. See also Tim Dean's crucial account of how this emphasis on desire and phallic wholeness skewed early receptions of Lacan in the Anglophone academy: Dean, *Beyond Sexuality*, intro., chap. 1.
4. See especially "The Deconstruction of the Drive" and "The Partial Drive and Its Circuit" in *Four Fundamental Concepts*. As I elaborate in the racializing of sexuality in chapter 5, the somatic indexicality of the drive has been central to queer theorists' development of it, especially Leo Bersani and Tim Dean.
5. See esp. Freud, *Beyond the Pleasure Principle*.
6. As Tim Dean's work shows again and again, sexual experiences cannot be folded neatly into any of the structures of the whole with which so many cultures freight them. They are disaggregating experiences, radically so, which is how Dean reads them through the Lacanian real. I return to Dean's work at length in chapters 4 and 5.
7. By calling it a background, I hope to evoke the phenomenological schema and its understanding of "prereflective" cognition through which individuals approach and interpret everyday occurrences. But unlike the phenomenological investment in objective and subjective truth claims, psychoanalytic approaches attune us to the crucial roles of the irrational—"beheaded," as Bataille would put it, from any rational purchase. My reading of fantasies in relation to the drive and the real hopes to sever them from the rational sublation that so many have read into the project of psychoanalysis.
8. See Nietzsche, *Genealogy of Morals*, esp. part 3, for his reading of power as correlated inversely with its visible, explicit expression; this also becomes germane

to one aspect of Foucault's concept of norms, when he argues that reproductive monogamy becomes most forceful as it falls silent and invisible in the nineteenth century in part 1 of *The History of Sexuality*, volume 1. Interestingly, I will develop a different aspect of Foucault's concept of norms—that is, statistics—in the chapter. Finally, given Anglo-American emphases on a phallic reading of Lacan, this kind of invisibility also resonates with the function of the phallus; I resist the collapse of the schema of fantasy into the structural role of the phallus because fantasies do not regulate the social through authority or even cathexis with authority. Fantasies are epistemological devices that offer interpretations of the social primarily through cathexis. I am interested in how there can be multiple, even clashing and discordant fantasies circulating in a society.

9. Bruce Fink offers the example of a man's gaze—"that look"—as inciting desire, rather than any particular man; of course, this generalized incitement of desire could never be admitted to the fantasy of romance and its individualization of desire.
10. While liberalism more publicly exalts equality, I focus on neutrality as the necessary condition of possibility for equality. Functioning as an epistemological structure, it is positioned as immune to ideological manipulation and thus implicitly undergirds other fantasies, as it were.
11. See Mills, *The Racial Contract*, which draws on Pateman's *Sexual Contract*, and has now been extended to an entire field of scholarship. With deep roots in Marx and Marxism, Mills's analyses exemplify an ideological critique of liberalism, one that is clearly still necessary, but also insufficient.
12. This helps to explain the cultural practice of easily dismissing pedestrian charges of xenophobia, especially of racism, as only so much "whining." I return to this phenomenon in the discussion of the law as the arbiter of neutrality.
13. See Melamed, "The Spirit of Neoliberalism" and *Represent and Destroy*.
14. As scholars, especially Nikhil Singh (but also Reddy and Melamed), are now showing, in addition to their work on the United States in the nineteenth-century eras of slavery and Reconstruction, the post–World War II and Cold War era embraces the Civil Rights Movement as proof of liberalism's ongoing claim to moral and cultural superiority, while continuing various neocolonial forms of violence. The aim of such scholarship is to expose the contradiction between this exalting of tolerance and the persistent violence against racialized (and implicitly sexualized) populations. Insofar as this scholarship enacts an ideological critique of liberalism, it will be insufficient, if still necessary, to dislodging the deep social cathexis to xenophobia. I hope this project will help to fill in some of the lacunae of its insufficiency.
15. See especially the pioneering work of Kimberlé Crenshaw and Ian Haney Lopez, both of whom understand their work as rooted explicitly in legal rationality and practices.
16. The emergent #BlackLivesMatter movement is exposing the gross violence of this internal self-correction of the law, especially the failure to indict police

officers who kill people of color. Ongoing litigation and questions about New York City's "Stop and Frisk" policy also serve as a recent example here.

17. I continue to be deeply informed by Georges Bataille's development of the epistemological and ontological moves to "a general economy." See Winnubst, *Queering Freedom*, for a prolonged elaboration, both hermeneutic and speculative.
18. This discussion draws on the much more extensive exploration of the role of utility in Locke's text and in contemporary stratifications of social difference in the United States that I developed in *Queering Freedom*, chaps. 1 and 5.
19. Mader, *Sleights of the Reason*, 56. Hereafter cited parenthetically in the text as SR.
20. Of course, this does not mean that statistics cannot still be effective in a binary, ideological manner from a range of ideological camps. The political Right mobilizes this kind of binary logic constantly, but it also pops up in leftist ideologies, such as we saw, for example, in the infamous "99% vs. 1%" of the Occupy Movement in 2011 and 2012.
21. My focus on statistics thus sympathizes with Miranda Joseph's recent argument that statistics are the technique of neoliberalism and thus not optional. Joseph reads statistics as hailing us and, explicitly developing an Althusserian and Marxian reading of their use, aims to find the "cracks" in this abstracted epistemology by pushing the abstraction/particularization contradiction to its extreme breaking point. Despite my critique of the limits of Althusserian-Marxian analysis, I am very interested in the possibility that the number (especially but not exclusively the statistical number) may be the sole remaining symbolic order interpellating us neoliberals. Joseph's work is critical to this angle of speculation. See Joseph, *Debt to Society*.
22. McWhorter, "Queer Economies," 68.
23. See especially hooks, "Eating the Other," in *Black Looks*.

INTERLUDE 3: NEOLIBERAL COOL

1. Simpson first wrote about the term in 1994 in the *Independent*, but it did not enter full popular culture circulation until the *Salon.com* essay in 2002.
2. Simpson, "Meet the Metrosexual." Hereafter cited parenthetically in the text as MM.
3. See Todd, "Is the Metrosexual Finally Dead?"
4. Bowers, "At Last: *American Hipster* Kills Hipsterism Dead."

4. "HOW COOL IS THAT?": GENDER AND THE NEOLIBERAL IMAGINARY

1. Susan Fraiman's work shows how this is always a masculinist "cool" that is defined by "a posture of flamboyant unconventionality [that] coexists

with highly conventional views of gender—i.e., is articulated through them." Fraiman, *Cool Men and the Second Sex*, xii. I agree that the posture of cool is always already masculinist (as is evident in my interludes of cool), but I am interested in the elasticity of gender as an expression of cool in these neoliberal times. The formalization and erasure of history involved in this cultural engagement of cool are more deeply transformative and troubling than any masculinizing effects. Moreover, I am attempting to move our analyses beyond these identity categories.

2. Hooks, *We Real Cool*, 150.
3. Ibid., 156. hooks traces this sellout of black cool to "the patriarchal black power movement [that] ushered in a politics of cool that was all about dominator culture, asserting power in the very ways righteous black men had criticized from the moment they touched earth in the so-called new world" (155).
4. Frank, *The Conquest of Cool*, 27. Hereafter cited parenthetically in the text as CC.
5. In this regard, Frank taps into a long trajectory of Marxist analysis of cool as the quintessential attitude of late capitalism. See Jameson, *Postmodernism*, 375; thanks to Jana Sawicki for bringing this text to my attention.
6. See Wendy Brown's classic essay "The Impossibility of Women's Studies," in *Edgework*, for the charges of *ressentiment* and the ensuing mechanisms of victim and guilt to police the fundamentally political character of feminist epistemologies. For a compelling argument that identity-based fields of knowledge, including the wide circulation of the concept of intersectionality, have been mired by ideological frameworks, see Wiegman, *Object Lessons*, esp. chap. 5, 239–300.
7. The literature on intersectionality is vast and still growing. For an excellent overview and critical assessment, especially on the grounds of differing epistemologies of identity and subject formation, with a particular concern for the normalizing effects of intersectionality, see Huffer, *Are the Lips a Grave?*, 13–20. Some of the central flashpoints of the debate include Kimberlé Crenshaw's coining of the phrase in "Demarginalizing the Intersection of Race and Sex" and "Mapping the Margins"; as well as the extensions and critiques in McCall, "The Complexity of Intersectionality"; Puar, *Terrorist Assemblages*, esp. "Conclusion: Queer Times, Terrorist Assemblages"; and Guidroz and Berger, "A Conversation with Founding Scholars on Intersectionality."
8. See Ferguson, "Reading Intersectionality."
9. The fields of Disability Studies and Trans* Studies seem particularly critical to the kinds of analysis I am advancing, especially the argument that somatic xenophobia persists through the neoliberal transformation of social difference and thereby offers an obstinate site from which to think resistance to it. The scholarly and activist fields are much too vast to cite here. For exemplars, see Kafer, *Feminist, Queer, Crip*, esp. chap. 3 and the discussion of the billboards of the Foundation for a Better Life; and Spade, *Normal Life*. See also notes 10 and 17 of this chapter.

10. I do not, thereby, address the emergence of trans* visibility and politics, including the burgeoning field of trans* studies, in this discussion of gender. Given the complex interactions with both the *soma* and the law, trans* embodiment, affect, and cultural representations also articulate the limits of this social difference-as-fungibility machine. Thankfully, there is much excellent scholarship already moving in this direction; see especially Spade, *Normal Life*; Clare, *Exile and Pride*; and the remarkable editorial work of Stryker.
11. On the exporting of Chicago School economics across the world, see Harvey, *A Brief History of Neoliberalism*, 8–9.
12. Friedman, *Capitalism and Freedom*, 5. Hereafter cited parenthetically in the text as CF.
13. Friedman consistently attempts to aestheticize and depoliticize all values as matters of individual choice, especially conflicting political and ethical values, such as racism; see *Capitalism and Freedom*, chapter 7. His rhetoric falls short of practice, however, even in this exemplary act of choosing a tie: Friedman regularly sported a spiffy "Adam Smith" tie—a preppy-colored, often striped tie with silhouettes of Adam Smith sprinkled across it that was, interestingly enough, worn throughout the Reagan White House.
14. As I noted in chapter 2, Althusser discusses the example of birth and the way that individuals are always already sexed subjects and thus always already interpellated. See Althusser, *Lenin and Philosophy*, 176.
15. By focusing on gender in the Lacanian register of the imaginary, I do not mean to imply that the symbolic and its enforcement of sexism are no longer functioning in neoliberal cultures. As the assault on reproductive rights continues to intensify, we must remain attentive to the persistence of this "old-fashioned" form of oppression in the sociohistorical fugue of liberalism-neoliberalism. The language of sexism and oppression, however, finds little to no traction in neoliberal social rationalities; to return to them may be part of a strategy of interrupting the neoliberal fungibility machine.
16. Dean, *Beyond Sexuality*, 70. Hereafter cited parenthetically as BS in this chapter.
17. Once more, I must emphasize my omission of trans* scholarship on gender from this discussion. First, while Dean's reading of transgender embodiment and identification is somewhat dated by now, his fundamental attempt to think it through the register of the real still seems quite worthwhile (and missing in contemporary trans* studies scholarship). Second, as is clear in the following section, I am focusing on contemporary mainstream US culture, where gender-as-accessory seems to reign; this is clearly a different concept of gender than the one under examination in trans* scholarship, activism, and communities. For a particularly incisive articulation of the resistance that the *soma* in trans* politics and embodiments presents to this neoliberal "playing" with gender, see Draz, *Transitional Subjects*.
18. Todd, "Is the Metrosexual Finally Dead?"

19. McRobbie, "Feminism and the Third Way," 103. The line of argument I am parodying here is most directly articulated by Janet Halley's calls for queer theorists, especially, to "take a break from feminism." For a thorough and incisive argument against Halley, see Huffer, *Are the Lips a Grave?*, chap. 1.
20. Simpson, "Meet the Metrosexual."
21. In his interview with himself in January 2004, "MetroDaddy Speaks!," Simpson writes: "Do metrosexuals have to be wealthy or middle class? This is a common fallacy, partly based on the idea that working-class equals authentic and middle-class equals inauthentic. It's actually a matter of spending priorities. Most metrosexuals in Britain, for example, are probably working class. David Beckham, like most of his male fans, is from a working-class family; he may have rather more money than most and get his togs for free, but this just means that he's been able to continue his metrosexuality longer and on a larger, more frightening scale than most working-class men." www.salon.com/2004/01/05/metrosexual_ii/.
22. For brief discussions of this widespread and persistent phenomenon, see Davis, *The Meaning of Freedom*, 47, and Thomas, "Soul," where he explains how the defiance of spending the equivalence of an entire month's rent on a pair of Nike Air Jordans is "the essence of Black cool" in poor communities (99–101).

INTERLUDE 4: THE BIRTH OF COOL

1. Carr, *Miles Davis*, 209.
2. This is how he describes his own impact in a nasty story he tells in his autobiography, *Miles*, of a horrible evening with ignorant white elites at a (Reagan) White House dinner for Ray Charles in 1984. Many critics concur with the impact; see, for example, both Blumenthal and Giddens in Kirchner, *A Miles Davis Reader*; and Palmer, "Miles Davis."
3. Kirchner, *A Miles Davis Reader*, 16.
4. Davis, *Miles: The Autobiography*, 59. Hereafter cited parenthetically in the text as M.
5. He does, however, see it as a damaging effect of internalized racism. As he puts it, "I wanted to see what was going on in all of music. Knowledge is freedom and ignorance is slavery, and I just couldn't believe someone could be that close to freedom and not take advantage of it. I have never understood why black people didn't take advantage of all the shit that they can. It's like a ghetto mentality telling people that they aren't supposed to do certain things, that those things are only reserved for white people. When I would tell other musicians about all this, they would just kind of shine me on. You know what I mean? So I just went my own way and stopped telling them about it" (M, 61).
6. Here's one example of how Miles understood musical creativity as first and foremost a collaborative undertaking, no matter the shared vocabularies involved:

"It was Dizzy who made me really learn how to play piano. I'd be over there watching Monk doing his weird shit with space and progressive chords. And when Dizzy would practice, man, I would be soaking up all that good shit. But then again, I showed Diz something that I'd learned at Juilliard, the Egyptian minor scales. With the Egyptian scale you just change the flats and sharps where you want the note flatted and where you want it sharp, so you have two flats and one sharp, right? That means you will play E flat and A flat and then the F will be sharp. You put in the note that you want, like in the C scale's minor Egyptian scale. The shit looks funny because you have two flats and a sharp. But it gives you the freedom to work with melodic ideas without changing the basic tonality. So I turned Dizzy on to that: it worked both ways. But I learned way more from him than he did from me" (M, 64).

7. Kirchner, *A Miles Davis Reader*, 66. Baraka was not alone in this kind of assessment. See, for example, Lhamon in Kirchner, *A Miles Davis Reader*, for an analysis of Davis as capturing the zeitgeist of the 1950s that he also locates in literature, poetry, painting, and photography—as well as in the nascent events and political consciousness of the Civil Rights Movement.
8. While mainstream white culture predictably tried to call this a form of racism, Miles never took that bigoted bait. Moreover, his long-standing friendship and collaboration with Gil Evans always served as an easy defense against such ignorant charges. For examples of his consistent critique of racism and commitment to the black community, see especially the *Rolling Stone* interview in 1969, the *Saturday Review* interview in 1971, and the *Jazz Magazine* interview in 1976, all collected in *A Miles Davis Reader*.
9. After beating his heroin addiction in 1954 and going relatively clean for fifteen years (he claimed to be a vegetarian, nonsmoker, and drinker in his interview with *Rolling Stone* in 1969), Miles fell in love with cocaine and struggled with various forms of substance abuse throughout the last two decades of his life. Michael Ullman calls his love for fashion and cars "one of most flamboyant lifestyles in the business. . . . A family of four could survive for a year on what he spent on sunglasses." Kirchner, *A Miles Davis Reader*, 13.
10. Every time I mentioned writing on Miles Davis to a black woman, she responded, "Have you read *Mad at Miles*?" Pearl Cleage persuasively argues that we must stop idolizing cool black men who are domestically violent. Using Miles's offhanded stories about "slapping the shit" out of Cicely Tyson, Cleage frames Miles as the exemplar of black masculinity not taking sexist violence seriously as a systematic problem of black culture and communities. Accordingly, she entices us to join her in a repeated mantra of denouncing Miles as "guilty of self-confessed violent crimes against women such that we should break his albums, burn his tapes and scratch up his CDs until he acknowledges and apologizes and agrees to rethink his position on The Woman Question." Cleage, *Mad at Miles*, 13, 14, 17, 18, 19. It is a passionate call never to ignore violence of any kind,

including the domestic sort that stains so many relationships and households across all racial boundaries.

5. READING RACE AS THE REAL: THE SECURITIES AND PUNISHMENTS OF NEOLIBERAL COOL

1. See Dean, *Beyond Sexuality*, 99–102, for a discussion of this mantra in Lacan's seminar and all of chapter 3 for Dean's provocative reading, through this insight, of the social function of AIDS in the United States.
2. Ibid., 86.
3. Dean largely reads race, like gender, as existing in the imaginary realm of identification. My crucial point of departure from his work is to insist here and in chapter 6 that we must read, especially in the United States, race as the real.
4. See the classic work, for example, of Davis, *Women, Race, and Class*; hooks, *Ain't I a Woman?*; hooks, *Feminist Theory*; and hooks, *Yearning*; and Spillers, *Black, White and in Color.*
5. Spillers, "Mama's Baby, Papa's Maybe," 206. Hereafter cited parenthetically in the text as MBPM.
6. Bersani, "Is the Rectum a Grave?," 215, 218.
7. See, for example, his graphic representation in seminar 11 that emphasizes the erogenous zone as an orifice: Lacan, *Four Fundamental Concepts*, 178. See also his famous explanation that distinguishes the circuit of the drive from the linearity of desire by a fundamental indifference to the object: "Even when you stuff the mouth—the mouth that opens in the register of the drive—it is not the food that satisfies it, it is, as one says, the pleasure of the mouth." Ibid., 167.
8. See especially Lacan, "The Deconstruction of the Drive" and "The Partial Drive and Its Circuit" in *Four Fundamental Concepts.*
9. This is also how, in a distinctly Foucaultian framework, Lynne Huffer challenges and extends Bersani's work into a feminist, queer ethics of eros that pivots on processes of desubjectivation. See Huffer, *Are the Lips a Grave?*, 27–49.
10. I am following Dean's critique of the Slovenian school for insufficient attention to sexuality here. See Dean, *Beyond Sexuality*, 19.
11. The parallel reductions and discountings are instructive: the Slovenians valorize proletarianization and discount race (for example, Jodi Dean in *The Communist Horizon*), whereas Tim Dean valorizes sexuality and discounts gender. I agree with Tim Dean, but lament the omission of race and argue that his account is still operating out of an exclusively liberal, not neoliberal, episteme; I disagree with Jodi Dean and insist that we must read race as the real. It is also important to note here that Lynne Huffer argues, in a Foucaultian lexicon, against the distinctly US reading of identity into Foucault's accounts of subjectivity, especially as they are taken up by "gay/lesbian" politics, thereby agreeing with the constraints of identity politics. Huffer, *Mad for Foucault*, 67–80.

12. Given the powerful forces of transnational capital as well as the wide legacy of colonialism, this arguably extends beyond any literal borders of the United States.
13. I have in mind most of the "foundational" texts of this field of scholarship: Muñoz, *Disidentifications*; Ferguson, *Aberrations in Black*; Puar, *Terrorist Assemblages*; and, more recently, Shah, *Stranger Intimacy*; Hong and Ferguson, *Strange Affinities*; and Reddy, *Freedom with Violence*.
14. Hall, "Race."
15. See Cacho, *Social Death*, esp. 20–23, for a discussion of the ways "impoverished African American citizens' consumption patterns are under constant scrutiny" (21) and how this feeds the criminalizing of people of color and the decriminalizing of unlawful corporate behavior.
16. For example, in addition to long-standing markets for home and community security devices, including the kinds of self-policing organizations that George Zimmerman volunteered for, I am also thinking of advertisements for credit cards via "security" (for example, American Express commercials airing in August 2013).
17. I cite data that the #BlackLivesMatter movement has put into global circulation since I first drafted this manuscript. In "Operation Ghetto Storm: 2012 Annual Report on the Extrajudicial Killings of 313 Black People by Police, Security Guards and Vigilantes," Arlene Eisen, of the Malcolm X Grassroots Movement (MXGM), found that 313 unarmed African Americans were killed by police, security guards, and self-appointed vigilantes in 2012. Overall, one black person was killed in an extrajudicial shooting every twenty-eight hours; in December 2014, activists are debating whether that ratio might now be once every twenty-four hours. See report at http://mxgm.org/operation-ghetto-storm-2012-annual-report-on-the-extrajudicial-killing-of-313-black-people. Trayvon Martin is in the list of "Memorial Pages" in report.
18. See Fry and Taylor, "A Rise in Wealth for the Wealthy; Declines for the Lower 93%," on the increase in wealth of the wealthy since the economic crisis in 2008. In the Great Recession of 2009–2011, the upper 7 percent of wealth distribution rose by 28 percent, while the lower 93 percent fell 4 percent. In dynamics that I explore regarding the racialized character of this accelerating wealth gap, the report analyzes how these disparities are caused by robust rebounds in financial markets, where the wealthiest locate their wealth, in contrast to the failing housing market, where the other 93 percent of the population ground the majority of their wealth assets. The report also explains that its data is restricted by its source, the US Census Bureau, and its demarcation of wealth categories; this helps to explain why it uses 7 percent and 93 percent rather than the more popularized (and catchy) 1 percent and 99 percent. See also Saez, "Striking it Richer," which I discuss in note 30.
19. Dimock, Kiley, and Suls, "King's Dream Remains an Elusive Goal."
20. Ibid.

21. Shapiro, Meschede, and Osoro, "The Roots of the Widening Racial Wealth Gap," 1.
22. Ibid.
23. See, for example, the film *Inequality for All*, in which Robert Reich, Clinton's labor secretary, shows how the levels of income inequality in 2007 matched those of 1928.
24. Fergus, "The Ghetto Tax," 279.
25. See ibid., 278. Fergus analyzes the auto insurance industry in California from 1986 to 2000 as an exemplar of a market's development and enforcement of a ghetto tax. Despite the passage of legislation (Proposition 103 in 1988) to render zip code redlining illegal, the auto insurance industry managed—through threatened boycotts and lobbyist manipulation directly tied to the blockage of campaign finance reform—not only to continue but also to intensify the practice. As Fergus concludes his essay, "In America, one's ZIP code may be used by local governments to apportion tax dollars (for example, for public education, rather than according to a parent's income); and despite the outlawing of racial redlining, banks and other members of the financial services industry still deny or charge extra for loans, credit, and insurance premiums to households in low-income or working-class neighborhoods as delineated by their ZIP codes." Ibid., "The Ghetto Tax," 306.
26. As Carolina Reid explains, "redlining" refers to the "residential security maps" that the Home Owner's Loan Corporation (HOLC) developed to advise real estate appraisers of "adverse influences" related to a property, including the presence of "inharmonious racial groups" in the neighborhood. As Reid explains, "The maps, which outlined minority neighborhoods in red, identified areas that were deemed 'too risky' to receive FHA financing." Reid, "Wealth Inequality," 78. The federal laws passed to address these inequalities include the Fair Housing Act (Title VIII of the Civil Rights Act of 1968), the Equal Credit Opportunity Act of 1974, the Home Mortgage Disclosure Act (HMDA) of 1975, and the Community Reinvestment Act (CRA) in 1977.
27. Ibid., 79.
28. Fergus calls these the "Step Acts to Deregulation," echoing the Step Acts to *Brown v. Board of Education*: Depository Institutions Deregulation and Monetary Control Act of 1980; Garn-St. Germain Depository Institutions Act of 1982; Tax Reform Act of 1986. Unpublished paper, presented at Ohio State University, November 18, 2011.
29. Fergus calculates that the racialized character of the subprime mortgage market of the late 1990s and early 2000s resulted in blacks receiving 3.5 times as many subprime mortgages as whites and Latinos receiving twice as many as whites. Unpublished paper, presented at Ohio State University, November 18, 2011. See also Reid, "Wealth Inequality," 80, for her details on this data.
30. Emmanuel Saez, an economist at UC Berkeley, has been tracking this since 2008 and is amassing information back to what he calls the "Clinton Expansion" in

1993. See "Striking it Richer," http://elsa.berkeley.edu/~saez/saez-UStopincomes-2012.pdf. Of all the unnerving data, perhaps the most astonishing is the gap between the real growth in income since 2009: 99 percent of the United States has seen a growth of 0.4 percent, while the wealthiest 1 percent of the United States has seen a growth of 95 percent.

31. Unpublished paper, presented at Ohio State University, November 18, 2011.
32. Since titled "A More Perfect Union" and granted its own website, this speech continues to garner much discussion. I do not pretend to do that discussion justice here. I am merely using this speech as exemplary of the kind of internalizing of neoliberal social rationalities and the barometer of class mobility. Hailed as the global public figure of a new postracial era, Obama embodies the neoliberal forms of racialization in unique manners. See http://constitutioncenter.org/amoreperfectunion. It is particularly telling that Obama is sometimes called "the cool President," a moniker that captures precisely the lingering anxiety about race in this celebratory "postracial" era. See Reed, "The President of the Cool."
33. The impetus for this "second speech on race" was the acquittal of George Zimmerman, the man who murdered Trayvon Martin. While Obama spoke more personally in this speech, suggesting that he could have been Trayvon Martin and locating his murder in the long history of violence and racial profiling against black men, he still concludes with three classically liberal responses: (1) the need to educate law enforcement on racial profiling, including better data collection; (2) a need to revisit "Stand Your Ground" laws; and (3) yet again, the ongoing work of "perfecting the nation," claiming that his daughters' generation is better on race and racism than his generation. As I noted in the introduction, Obama has since given several more statements and interviews responding to the protests to the failure to indict the police officers who killed Michael Brown, John Crawford, and Eric Garner. Each of these includes his identification with young black men, rendering his otherwise classically liberal response ambivalent.
34. In "Race-ing Homonormativity: Citizenship, Sociology and Gay Identity," Roderick Ferguson argues that homosexuality becomes normalized through the privatizing schemas of citizenship, just as Marx shows that religious difference is also normalized through privatization. Ferguson examines the sociological construction of ethnicity as a socially constructed category—as opposed to race as a biological category—as serving these privatizing schemas.
35. Or what Žižek, tellingly, calls "that kernel of jouissance" in "Love Thy Neighbor? No, Thanks!"
36. See Sullivan, *Good White People*, esp. chap. 1, for a compelling analysis of how "good white middle-class liberals" disavow all explicit forms of racism and bigotry by projecting it onto "white trash," who are always characterized as ignorant and thus caught in eras long past.

37. For one of the most incisive and direct performances of "the hoodie" as absurd racial profiling, see the video produced by Howard University, "Am I Suspicious?," March 25, 2012, www.youtube.com/watch?v=rH5bB8HUWFs.
38. There is much more to say about how and when and where the neoliberal intensification of liberalism tears open, exposing the precious *objet a* of xenophobia without a symbolic apparatus sufficient to sublate it. I emphasize three registers here: (1) the recathecting to racism through the classic position of disavowal, which lays at the heart of the fantasy of tolerance; (2) the condemnation of racism as an archaic historical hangover, enacting the "new" syntax of progress as diversity; (3) the remarkably clever and enjoyable aestheticizing of difference, which we can all simply purchase and don.
39. Foundational texts on the carceral state include Davis, *Are Prisons Obsolete?* and *Abolition Democracy*; Gilmore, *The Golden Gulag*; Roberts, *Killing the Black Body*; and Wacquant, "From Slavery to Mass Incarceration." Foundational texts on the queer critique of homonormativity and homonationalism include Warner, *Fear of a Queer Planet*; Duggan, *The Twilight of Equality*; and Puar, *Terrorist Assemblages*.
40. Winnubst, *Queering Freedom*, 202.
41. The first answer to this question is direct and simple: white supremacy. To be clear: I am arguing that the neoliberal episteme keeps the historical schematic of white supremacy that it overlays in liberalism structurally intact. But since it strips us of a vocabulary for such speech, I am interested in finding new ways to speak of this. The answer "white supremacy" falls on deaf ears, cast back into that long-ago time when the bigots were also still live. Neoliberalism conquered white supremacy with diversity: good color-blind neoliberals cannot speak or hear or understand the meaning of calling this out as the ongoing victory of white supremacy. I return to this in chapter 6 as a call to move beyond identity categories in our thinking about race.
42. Again, this concept of gender changes immensely when taken up through the axis of trans* scholarship, activism, and communities.
43. I thank Kimberly Springer for immediately seeing this unnerving connection. Data for total number of persons incarcerated in the United States after 2011 is not yet available; therefore, my flatlined depiction at seven million is likely an undercounting. The following are the sources for various data included in this chart. For total numbers of persons incarcerated in United States: Sourcebook of Criminal Justice Statistics Online, table 6.1.2011, www.albany.edu/sourcebook. For legalization of same-sex marriage: www.gaymarriage.procon.org (I listed Hawaii, Vermont, and California at the times of their respective initial legalization, rather than the final legalization as of 2013). For estimates of state populations: www.quickfacts.census.gov and www.worldpopulationstatistics.com.
44. Harcourt, *The Illusion of the Markets*, 52. Hereafter cited parenthetically in the text as IM.

45. Alexander, *The New Jim Crow*, 9.
46. See Rodolphe Gasché's remarkable book on Bataille (Gasché, *Georges Bataille*) for a discussion of Schelling's *katabole* as a kind of destructive opening that grounds all epistemologies of representation. Related to the twentieth-century meanings of the metabolic function (catabolism) whereby molecules are destroyed and release energy to the organism, the *katabole* signifies the endless movement of an energy that must expend itself and, in so doing, render all formations unstable.

INTERLUDE 5: REAL COOL, NOW

1. In honor of the 2010 World Cup, Puma commissioned Wiley to paint four portraits of prominent African football players—a partnership that Wiley called, "a perfect marriage," especially because it focuses on the joy of Africa. See www.youtube.com/watch?v=NwNbQR_yIn8. Patterns from his paintings were incorporated into Puma athletic gear. The complete series, *Legends of Unity: World Cup 2010*, was exhibited in early 2010 at Deitch Projects in New York City.
2. Robert Mapplethorpe's hugely controversial *The Black Book* (published in 1988), for example, is part of an emergent vocabulary that turns to this asignifying phenomenon, blackness. The work of Kobena Mercer and Stuart Hall and a return to Frantz Fanon also follow out this trajectory. Wiley himself often positions his work in the lineage set forth by Thelma Golden's curating of the exhibit *The Black Male* in 1994. (It was Golden who selected Wiley to work at the Harlem Museum in 2001 after his MFA at Yale.) There are, unsurprisingly, many contemporary artists pursuing this vexed and vexing subject in a wide array of manners and inflections: Glenn Ligon, Adrian Piper, Kara Walker, and Carrie Mae Weems, among others.
3. See especially Wiley's interview with C. C. H. Pounder during his exhibit *The World Stage: Israel* at the Jewish Museum in New York City: www.youtube.com/watch?v=XluSaO8P_qA. See also his interview with *Bad at Sports*: "Interview with Kehinde Wiley," www.artpractical.com/column/interview_with_kehinde_wiley/.

6. STOP MAKING SENSE: THE APORIA OF RACE AND ETHICS

1. Additionally, by trying to reconceptualize race away from identity categories in a manner that insists on the persistence of racism, I offer a kind of end run around some of the "category fatigue" that plagues intersectional analyses, while still committed to the spirit of intersectionality.
2. Ligon, *Yourself in the World*, 43.
3. In the 1962–63 seminar that I turn to at length, Lacan situates embarrassment—or what I am also calling shame—in the same neighborhood as anxiety. In this vein, to fear the shame of being called out as a racist signals something decid-

edly different from being caught as guilty for actually being a racist. While the classically liberal lexicon might read this as a split between private and public, whereby we allow ourselves to harbor all kinds of racist convictions privately so long as they do not become public, I want to follow out a Lacanian reading that exposes different dynamics about the blocking of history at work in the neoliberal anxiety around race.

4. I invoke the house of mirrors to place this in the vicious space of ideology, shorn of a symbolic, that I elaborated in chapter 2. For example, thinking of the kinds of debates spurred by the killing of Jordan Davis or of Trayvon Martin (prior to the emergence of #BlackLivesMatter in the fall of 2014), I easily read the inability to recognize racism along identity fault lines, with whites on one side and people of color on the other. This is the ideological house of mirrors, where whites cannot see racism at all in anything, people of color can only see racism in everything, and a clearly racist act becomes a site of contention that goes unpunished in the legal system. This ideological problem calls for political intervention that is itself restricted to the ideological house of mirrors. The kind of analysis I am advancing cuts to the ethical question of how this profound inability to recognize (which is different from the *meconnaissance* of signification, as I will develop) that lies at the heart of the ideological confusion came into being at all.
5. Lacan, *Anxiety*, 173. Hereafter cited parenthetically in the text as A.
6. Lacan, *The Ego in Freud's Theory*, 164.
7. This does not mean that we are not developing new ways to speak of this history; it means that the old language of explicit racism is fading with the eclipsed symbolic. For example, scholarship in both Afro-pessimism and decolonial feminism is developing very interesting new manners of language; I am sadly too new to this scholarship to elaborate these connections here.
8. This distance from the structure of desire leads Lacan to dismiss existentialist accounts of anxiety from the outset, especially those of Kierkegaard, Sartre, and Heidegger. He insists, however, that anxiety is an affect and thereby offers a snapshot of a desubjectified account of affect: "It's unfastened, it drifts about. It can be found displaced, maddened, inverted, or metabolized" (A, 14).
9. Evans, *An Introductory Dictionary*, 12.
10. This kind of approach to anxiety and trauma spins the swirling debates of 2014 about "trigger warnings" in university classrooms, especially feminist classrooms, into considerably different registers.
11. See Dean, *Beyond Sexuality*, 7, for Tim Dean's elaboration of Lacan's writing on the unconscious as "the censored chapter."
12. Lacan, *Four Fundamental Concepts*, 41.
13. Many social theorists have turned to an ethics of the real in recent years, particularly under the influence of Alain Badiou and Slavoj Žižek, two suspiciously cool male theorists. To rehearse those scholarly debates and dialogues would involve a book-length study that outstrips the scope of my final meditation on

ethics. Taking this emergent trend as a common point of departure, however, substantiates my belief that a Lacanian lexicon of the real speaks effectively to many of the sociopsychic transformations underway in the neoliberal episteme. In my final turn to articulate an ethics of the real as an ethics of racialized justice in the United States, I draw particularly on the work of Alenka Zupančič and Tim Dean.

14. Zupančič, *Ethics of the Real*, 3. Hereafter cited parenthetically in the text as ER.
15. See ER, 236, and Žižek, *Welcome to the Desert of the Real*, on how making the real an object turns it into a strange desire for catastrophe and terror.
16. By suggesting that we can attune ourselves to these effects, I hope to resignify the Heideggerian roots of this term to capture a process of consciously retraining unconscious habits of response. I am, however, still frustrated with this formulation and hope to research atonality as a better formulation in future projects.
17. Hollywood, *Sensible Ecstasy*, 65. For a longer discussion of Hollywood and Zupančič, as well as of Lacan in relation to Bataille, see Winnubst, "Sacrifice as Ethics." Recuperative narratives continue to dominate cultural representations of chattel slavery, such as the recent film *Twelve Years a Slave*, and settler colonialism. This resistance to recuperative narratives also structures Ann Cvetkovich's project of reclaiming cultural expressions of trauma and depression as sites of meaning, rather than as in need of salvation; see Cvetkovich, *An Archive of Feelings*, and Cvetkovich, *Depression*.
18. See Dean, "The Biopolitics of Pleasure," for a provocative reading of Foucault's understanding of pleasure, especially in *History of Sexuality*, volume 2, as an enactment of *jouissance*. In this vein, *jouissance* is clearly that which has to be suppressed in lesbian and gay communities for same-sex marriage to be legalized and thus animates most queer critiques of homonormativity.
19. For a reading of *jouissance* as at the heart of racism as configured through the Other, see Žižek, "Love Thy Neighbor? No, Thanks!"
20. I argued this explicitly in the register of nightmares and anxiety, albeit not in their Lacanian iterations, in Winnubst, "Vampires, Anxieties and Dreams."
21. I call them denizens, rather than citizens, to emphasize the racialized limits to citizenship afforded residents of New Orleans. Before abolition, "denizen" connoted "a free Negro" who had rights somewhere between those of a full citizen and those of a resident alien.
22. See Žižek, *First as Tragedy, Second as Farce*, 53–54.
23. CBSNEWS.com, "Katrina Victims Are Buried, 3 Years After," August 28, 2008, www.cbsnews.com/news/katrina-victims-are-buried-3-years-after.
24. "Displaced by Katrina, Most Stay Near: Poor Evacuees Found Settling Farther Away," *Boston Globe*, December 18, 2005, www.boston.com/news/nation/articles/2005/12/18/displaced_by_katrina_most_stay_near/?page=full.
25. See PolicyLink: www.policylink.org/site/c.lkIXLbMNJrE/b.5160103/k.6C6A/New_Orleans_and_Gulf_Coast__Overview.htm.

26. The argument that Hurricane Katrina was largely human-made, due to the effects of global climate change and the local negligence of levees, is widely known and accepted by now. See Adams, *Markets of Sorrow, Labors of Faith*, and Johnson, *The Neoliberal Deluge*, for a wide range of excellent analyses and overviews of this extensive scholarship.
27. In *After the Deluge*, Walker curated images from the vast Metropolitan Museum archive of eighteenth- and nineteenth-century paintings to show how the white European and American imaginary has consistently scripted the ocean, which is either fearsomely beyond control or conquered for smooth commerce, in a metonymic relation with the powerful black body. From these historical images, Walker then pairs her infamous cut-outs with iconic images from media representations of Katrina to show how two iconic options emerge for the white imaginary's confrontation with Katrina: the happy-go-lucky, if also pitiful and pathetic, "Aunt Jemima" figure, who is portrayed as both so dumb and so passive that she cannot help but resign herself to *her natural condition* of being at the whim of the raging waters; and the conniving, threatening "Coon," violent and hypersexualized, that was the Katrina looter (and quickly a spoofed "beer looter" across various media). For an incisive reading of the racist media representations of the looter images, as well as the labels of refugee/evacuee, the neoliberal rewriting of Katrina as offering "a clean sheet" for enterprise, and the need for comparative racialization analytics, see Cacho, *Social Death*, esp. the introduction.
28. Reports of widespread looting, street gangs, and rape filled the airwaves as the nightmare of a Superdome ill-equipped to house so many bodies for so long unfolded. The reports became self-fulfilling racist fantasies, as evacuation and medical relief workers began to shut down services due to fears of the violence. For Slavoj Žižek's analysis of these lies and their material effects, see Žižek, "The Subject Supposed to Loot and Rape," http://inthesetimes.com/article/2361/the_subject_supposed_to_loot_and_rape.
29. As Freud explains in his essay "Fetishism," the role of the fetish is to protect the little boy from the fear of castration upon encountering his mother's infamous "horror of nothing to see." To heal this splitting of his subjectivity between a horrified threat and an adamant disavowal, the boy creates a fetish to function as a compromise between the two conflicting poles. The function of the fetish is to memorialize the horrifying threat of castration, while ensuring the boy's victory over it: as Freud tells us, "[The fetish] remains a token of triumph over the threat of castration and a protection against it." Freud, "Fetishism," 154. Reenacting the conquering of the threat in every act of fetishism, the fetish enlivens the memory trace of a vanquished threat.

BIBLIOGRAPHY

Adams, Vincanne. *Markets of Sorrow, Labors of Faith*. Durham: Duke University Press, 2013.

Agamben, Giorgio. *Homo Sacer: Sovereign Power and Bare Life*. Stanford: Stanford University Press, 1998.

Alarcón, Norma. "The Theoretical Subject(s) of *This Bridge Called My Back* and Anglo-American Feminism." In *The Second Wave: A Reader in Feminist Theory*, edited by Linda Nicholson, 288–317. New York: Routledge, 1997.

Alexander, Michelle. *The New Jim Crow: Mass Incarceration in the Age of Colorblindness*. New York: New Press, 2010.

Alexander, M. Jacqui, and Chandra Talpade Mohanty, eds. *Feminist Genealogies, Colonial Legacies, Democratic Futures*. New York: Routledge, 1996.

Althusser, Louis. *Lenin and Philosophy, and Other Essays*. New York: Monthly Review Press, 1971.

Bataille, Georges. *The Accursed Share*. Vol. 1. Translated by Robert Hurley. New York: Zone Books, 1991.

Becker, Gary S. *Human Capital: A Theoretical and Empirical Analysis with Special Reference to Education*. Chicago: University of Chicago Press, 1964.

Berlant, Lauren. *Cruel Optimism*. Durham: Duke University Press, 2011.

Bersani, Leo. "Is the Rectum a Grave?" *October* 43 (1987): 197–222.

Bowers, Keith. "At Last: *American Hipster* Kills Hipsterism Dead." *SFWeekly* blog, March 15, 2002. http://blogs.sfweekly.com/exhibitionist/2012/03/at_last_american_hipster_kills.php.

Brown, Wendy. *Edgework: Critical Essays on Knowledge and Politics*. Princeton: Princeton University Press, 2005.

——. *Regulating Aversion: Tolerance in the Age of Identity and Empire*. Princeton: Princeton University Press, 2006.

Butler, Judith. *Gender Trouble: Feminism and the Subversion of Identity*. New York: Routledge, 1989.

——. *Precarious Lives: The Powers of Mourning and Violence*. New York: Verso, 2006.

Cabezas, Amelia L., Ellen Reese, and Marguerite Waller, eds. *The Wages of Empire: Neoliberal Policies, Repression, and Women's Poverty*. Boulder, Colo.: Paradigm, 2007.

Cacho, Lisa Marie. *Social Death: Racialized Rightlessness and the Criminalization of the Unprotected*. New York: New York University Press, 2012.

Calderon, Hector, and Jose David Salvidar, eds. *Criticism in the Borderlands: Studies in Chicano Literature, Culture and Ideology*. Durham: Duke University Press, 1991.

Camoroff, Joan, and John L. Camoroff. *Millennial Capitalism and the Culture of Neoliberalism*. Durham: Duke University Press, 2001.

Carr, Ian. *Miles Davis: A Critical Biography*. New York: Quartet Books, 1982.

Chaiken, Jennifer, Sebastian Dungan, Jacob Kornbluth, Robert B. Reich, Svetlana Cvetko, Dan Krauss, Marco D'Ambrosio, and Robert B. Reich. *Inequality for All*. 72 Productions: San Francisco and Los Angeles, 2014.

Cherniavsky, Eva. "Neocitizenship and Critique." *Social Text* 99 27, no. 2 (2009): 1–23.

Clare, Eli. *Exile and Pride: Disability, Queerness and Liberation*. New York: South End Press, 1999.

Cleage, Pearl. *Mad at Miles: A Blackwoman's Guide to Truth*. Southfield, Mich.: Cleage Group, 1990.

Copjec, Joan. *Read My Desire: Lacan Against the Historicists*. Cambridge, Mass.: MIT Press, 1994.

Crenshaw, Kimberlé. "Demarginalizing the Intersection of Race and Sex: A Black Feminist Critique of Antidiscrimination Doctrine, Feminist Theory, and Anti-Racist Politics." *University of Chicago Legal Forum* (1989): 139–67.

——. "Mapping the Margins: Intersectionality, Identity Politics, and Violence Against Women of Color." *Stanford Law Review* 43 (1991): 1241–99.

Cvetkovich, Ann. *An Archive of Feelings: Trauma, Sexuality, and Lesbian Public Cultures*. Durham: Duke University Press, 2003.

——. *Depression: A Public Feeling*. Durham: Duke University Press, 2012.

Davis, Angela. *Abolition Democracy: Beyond Empire, Prisons and Torture*. New York: Seven Stories, 2005.

——. *Are Prisons Obsolete?* New York: Seven Stories, 2003.

——. *The Meaning of Freedom, and Other Difficult Dialogues*. San Francisco: City Lights, 2012.

——. *Women, Race, and Class*. New York: Vintage, 1983.

Davis, Miles. *Miles: The Autobiography*. New York: Simon and Schuster, 1990.

Dean, Jodi. *The Communist Horizon*. Brooklyn: Verso, 2012.

——. *Democracy and Other Neoliberal Fantasies: Communicative Capitalism and Left Politics*. Durham: Duke University Press, 2009.

——. "Drive as the Structure of Biopolitics: Economy, Sovereignty, and Capture." *Krisis: A Journal for Contemporary Philosophy* 2 (2010): 2–15.

——. "Enjoying Neoliberalism." *Cultural Politics* 4, no. 1 (2008): 47–72.

Dean, Tim. *Beyond Sexuality*. Chicago: University of Chicago Press, 2000.

——. "The Biopolitics of Pleasure." *South Atlantic Quarterly* 111, no. 13 (2012): 477–96.

——. *Unlimited Intimacy: Reflections on the Subculture of Barebacking*. Chicago: University of Chicago Press, 2009.

Delaney, Samuel. *Times Square Red: Times Square Blue*. New York: New York University Press, 1999.

Dilts, Andrew. "From 'Entrepreneur of the Self' to 'Care of the Self': Neo-Liberal Governmentality and Foucault's Ethics." *Foucault Studies* 12 (2011): 130–46.

Dimock, Michael, Jocelyn Kiley, and Rob Suls. "King's Dream Remains an Elusive Goal; Many Americans See Racial Disparities." Pew Research Center, Washington, DC. August 22, 2013. www.pewsocialtrends.org/2013/08/22/kings-dream-remains-an-elusive-goal-many-americans-see-racial-disparities/.

Draz, Marie. *Transitional Subjects: Gender, Race, and the Politics of Temporality*. PhD diss., DePaul University, 2014.

Duggan, Lisa. *The Twilight of Equality? Neoliberalism, Cultural Politics, and the Attack on Democracy*. Boston: Beacon, 2003.

Dworkin, Ronald. *Justice for Hedgehogs*. Cambridge, Mass.: Harvard University Press, 2011.

Ehrenreich, Barbara, and Arlie Russell Hochschild, eds. *Global Woman: Nannies, Maids, and Sex Workers in the New Economy*. New York: Owl Books, 2002.

Eisen, Arlene. *Operation Ghetto Storm: 2012 Annual Report on the Extrajudicial Killings of 313 Black People by Police, Security Guards, and Vigilantes*. April 28, 2013. http://mxgm.org/operation-ghetto-storm-2012-annual-report-on-the-extrajudicial-killing-of-313-black-people/.

Esposito, Roberto. *Bios: Biopolitics, and Philosophy*. Translated by Timothy Campbell. Minneapolis: University of Minnesota, 2008.

Evans, Dylan. *An Introductory Dictionary of Lacanian Psychoanalysis*. New York: Routledge, 1996.

Fergus, Devon. "The Ghetto Tax: Auto Insurance, Postal Code Profiling, and the Hidden History of Wealth Transfer." In *Beyond Discrimination: Racial Inequality in a Post-Racist Era*, edited by Frederick C. Harris and Robert C. Lieberman, 277–316. New York: Russell Sage Foundation, 2013.

Ferguson, Roderick. *Aberrations in Black: Toward a Queer of Color Critique*. Minneapolis: University of Minnesota Press, 2003.

——. "Race-ing Homonormativity: Citizenship, Sociology and Gay Identity." In *Black Queer Studies: A Critical Anthology*, edited by Patrick E. Johnson and Mae G. Henderson, 52–67. Durham: Duke University Press, 2005.

——. "Reading Intersectionality." *Trans-Scripts* 2 (2012): 91–99.

Fink, Bruce. *The Lacanian Subject: Between Language and Jouissance*. Princeton: Princeton University Press, 1995.

Floyd, Kevin. *The Reification of Desire: Towards a Queer Marxism*. Minneapolis: University of Minnesota Press, 2009.

Foucault, Michel. *The Birth of Biopolitics: Lectures at the Collège de France, 1978–79*. Translated by Graham Burchell. New York: Palgrave MacMillan, 2008.

——. "Discourse on Language." In *The Archeology of Knowledge and the Discourse on Language*. Translated by A. M. Sheridan Smith. New York: Pantheon, 1971.

——. *History of Sexuality*. Vol. 1, *An Introduction*. Translated by Robert Hurley. New York: Vintage, 1990.

——. "Truth and Power." In *Power/Knowledge: Selected Interviews, and Other Writings, 1972–1977*, edited by Colin Gordon. New York: Harvester, 1980.

Fraiman, Susan. *Cool Men and the Second Sex*. New York: Columbia University Press, 2003.

Frank, Tom. *The Conquest of Cool: Business Culture, Counterculture, and the Rise of Hip Consumerism*. Chicago: University of Chicago Press, 1997.

Freeman, Carla. "The 'Reputation' of Neoliberalism." *American Ethnologist* 34, no. 2 (2007): 252–67.

Freud, Sigmund. "Beyond the Pleasure Principle." In *Standard Edition of the Complete Psychological Works*, vol. 18, translated by James Strachey. London: Hogarth Press, 1986.

——. "Fetishism." In *Standard Edition of the Complete Psychological Works*, vol. 21, translated by James Strachey. London: Hogarth Press, 1986.

Friedman, Milton. *Capitalism and Freedom*. Chicago: University of Chicago Press, 1962.

Fry, Richard, and Paul Taylor. "A Rise in Wealth for the Wealthy; Declines for the Lower 93%: An Uneven Recovery, 2009–2011." *Pew Research: Social and Demographic Trends*. April 23, 2013. www.pewsocialtrends.org/2013/04/23/a-rise-in-wealth-for-the-wealthydeclines-for-the-lower-93/.

Fukuyama, Francis. *The End of History and the Last Man*. New York: Free Press, 1992.

Gasché, Rodolphe. *Georges Bataille: Phenomenology and Phantasmology*. Translated Roland Vesgo. Stanford: Stanford University Press, 2012.

Gilmore, Ruth. *The Golden Gulag: Prisons, Surplus, Crisis and Opposition in Globalizing California*. Berkeley: University of California Press, 2007.

Giroux, Henry. *Against the Terror of Neoliberalism: Politics Beyond the Age of Greed*. Herndon, Va.: Paradigm, 2008.

Goldberg, David Theo. *The Threat of Race: Reflections on Racial Neoliberalism*. Malden, Mass.: Wiley-Blackwell, 2009.

Goyette, Desirée. "Joe Cool." 1971.

Guidroz, Kathleen, and Michele Tracy Berger. "A Conversation with Founding Scholars on Intersectionality: Kimberle Crenshaw, Nira Yuval-Davis, and Michelle Fine." In *The Intersectional Approach: Transforming the Academy Through Race, Class and Gender*, edited by Guidroz and Berger, 61–79. Asheveille: University of North Carolina Press, 2009.

Habermas, Jurgen. "Toward a Cosmopolitan Europe." *Journal of Democracy* 14, no. 4 (2003): 86–100.

Hall, Stuart. "The Problem of Ideology: Marxism Without Guarantees." In *Stuart Hall: Critical Dialogues in Cultural Studies*, edited by David Morley and Kuan-Hsing Chen, 25–46. London: Routledge, 1996.

——. *Race: The Floating Signifier*, directed by Sut Jhally, Media Education Foundation, 1997.

Halley, Janet. *Split Decisions: How and Why to Take a Break from Feminism*. Princeton: Princeton University Press, 2006.

Han, Beatrice. *Foucault's Critical Project: Between the Transcendental and the Historical*. Stanford: Stanford University Press, 2002.

Harcourt, Bernard, ed. *Carceral Notebooks*. Vol. 4, 2008. www.thecarceral.org/journal-vol4.html.

——. *The Illusion of Markets: Punishment and the Myth of Natural Order*. Cambridge, Mass.: Harvard University Press, 2011.

Harvey, David. *A Brief History of Neoliberalism*. Oxford: Oxford University Press, 2005.

Hawkesworth, Mary. *Globalization and Feminist Activism*. New York: Roman and Littlefield, 2006.

Hennessey, Rosemary. *Profit and Pleasure: Sexual Identities in Late Capitalism*. New York: Routledge, 2000.

Hollywood, Amy. *Sensible Ecstasy: Mysticism, Sexual Difference and the Demands of History*. Chicago: University of Chicago Press, 2002.

Hong, Grace Kyungwon, and Roderick Ferguson, eds. *Strange Affinities: The Gender and Sexual Politics of Comparative Racialization*. Durham: Duke University Press, 2011.

hooks, bell. *Ain't I a Woman? Black Women and Feminism*. Cambridge, Mass.: South End Press, 1981.

——. *Black Looks: Race and Representation*. Cambridge, Mass.: South End Press, 1992.

——. *Feminist Theory: From Margin to Center*. Cambridge, Mass.: South End Press, 1984.

——. *We Real Cool: Black Men and Masculinity*. New York: Routledge, 2004.

——. *Yearning: Race, Gender and Cultural Politics*. Cambridge, Mass.: South End Press, 1990.

Huffer, Lynne. *Are the Lips a Grave? A Queer Feminist on the Ethics of Sex*. New York: Columbia University Press, 2013.

——. *Mad for Foucault: Rethinking the Foundations of Queer Theory*. New York: Columbia University Press, 2010.

Jameson, Frederick. *Postmodernism, or, The Cultural Logic of Late Capitalism*. Durham: Duke University Press, 1990.

Johnson, Cedric, ed. *The Neoliberal Deluge: Hurricane Katrina, Late Capitalism, and the Remaking of New Orleans*. Minneapolis: University of Minnesota Press, 2011.

Johnson, Rheta Grimsley. *Good Grief: The Story of Charles M. Schulz*. New York: Pharos Books, 1989.

Joseph, Miranda. *Debt to Society: Accounting for Life Under Capitalism*. Minneapolis: University of Minnesota Press, 2014.

Kafer, Alison. *Feminist, Queer, Crip*. Bloomington: Indiana University Press, 2013.

Kirchner, Bill, ed. *A Miles Davis Reader*. Washington: Smithsonian Institution Press, 1997.

Lacan, Jacques. *Anxiety: The Seminar of Jacques Lacan, Book X*. Edited by Jacques-Alain Miller. Cambridge: Polity, 2014.

——. *Écrits: The First Complete Edition in English*. Translated by Bruce Fink. New York: Norton, 2002.

——. *The Ego in Freud's Theory and the Technique in Psychoanalysis*. Edited by Jacques-Alain Miller. New York: Norton, 1999.

——. *The Four Fundamental Concepts of Psycho-Analysis, Book XI*. Edited by Jacques-Alain Miller. New York: Norton, 1981.

Lemke, Thomas. "'The Birth of Bio-Politics': Michel Foucault's Lecture at the Collège de France on Neo-Liberal Governmentality." *Economy and Society* 30, no. 2 (May 2001): 190–207.

Ligon, Glenn. *Yourself in the World: Selected Writings and Interviews*. Edited by Scott Rothkopf. New Haven: Yale University Press, 2011.

Lopez, Ian Haney. *White by Law: The Legal Construction of Race*. New York: New York University Press, 1997.

Lugones, María. "Heterosexualism and the Colonial/Modern Gender System." *Hypatia: A Journal of Feminist Philosophy* 22, no. 1 (Winter 2007): 186–209.

——. "Toward a Decolonial Feminism." *Hypatia: A Journal of Feminist Philosophy* 25, no. 4 (Fall 2010): 742–59.

Mader, Mary Beth. *Sleights of the Reason: Norm, Bisexuality, Development*. Albany: State University of New York Press, 2012.

Marx, Karl. "Economic and Philosophic Manuscripts of 1844." In *Marx-Engels Reader*, edited by Robert Tucker. New York: Norton, 1978.

——. *Grundrisse: Foundations of the Critique of Political Economy*. Translated by Martin Nicolaus. New York: Penguin, 1993.

McCall, Leslie. "The Complexity of Intersectionality." *Signs* 30, no. 3 (Spring 2005): 1771–800.

McQueen, Steve. *12 Years a Slave*. Fox Searchlight Pictures: Los Angeles, 2013.

McRobbie, Angela. "Feminism and the Third Way." *Feminist Review* 64 (2000): 97–112.

McWhorter, Ladelle, ed. "Foucault and Race." *Foucault Studies* 12 (2011).

——. "Queer Economies." In "Foucault and Queer Theory," edited by Jana Sawicki and Shannon Winnubst, special issue, *Foucault Studies* 14 (2012): 61–78.

——. *Racism and Sexism in Anglo-America: A Genealogy*. Bloomington: Indiana University Press, 2009.

Melamed, Jodi. *Represent and Destroy: Rationalizing Violence in the New Racial Capitalism*. Minneapolis: University of Minnesota Press, 2011.

——. "The Spirit of Neoliberalism: From Racial Liberalism to Neoliberal Multiculturalism." *Social Text* 89, vol. 24, no. 4 (Winter 2006): 1–24.

Mendelson, Lee, and Bill Melendez. *There's No Time for Love, Charlie Brown*. March 11, 1973.

Mies, Maria. *Patriarchy and Accumulation on a World Scale: Women in the International Division of Labor*. London: Zed, 1999.

Mills, Charles. *The Racial Contract*. Ithaca: Cornell University Press, 1999.

Mirowski, Philip, and Dieter Plehwe, eds. *The Road from Mont Pelerin: The Making of the Neoliberal Thought Collective*. Cambridge, Mass.: Harvard University Press, 2009.

Montag, Warren. *Althusser and His Contemporaries: Philosophy's Perpetual War*. Durham: Duke University Press, 2013.

Moraga, Cherríe, and Gloria Anzaldúa, eds. *This Bridge Called My Back: Writings by Radical Women of Color*. New York: Kitchen Table, Women of Color Press, 1991.

Muñoz, José. *Disidentifications: Queers of Color and the Performance of Politics*. Minneapolis: University of Minnesota Press, 1999.

Nealon, Jeffrey. *Foucault Beyond Foucault: Power and Its Intensifications Since 1984*. Stanford: Stanford University Press, 2008.

Nietzsche, Friedrich. *On the Genealogy of Morals*. Edited by Walter Kaufmann and R. J. Hollingdale. New York: Vintage, 1967.

——. "On Truth and Lying in an Extramoral Sense." In *Friedrich Nietzsche on Rhetoric and Language*, translated by Sander L. Gilman, Carole Blair, and David J. Parent. New York: Oxford University Press, 1989.

Obama, Barack. "A More Perfect Union." Speech at Constitution Center. March 18, 2008. http://constitutioncenter.org/amoreperfectunion/.

——. "Speaks on Trayvon Martin." Speech at White House. July 19, 2013. www.whitehouse.gov/photos-and-video/video/2013/07/19/president-obama-speaks-trayvon-martin.

Ong, Aiwha. *Neoliberalism as Exception: Mutations in Citizenship and Sovereignty*. Durham: Duke University Press, 2006.

Palmer, Robert. "Miles Davis: The Man Who Changed Music." *Rolling Stone* 617 (November 14, 1991).

Parrenas, Rhacel Salazar. *Servants of Globalization: Women, Migration and Domestic Work*. Stanford: Stanford University Press, 2001.

Passavant, Paul. "The Strong Neo-Liberal State." *Theory and Event* 8, no. 3 (September 2005): 1–48.

Pateman, Carole. *The Sexual Contract*. Stanford: Stanford University Press, 1988.

Peterson, Spike. *A Critical Rewriting of Global Political Economy: Integrating Reproductive, Productive, and Virtual Economies*. New York: Routledge, 2003.

Povinelli, Elizabeth. *Economies of Abandonment: Social Belonging and Endurance in Late Liberalism*. Durham: Duke University Press, 2011.

Puar, Jasbir. *Terrorist Assemblages: Homonationalism in Queer Times*. Durham: Duke University Press, 2007.

Reddy, Chandan. *Freedom with Violence: Race, Sexuality, and the US State*. Durham: Duke University Press, 2011.

——. "Time for Rights? *Loving*, Gay Marriage, and the Limits of Comparative Legal Justice." In *Strange Affinities: The Gender and Sexual Politics of Comparative Racialization*, edited by Hong and Ferguson. Durham: Duke University Press, 2011.

Reed, Ishmael. "The President of the Cool." *New York Times*, December 18, 2013.

Reid, Carolina. "Wealth Inequality in the 'Land of the Fee': A Conversation with Devin Fergus." *Berkeley Planning Journal* 26 (2013): 75–85.

Roberts, Dorothy. *Killing the Black Body: Race, Reproduction and the Meaning of Liberty*. New York: Vintage, 1997.

Rosenberg, Jordana, and Amy Villarejo, eds. "Queer Studies and the Crisis of Capitalism." *glq*, 18, no. 1 (2012).

Sachs, Jeffrey. *The End of Poverty: Economic Possibilities for Our Time*. New York: Penguin, 2005.

Saez, Emanuel. "Striking it Richer." http://elsa.berkeley.edu/~saez/saez-UStopincomes-2012.pdf.

Satz, Debra. *Why Some Things Should Not Be for Sale: The Moral Limit of Markets*. Oxford: Oxford University Press, 2010.

Sedgwick, Eve Kosovsky. *Tendencies*. Durham: Duke University Press, 1993.

Shah, Nayan. *Stranger Intimacy: Contesting Race, Sexuality and the Law in the North American West*. Berkeley: University of California Press, 2012.

Shapiro, Thomas, Tatjana Meschede, and Sam Osoro. "The Roots of the Widening Racial Wealth Gap: Explaining the Black-White Economic Divide." *Institute on Assets and Social Policy Research and Policy Brief*, February 2013.

Sheth, Falguni. *Toward a Political Philosophy of Race*. Albany: State University of New York Press, 2009.

Simpson, Mark. "Meet the Metrosexual: He's Well Dressed, Narcissistic and Obsessed with Butts. But Don't Call Him Gay." *Salon.com*, July 22, 2002. www.salon.com/2002/07/22/metrosexual/.

——. "MetroDaddy Speaks." *Salon.com*. January 5, 2004. www.salon.com/2004/01/05/metrosexual_ii/.

Singh, Nikhil. *Black Is a Country: Race and the Unfinished Struggle for Democracy*. Cambridge, Mass.: Harvard University Press, 2005.

Spade, Dean. *Normal Life: Administrative Violence, Critical Trans Politics, and the Limits of the Law*. New York: South End Press, 2011.

Spillers, Hortense J. *Black, White and in Color: Essays on American Literature and Culture*. Chicago: University of Chicago Press, 2003.

——. "Mama's Baby, Papa's Maybe: An American Grammar Book." In *Black, White and in Color*.

Stiglitz, Joseph. *Globalization and Its Discontents*. New York: Norton, 2003.

Stryker, Susan, and Aren Z. Aizura, eds. *Transgender Studies Reader*. Vol. 2. New York: Routledge, 2013.

Stryker, Susan, and Paisley Currah, eds. *TSQ: Transgender Studies Quarterly*. Durham: Duke University Press, 2014– .

Stryker, Susan, and Stephen Whittle, eds. *Transgender Studies Reader*. New York: Routledge, 2006.

Sullivan, Shannon. *Good White People: The Problem with Middle-Class White Anti-Racism*. Albany: State University of New York Press, 2014.

Thomas, Hank Willis. "Soul." In *Black Cool: One Thousand Streams of Blackness*, edited by Rebecca Walker, 97–109. Berkeley: Soft Skull, 2012.

Todd, Michael. "Is the Metrosexual Finally Dead?" *Salon.com*, November 21, 2012. www.salon.com/2012/11/21/is_the_metrosexual_finally_dead/.

Viego, Antonio. *Dead Subjects: Towards a Politics of Loss in Latino Studies*. Durham: Duke University Press, 2007.

Wacquant, Loic. "From Slavery to Mass Incarceration: Re-Thinking the 'Race Question' in the US." *New Left Review* 13 (January–February 2002). http://newleftreview.org/II/13/loic-wacquant-from-slavery-to-mass-incarceration.

——. "Three Steps to a Historical Anthropology of Actually Existing Neoliberalism." *Social Anthropology* 20 (2012): 66–79.

Walker, Kara. *After the Deluge*. New York: Rizzoli, 2007.

Walker, Rebecca, ed. *Black Cool: One Thousand Streams of Blackness*. Berkeley: Soft Skull, 2012.

Wiegman, Robyn. *Object Lessons*. Durham: Duke University Press, 2012.

Wiegman, Robyn, and Elizabeth A. Wilson, eds. "Queer Theory Without Antinormativity." Special issue, *differences: A Journal of Feminist Cultural Studies* 26, no. 1 (October 2014).

Wiley, Kehinde. "Interview with Kehinde Wiley." *Bad at Sports*. January 15, 2013. http://www.artpractical.com/column/interview_with_kehinde_wiley/.

——. "The World Stage: Israel, An Interview with C. C. H. Pounder." February 27, 2013. www.youtube.com/watch?v=XluSaO8P_qA.

Winnubst, Shannon. *Queering Freedom*. Bloomington: Indiana University Press, 2006.

——. "The Queer Thing About Neoliberal Pleasure: A Foucaultian Warning." *Foucault Studies* 14 (2012): 79–97.

——. "Sacrifice as Ethics: The Strange Religiosity of Neoliberalism." In *Negative Ecstasies*, edited by Jeremy Biles and Kent Brintnall. New York: Fordham University Press, 2015.

——. "Vampires, Anxieties and Dreams." *Hypatia: A Journal of Feminist Philosophy* 18, no. 3 (2003): 1–20.

Zack, Naomi. "The American Sexualization of Race." In *Race/Sex: Their Sameness, Difference, and Interplay*, edited by Naomi Zack. New York: Routledge, 1997.

Žižek, Slavoj. *First as Tragedy, Then as Farce*. London: Verso, 2009.

——. "Love Thy Neighbor? No, Thanks!" In *The Psychoanalysis of Race*, edited by Christopher Lane, 154–75. New York: Columbia University Press, 1998.

——. "The Subject Supposed to Loot and Rape." *In These Times*. October 20, 2005.

——. *Welcome to the Desert of the Real*. New York: Verso, 2002.

Zupančič, Alenka. *Ethics of the Real: Kant, Lacan*. London: Verso, 2000.

INDEX

Page numbers in italics signify graphics.

GPSR Authorized Representative: Easy Access System Europe, Mustamäe tee 50, 10621 Tallinn, Estonia, gpsr.requests@easproject.com

www.ingramcontent.com/pod-product-compliance
Lightning Source LLC
Chambersburg PA
CBHW072104040426
42334CB00042B/2299

* 9 7 8 0 2 3 1 1 7 2 9 5 0 *